Founding Mother

Frances Kellor and the
Creation of Modern America

Founding Mother

Frances Kellor and the Creation of Modern America

John Kenneth Press, Ph.D.

Social Books
New York, New York

Copyright © 2012
by John Kenneth Press, Ph.D.

Social Books
pressjohn@hotmail.com
www.franceskellor.com

All rights reserved. No part of this publication may be reproduced, stored in a retrieval system or transmitted, in any form, or by any means, electronic, mechanical, recorded, photocopied, or otherwise, without the prior permission of the copyright owner, except by a reviewer who may quote brief passages in a review.

ISBN: 0978-0-9785777-2-8

Printed in the United States of America

Cover design by Divine Tree
www.vedicdesign.com

To my grandparents,
Edwin and Marion Levine,
whose level of Americanization
was perfect.

Table of Contents

Acknowledgements i
Introduction iii
Note on Pronouns xi

CHAPTER ONE
People in a Small Town 1

CHAPTER TWO
Cornell, Basketball, and Women's Americanization 23

CHAPTER THREE
Southern Female African-American Prisoners and White Women 51

CHAPTER FOUR
For the Love of Women 69

CHAPTER FIVE
Kellor Crosses the Color Line 89

CHAPTER SIX
Americanization from the Trenches 104

Selected Photos 126

CHAPTER SEVEN
The Nation Sours and New Nationalism is Born 136

CHAPTER EIGHT
Multicultural Nationalism 158

CHAPTER NINE
Living in a Material World 175

CHAPTER TEN
Forced Activism 190

CHAPTER ELEVEN
Taking it to the Streets 210

CHAPTER TWELVE
Wartime Americanization 231

CHAPTER THIRTEEN
Media Americanization 259

CHAPTER FOURTEEN
Internationalism Versus Americanism 277

CHAPTER FIFTEEN
Kellor Takes Off 295

Kellor Life Timeline 312
Index 314
Bibliography 319

Acknowledgements

Above all else, I want to thank Jon Zimmerman for helping me put my work into the context of the literature of the field. Also from New York University, I would like to thank Sandra DeVera. Her endless academic curiosity inspired me. Input from our History of Education writing group provided much needed criticism. Additionally, I would like to thank my readers, Jim Fraser, Harold Wechsler, Erich Dietrich and, Joan Malczewski.

Throughout this adventure, many people have provided small acts of essential help. Nola Baker, provided intense help in Coldwater, Michigan's Branch District Library. Phyllis Holbrook's historical work at the same library proved invaluable. Ellen Fitzpatrick sending me her archives showed great collegiality. And, most significantly, Dr. William J. Maxwell deserves recognition. His research into Kellor's early life shed light on all of her subsequent work.

More personally, the interest and playtime provided by my sister's family, Samantha, Jason, Moshe, and Chana Fink kept my spirits renewed. Special thanks need to go to Soo Hee Lee, without whose encouragement and emotional support I would not have gone to NYU or gotten through it. My mother and father's lifelong encouragement has been instrumental in all I have achieved. Steve Essig's friendship and editing efforts were both greatly appreciated throughout the writing process. And many thanks also go to Holly Bowers, who sprinkled cool patience when I began to race towards the finish line.

Finally, I would like to thank Frances Alice Kellor. Any merit in this work only reflects her extraordinary energy and efforts.

Introduction

Upon entering New York University, I intended to study the Americanization movement. During the enormous immigration wave of the Progressive era, the Americanization movement (1906 to 1921) crusaded to turn immigrants into "good Americans." This popular movement garnered enthusiastic support from Presidents, Mayors, Chambers of Commerce, Captains of Industry, average American citizens, and – as I found out – many immigrants themselves. Academics have roundly condemned the Movement for using coercion to create cultural conformity. As I personally think unity has some benefits that diversity overshadows, I determined to study the Americanization Movement to understand why an earlier generation supported cultural unity.

In researching the Americanization Movement, one name popped-up over and over again – that of Frances Alice Kellor (1873 – 1952). Most books on the subject of Americanization take the time to acknowledge Kellor as the movement's leader. I was surprised, therefore, to find out that no one had ever written a book about this leader in immigration relations. Happily, I had found the perfect subject for my dissertation. Writing Kellor's biography would help me grasp the reasons a huge national movement sought to "Americanize" immigrants.

Yet the moment I began researching Kellor, her story challenged my assumptions. Far from conservative, she sat at the heart of the Progressive Movement. The Progressive Movement got closer to winning a presidential election than any third party ever had with Theodore Roosevelt's 1912 attempt to recapture the White House. Kellor held a high position in Roosevelt's presidential campaign. She wrote the Progressive Party's platform on immigration. And, at one point, she even headed half of the national Progressive Party. Today's "progressive" politicians get their label from the Progressive Movement of Kellor's era. I had not expected the Americanization Movement to be so intimately tied to the origin of modern liberal politics.

As I continued to study Kellor she continued to explode my expectations. In 1898 she undertook a two-year study of African - American women in southern penitentiaries. She did this in order to challenge the racism and sexism of the world's leading criminal sociologist, Cesare Lombroso. In doing so, Kellor vindicated incarcerated African – American women. She then became the leading white activist for African-American women in New York of her time. She set up a national network to assist African – American workers coming to the North; an effort that parallels, though it is different than, the Underground Railroad. Kellor co-founded the National Urban League. Who could have guessed that the head of a movement maligned for being hostile to immigrants and their cultures would have been a seminal civil rights activist?

Just as remarkable was the discovery of Kellor's status as a transgender lesbian. In feminist terms, she herself was an oppressed minority. While becoming the third woman to ever receive a law degree from Cornell, she led a battle for women's athletics. When working with the Progressive Party, she got Roosevelt to put suffrage on the National Progressive Party platform. When Kellor undertook her presidential political campaigns, she herself could not yet vote. And, she largely undertook the campaigns to publicize the fact that women could engage in public political expression and "masculine" battles. As a person totally aware of her own status as an oppressed minority, Kellor seemed an unlikely candidate for an immigrant oppressor.

I also began to wonder why more had not been written about Kellor. I had thought her worthy of study just for having led a huge national movement addressing the hot topic of immigration. But the more I read of her, the more I became amazed at Kellor's breadth. She developed innovative theories and took action in the fields of sports, race, gender politics, political science, criminology, immigration, media, labor theory, education, and international arbitration. The sociology of Kellor's time taught how to control all of society via its mechanisms. It was as one of the best-trained sociologists in the nation, that Kellor sought to change America's basic nature. Many of her attempts to act as a Founding Mother to our modern era succeeded. One would have thought that, at very least, an intellectual or cultural historian would have written a book exploring her ideas.

In studying American intellectual history, I began to develop some theories concerning Kellor's neglect. First of all, her intimate link with the vilified Americanization Movement means that taking her seriously requires taking the

Americanization Movement seriously. Jane Addams was a colleague of Kellor's and the most famous female activist of her time. Addams was banished to obscurity and later won the Nobel Peace Prize for opposing our entry into World War I. But, rather than pacifism, Kellor actively and publically supported U.S. military preparedness for World War I. I have thought that not taking the anti-war stance that Addams and other women's movement leaders took, could make Kellor an awkward role model for some feminists.

Ultimately, however, I came to the conclusion that lingering sexism had mostly banished our world-shaper to obscurity. Whereas male intellectuals developed pristine ideals in books, Kellor actually implemented her ideas. By the definition of an intellectual as someone who writes books rather than take action, Kellor is not an intellectual. Rather, as a woman activist, Kellor gets labeled as a "social worker." And so, while volumes get written about the male intellectuals Kellor worked with, we have been thus far been deprived of any in-depth look into how Kellor's thoughts *and actions* have shaped our world. I feel a sense of pride in breaking down this gender wall for Kellor. And, I think this exploration of Kellor's thoughts *and actions* will make an important contribution to U.S. cultural and intellectual history.

Were Kellor more widely known and studied, we would learn a lot about ourselves. Kellor based her brand of Americanization in aspirations for social justice. A well-taken-care-of immigrant, protected from abuse and exploitation, would feel loyalty to this nation. And rather than making immigrants disloyal, Kellor thought getting immigrants involved in public protest made immigrants more American. Kellor's Americanization Day celebrations got hundreds of thousands of immigrants parading in ethnic costumes every Fourth of July. With these efforts and others, Kellor created a sort of "Multicultural Nationalism." Today the left would sour at the nationalism while the right would reject the multicultural parts. Taking Kellor's thought seriously provides us with a whole new way to configure assimilation. Rather than reinforce my pre-existing beliefs, studying Kellor brought me face-to-face with the limits of my thinking on assimilation. I got much more than I bargained for when I chose Kellor as a subject of study.

Immigration issues are just one of many arenas in which Kellor stimulates us to reflect on our own thinking and time. Kellor promoted sports as a way to consciously shape women's character. She found it sad that people studying to become physical education teachers did not consider the cultural impact of sports. In watching Kellor run a parallel Federal government based on activism, we come to realize the limits of elections as indicators of how democratic we are. Kellor's status as an LGBT leader and role model inspires youth and makes us rethink who belongs in U.S. history courses. Each of Kellor's battles tells us something about our assumptions and the limits of our imagination.

The title of this book, "Founding Mother," applies to Kellor in numerous ways. Its contrast with the phrase "Founding Fathers" brings ironic attention to Kellor's obsession with gender.

And again, as a highly trained sociologist she consciously strove to remake society and largely succeeded. Kellor's policies led to a larger Federal government that provides support without judgment. Herein I think Kellor's hopes as an LGBT person and the world she created overlap. Kellor wanted people to be able to engage in activism no matter who they were. This instinct, in turn, fed into her form of multiculturalism. As a seminal figure in the creation of modern America, understanding Kellor as a person helps us understand who we are.

In the end, Kellor rejected the Americanization Movement. She denounced its bullies for making immigrants see America as a hostile place. In her last writings on the topic, Kellor argued that we had to stop thinking in terms of immigration; people now traveled internationally for work. Instead of immigration, she preferred to discuss the legal status of what she called the "International Human Being." Laws in 1921 and 1924 greatly restricted the flow of immigrants into America. At that point she discontinued her Americanization work and began creating our current system of international arbitration. During this transition, creating a vision America rejected, Kellor argued for global treaties to protect the commuting international humans.

This book will follow Kellor as she imaginatively takes on many issues. As a modernist, her issues are still not remote. The protection of "International Human Beings," and the level of globalism that entails, continues to fuel skirmishes. America sometimes seems obsessed with the LGBT and gender issues Kellor raised. In politics we largely fight over her work aimed at having the Federal government take more responsibility for the economy. Race relations continue to matter in our nation. And, citizens still passionately debate the secular trends in national identity she championed with her Americanization Movement. Watching Kellor raise and address these and other issues, makes us aware that, as she created modern America, Kellor created us.

Note on Pronouns

Throughout this text, though transgender, Frances Kellor will be referenced with the feminine pronouns, "she," "her," and, "herself." Kellor was the male persona in her lifelong relationship with Mary Dreier, argued publically that women needed to take on more "masculine" characteristics, changed her name from the feminine "Alice" to the more ambivalent "Frances," and dressed in men's clothes. Within the broad parameters of today's language, Kellor was transgender. In her ongoing focus on gender roles, Kellor called herself "masculine," but she never called herself "male." Therefore, throughout this text, feminine pronouns will be used when referring to Kellor.

– CHAPTER ONE –

THE PEOPLE IN A SMALL TOWN

Alice Kellar's America [*]

Shortly after Frances Alice Kellar came into this world, in Columbus, Ohio, on October 20th, 1873, her mother moved her to Coldwater, Michigan. Alice, as she was called in Coldwater, stayed in this town through her twenty-first birthday. And, as luck would have it, around the age of seventeen Alice got a job describing the town's very active social life for the biggest local newspaper, *The Coldwater Republican*. That means we not only have a thorough and engaging depiction of Coldwater, we have a glimpse into how young Alice saw this proud small town.

The inhabitants, social life, and activism of Coldwater made young Alice the woman she became. People often ask those of us who study Americanization, "What was the ideal to

---

[*] In her hometown, Kellor was known as "Alice Kellar." In this chapter, when referring to her life in her hometown, her original name wil be used. When referring to later events, the name "Frances Kellor" will be used.

Chapter One

which Americanizers aimed?" Kellor's Americanization ideal often looked like an attempt to recreate her hometown of Coldwater, Michigan in the big cities of the industrial era.[1]

Coldwater sits about fifty miles north of the Indiana border between Hillsdale and Kalamazoo. The first dirt roads and bridges going into Coldwater appeared in the 1820s and 1830s. By 1890 Coldwater had around five thousand residents and did over two million dollars in business annually. An early chronicler called Coldwater a "boomtown" and then, tellingly, rejected the label. "Boom," he explained, is associated with "speculators" in the "stock market."[2] A sense of Protestant morals and ideals of self-reliance permeated this popular description of Coldwater.

In fact, Coldwater was not just a boomtown whose rise reflected the lucky fortune of a single commodity. It had a staid and diversified economy, laid on a steady foundation of businesses, informed by a "general spirit of progress."[3] Indeed, they had an astonishing variety of businesses. In addition to the regular agriculture, grocery stores and restaurants, Coldwater had sewing machine and musical instrument manufacturers, printing and engraving enterprises, cigar and cigar box makers, marble works, carriage makers and even a stove manufacturer.[4] Coldwater personified the promise of American enterprise.

Coldwater not only had pride in its manufacturers; it had plans to put itself on the cultural map. This ambition manifest itself in Tibbit's Opera House and the Lewis Art Gallery. The author of the 1889 book, *Coldwater Illustrated,* noted that,

"Nothing has given to Coldwater a more enviable reputation with people of culture throughout this *whole country* than the possession of this celebrated gallery."[5] [Italics added]

As overblown as this self-estimation of community pride seems, Coldwater had reasons for its pretentions. Henry C. Lewis, who founded the Lewis Art Gallery, ran a mercantile manufacturing operation and engaged in milling pursuits before becoming the president of one of Coldwater's three banks. He traveled to Europe often and served as an art juror at both the Vienna and Paris Expositions. The *New York Times* wrote that some thought Lewis' the largest private art collection in the country and noted that it drew visitors from all over the nation.[6] Striving civic pride surrounded this future Americanizer.

Coldwater's Connection

In her seventeenth year, Alice started writing a gossip column that covered Coldwater's vibrant social scene. Her August 22nd, 1893 article alone announced that, "Mrs. Clarence Loveridge gave a party in honor of her little friend, Grace Dennis." In addition, Mr. and Mrs. Lilly entertained friends with cards and refreshments and Mrs. Stevens had a tea party. Meanwhile, there were forty invited guests of honor at the "zoological party." At this party people drew animals they were assigned. "Helen Branch and Ralph Andrews carried off first prizes by guessing [animals] correctly the greatest number of times." For more strenuous edification, Dr. Will Ford and Mell Peters announced they would "represent the medical and legal professions at the fair" coming at the end of the week.[7] If you preferred moral uplift, the local prohibitionists held a contest and, separately, a lecture with a large audience. And, the same day, the young writer told her readers, both the Coldwater marine band and the mandolin club announced they would soon be playing on a barge attached to two boats strewn with Japanese lanterns.

"Social capital" is a term sociologists use to measure how many people to whom the average person in a society is connected.[8] Coldwater had high levels of social capital. And, as a reporter, Kellar would have been at the center of that human capital. She must have had some social connections to know that "Eva squires, residing on Harrison street, was given a very enjoyable surprise party on Wednesday evening by a number of her young friends. A very delightful evening was passed, and Eva invites all to come again – but not so unexpectedly."[9]

In this context we should also note that each person in Alice's articles gets referred to by name. The subjects are not strangers to the readers. If they are, she introduces them. When A Mr. M. Loveland was visiting Coldwater, Alice informed her readers that he was "an uncle of Mrs. S. H. Loveland of Los Angeles, Cal., formerly of Quincy, and now visiting her niece, Mrs. Laura brown on north Hudson street."[10] Notice the wording in this death announcement: "The remains of Erastus Hathaway of Union City were brought here Tuesday and shipped on the noon train to Girard, Pa, where they were buried. He was not unknown in this city."[11] Human connection sat at the center of Kellor's Americanization project and it permeated Coldwater.

We also see the roots of Kellor's extreme savvy in cultivating business and government connections in Coldwater. On February 23rd of 1894 she reported that after a vacation, "The Blodgett and Son undertaking business is continued at the old place of business."[12] If Blodgett did not seek her out, he must have been glad to have had that information known and printed. People must have often been seeking her out to pass on information they would want printed. In Coldwater business was personal. Alice told us, "M. E. Wattles received $76 for two cans of peppermint oil last week, E. R. Clark & Co. paying that amount. The peppermint was grown on his farm in Matteson." Even the government was personal. Young Kellor informed her readers that, "Marshal Swaffield is now ready to receive city taxes. He can be found every Friday at the council building."[13]

For Kellor, Americanization mostly meant breaking down the walls that separated people. She wanted long-term Americans to understand and accept immigrants. She repeatedly bragged that immigrants in her Americanization Day celebrations said it was the "first time they had shaken hands with an American!"[14] She wanted employers and employees to understand each other. In Coldwater, employees and employers, neighbors, reformers, and government officials knew each other. Much of the Americanization movement can be explained as Kellor's attempt to recreate the small town intimacy of Coldwater in an industrial setting.

Chapter One

Kellor's Personality

All facets of life appear in these Coldwater articles. It was newsworthy that "Mr. A Bunnell has laid a new sidewalk in front of his residence on Grand street."[15] And, one cannot help but raise a hint of a smile as we read that "A double pant race is on the slate for Thursday forenoon, Sept. 28th, at the county fair."[16] Yet for all the glee, on July 27th of 1894, Kellar wrote, "Mrs. L. M. Nye, residing two miles south of the city, lies critically ill at home, having had several light strokes of paralysis resulting from grippe. Her recovery is doubtful."[17] And she showed sensitivity beyond her years when writing of a Civil War reunion where veterans enjoyed war stories, "but each showed the encroachment of age, and the hardship of the camps, in stooping form and silvered hair."[18]

And all was not sweetness and light in Coldwater. Homes were broken into, people got held up at gunpoint, and Kellar even reported on a shoot-out on the mean streets of Coldwater. In one crime in nearby Somerset, an elderly couple was beaten and the wife had a piece of firewood forced down her throat.[19] Remarkably, Kellar found humor in crime. Mimicking her social announcement format she wrote, "Lewis Phinney of Bronson will be the guest of Sheriff Sweet for three months. He is charged with stealing $12 from a Polish woman in Bronson."[20] We can hear coldness in some of her precocious quips. When a conviction of a man for cruelty to animals helped spur the formation of a humane society she gleefully exclaimed, "He may be of some benefit to humanity yet."[21] When prisoners complained of heat in the jail, she curtly reported that they "could have enjoyed the outside if they had acted wisely, no sympathy is extended."[22] Alice was warm yet tough.

Skirting darkness, Kellar often reported on injuries, and sometimes seemed to take pleasure in it. When a woman fell out of a tree, Kellar wrote, "One of Coldwater's most popular former science teachers . . . now boasts of a badly bruised body . . . She insists that she was studying astronomy and saw several new species of luminaries upon her descent."[23] Sometimes she was overly droll. When a man cut off the tips of his fingers working at Johnson's cooper shop, she reported that "It was not intentional and care will be taken that it is not repeated."[24] And Kellar routinely shared gore-filled details, such as the fact that "John Shaw . . . cut his left hand with a cleaver yesterday forenoon"[25] and that Mrs. Godfrey "slipped on the stone step, falling backward and striking her head, cutting quite a gash in the back of it."[26]

For every benevolent reformer in Coldwater, there seems to have been a hooligan. Those in Coldwater who strove for civic improvement were wealthy. Kellor could have made her Americanization programs about a need to "fix" those at the bottom. To the extent that she had such an attitude we will investigate it. But, overall, she accepted people. In fact, the upper strata got the vast majority of her wrath. And she routinely unleashed her wrath on them for the exact crime of looking down upon those who were less fortunate or different from them. A perverse delight in people lay behind her acceptance of them.

Chapter One

Alice Kellar's Household

People who hear that Kellor lead the Americanization movement often inquire into her ethnic background. On this score, we know little. Young Alice never met her father. She had a sister twenty-four years her senior. But, if the sister ever moved to Coldwater, she did not stay long. Alice grew up in a household headed by her single mother, Mary Sprau Kellar.

No one knows why Mary chose Coldwater or why the father, Daniel, did not follow. There has been speculation that Kellar's mother was not her mother. A circumstantial case could be made that Kellar was the illegitimate spawn of her father and her much older sister. That would explain the move to Coldwater right after Kellar's birth. It would explain her sister's tenuous ties to Coldwater. It would explain the anomaly of Kellar's mother having a second child when she had already finished raising her twenty-four-year-old daughter. It would account for the very private nature of Mary Sprau Kellar. But, most of all, it would explain the complete disappearance of Kellar's father from the public record.

The fact that Kellor's last name had two spellings obscures her roots. In Coldwater Kellor published under the name of "Alice Kellar." Thus, we do not ultimately even know the exact spelling of Kellor's name, we know nothing of her father, and her mother's presence went virtually unnoticed in Coldwater. Starting in her teens, Kellar attended a Presbyterian church under the leadership of an unorthodox minister. With her mother hard at work, she was largely raised by the community of Coldwater.[27]

Before joining the church she did not seem to have had much of a specific cultural heritage to draw upon.

To make ends meet, Mary Sprau Kellar took in clothes and did domestic work. And young Alice had to alternate between working with her mother part-time and full-time, depending on the school schedule, and financial needs. Progressive reformers have been typified as coming from elite backgrounds.[28] For many reformers that was true. But when Alice wrote about the pain of poverty and the limitations it enforced, it was based on personal knowledge. Her clothes as a child were said to be faded from many washings.[29] Many years later she would say learning to enjoy Christmas was very difficult for her because it always reminded her of the deprivation of her childhood.[30] And poverty could have fatally limited young Alice's upward mobility as well. After two years of high school, economic necessity made her leave school to devote herself to full-time domestic work with her mother.

Kellar's public poverty in Coldwater accounts for the Americanization movement's accent on social justice. Kellor's first two books sought reform in order to protect the poor. Working with her mother likely contributed to Kellor's choice to make her second book specifically about the plight of domestic workers. When she went undercover as a domestic worker for that project she must have drawn on personal experience. The historical scholarship on Americanization has yet to really acknowledge the strong social justice orientation behind many of the

Chapter One

Americanization efforts. In a small town everyone knows your position. Your poverty is a shame that cannot be hidden by the anonymity of the big city. Noting that the leader of the Americanization movement grew up in visible public poverty should help historians to notice its emphasis on social justice.

Kellor's early poverty helps us understand her concern with the poor generically. Her coming from a single-mother-headed home helps explain why her work so exactly targets challenges facing women. Her first book concerned African - American women in southern penitentiaries. One would be hard pressed to find a group of women with less power. Her second work, again, concerned the exploitation of domestic servants. Her third book concerned the limits society put on women and how sports could overcome them.

After her first three books, Kellor never again exclusively focused on women. The public face of immigration was a male face. Thus, as she adopted a national position on Americanization, she came to emphasize men. But even in her later books, she had chapters and sections especially devoted to women. She also wrote articles that highlighted special challenges facing female immigrants and devised techniques tailored to meet their needs. Kellor nearly always approached Americanization with a consciousness of gender. Her mother's predicament likely contributed to her long attention to vulnerable women.

Tomboy

The October 4, 1911 edition of the *Coldwater Courier* bragged about the "former Coldwater Girl" getting a big government position in New York City. The article tells of an incident wherein a sixteen-year-old Kellar was hunting and her gun accidentally discharged. "The bullet," the writer told the readers, "passed through the flesh of the two fingers of the left index hand and lodged in the index finger."[31] While running through the streets, unable to find her mother, the Eddy sisters encountered the teen, got her to a doctor and, some time later, adopted her. Thus Mary and Frances Eddy, the article claimed, rescued young Alice from obscurity.

There is little evidence for and convincing evidence against this exciting story.[32] It is true that Alice supplemented the family income by hunting. She greatly enjoyed fishing. And whenever possible "off she would slip with a pole over her shoulder and a can of worms in her hand."[33] While other mothers were nervously trying to ensure their daughters became proper little ladies, young Alice ran wild through the streets and prairies. An unredeemable tomboy, she was said to have been able to hit anything she aimed at with a slingshot.[34] Often unsupervised, one historian wrote, "in many important respects she was as much a child of the community as she was of her natural mother."[35] So the 1911 article seems to correctly capture the spirit of the "young Diana."[36] Contrary to the dramatic accident story, however, Kellar's spending so much of her free time at the library likely led to her meeting the Eddy sisters.

Kellor's activism was inextricably mixed with her masculinity. Kellor donned aspects of male attire in nearly all of her photos. We will see her carve out a masculine place in society for women, in the name of women. Her several firsts included doing jobs that had been previously reserved for men. And Kellor wrote about gender and so deployed her gender consciously. But her deployment of gender identity politics was not purely an artificial strategy choice. A fellow Coldwater resident with young Alice remembered disapproving of her because she "wore her hair shingled and walked and talked like a boy."[37] Kellor's cross-dressing had early roots.

Uplift

The Eddy sisters were spinsters who came from a respected and well-to-do family. If the sisters adopted Kellar at the age of sixteen, as the article states, Mary would have been about thirty-six years old. Frances was older yet. And a report just after Kellar's 19th birthday confirmed that she still lived with them when it announced, "Alice Kellar is quite sick with bilious fever at her home with the Misses Eddy on Marshal street."[38] Both sisters participated in the sorts of social events described above, but Mary also provided young Kellar with her first intimate look at a strong activist woman.

Both sisters helped to found Coldwater's "ladies library."[39] This lending library had over 2,000 books.[40] Coldwater's Senator Morgan had been responsible for the state library law of 1877 that gave state recognition to local public libraries. And the Ladies'

Library group lobbied for the building of a full-fledged library under this provision. And when, in 1886, Coldwater's new library opened its doors, they made Mary head librarian in honor of her leadership. In 1891, on a train ride back from the American Library Association meeting, Mary suggested the founding of the Michigan Library Association (MLA). She then set to work rallying thirty-seven people to attend a meeting to consider launching the organization.

Mary was nervous about the first MLA meeting. She wrote a co-organizer, "It will be no small job to make the first meeting interesting and instructive so that they will want to come again."[41] In the same letter she explained why she thought the MLA necessary. She lamented that the nearby town of Hillsdale had no free public library despite the fact that it too had a Ladies' Library. Ultimately, she hoped their actions would result in a state organization that promoted library formation. At the meeting Mary organized, Senator Morgan noted that very few students continued into college. All attending agreed that this meant that the public library must become the People's University.[42] The MLA came into being, Mary's dream of state support for public libraries became a reality, and the MLA website still honors Mary Eddy as its founder. Thus Mary Eddy provided young Alice with a model of a woman who established local and statewide social improvement agencies.

Kellor's writing contained a bias that has gone unnoticed. The vast bulk of Kellor's moral exhortations got aimed at long-

Chapter One

term Americans and the rich. Kellor not only tries to get industries to stop exploiting workers throughout her career, she tries to get them to provide great facilities for workers. She relentlessly asked the wealthy to take responsibility for the poor. The situation of the poor, she held, did not reflect their moral character. This does not mean that she totally ignored immigrants' character. She wanted them to become American by participating in progressive activism. But she spent the vast bulk of her time pleading with the rich and powerful to fulfill their duty to the poor. In addition to lifting Kellar up, the Eddy sisters taught her about lifting people up.

Women's Christian Temperance Union

Progressives have been characterized as moralizers. Some of young Alice's attitudes towards morality can be seen in her reporting on arrests for drunkenness. Kellar's constant reporting on the Women's Christian Temperance Union (WCTU) reflected the fact that it was the most active political reform group in Coldwater. As the name indicates, the WCTU was a Christian women's organization dedicated to eradicating alcohol consumption in America. Today's we denounce prohibition pushers as nosey, unrealistic, condescending moralizers. Kellar would seem to share some of our sentiment. Kellar herself was incredibly straight-laced, but she bucked the trend of moralizing about drinkers.

When the German Benevolent Society had a parade and picnic that featured beers, our young journalist called it "undoubtedly the jolliest picnic of the season."[43] This evaluation could not have pleased the WCTU. More impressively, she attacked another newspaper for calling someone defending a liquor salesman a "whisky lawyer." This sort of logic, the young future lawyer Kellar argued, would make the whole State Supreme Court "whisky judges." Utilizing her sharp humor, Alice worried that if the other newspaper were to judge us on the last day, "What a small heaven and large hades there would be."[44] Kellar clearly did not share in the ubiquitous WCTU members' zeal for temperance. Rather than absolute moral codes, Kellar championed pragmatic values.

Coldwater had many male-dominated lodges. But you do not read about them much in the town's newspapers. These groups, if we trust Kellar's reporting, did not engage the public publically. Instead, Kellar's reporting mostly depicted female-led organizations headed by people she knew. The aforementioned Ladies' Library provides one example. Mary Eddy also organized a Columbian Circle. These reading groups were popular then. Coldwater's branch led off by reading "Famous American Women."[45] Mary Eddy also ran the female dominated Rainbow Club. Frances Eddy participated in both of these organizations.

As early as 1892, Coldwater's WCTU also started working for women's suffrage. They asked women to work for the election of women and urged "special attention be given to the work of the franchise."[46] The Michigan branches of the WCTU backed suffrage more than other chapters. Nearby Hillsdale even sent a temperance delegation to the state suffrage convention.[47] In Coldwater the WCTU were widely seen as activists for women's rights. The stage at one of Coldwater's many fairs featured a WCTU banner on the left side and one sponsored by liquor interests on the right. The latter read, "The ballot in the hands of women will be the death blow to our country."[48] Adopting this WCTU-backed crusade, Kellar played an important role in getting women the vote.

Outside of her reporting, Kellar's social circle overlapped with that of the WCTU. The Eddy sisters and Alice were members of H. P. Collin's Presbyterian church. This church hosted many WCTU events. In 1892 Rev. Collin delivered a series of lectures on social purity at the request of the WCTU. Transcending the alcohol issue, he said the WCTU acted, "Wherever they see anything that is harming men or women in body, mind or spirit." Far from only being a temperance organization, he noted that they have committees on "heredity, health, scientific temperance instruction, kindergarten work, the press, purity in literature and art, narcotics, work in prisons, jails, police stations and almshouses, social purity and the white cross, mothers meetings" and more.[49] As Kellar attended Collin's church, she likely had personal contact with this all-encompassing female-dominated social reform group.

Early Philosophical Grooming

As Mary Eddy, Rev. Collin also served as a trainer in social action for young Alice. In reference to Collin, a modern

Coldwater's librarian called Kellor "His masterpiece."[50] Though it failed to credit the Eddy sisters enough, this remark had justification. Indeed, Collin knew the Eddy sisters well. He accompanied Mary Eddy to the meeting in which they formed the MLA. Kellar, as others, took classes from Collin that he taught both at the church and in Mary Eddy's library. And, when Alice was nineteen she traveled alone with Collin and Frances Eddy to Bay View, Michigan for a three-week Chautauqua.[51] These were events where people came to learn and hear lectures. Unlike his library classes, young Alice was the only youth who attended the distant Chatauquas with him.

When she went to the Chautauqua, the often-wry Alice laughed at all those there who had "the craze" for stone collection. These were, "worthless pebbles presented to wise judges."[52] The Chautauqua was run by one of the leading Social Gospel teachers ever, Richard T. Ely. Embodying the Social Gospel, Ely wrote of Jesus' admonition to love thy neighbor as obligating us to work towards creating a "prosperous, righteous, and progressive state of society."[53] Rev. Collin's philosophy of socially active Christianity mirrored Ely's. Yet Ely wrote about more industry-oriented projects than Collin did. For example, the more famous lecturer denounced the Church for not fighting child labor. But both men preached the Social Gospel and publically stated that fifty percent of clergy's training should consist of sociology courses.

Chapter One

Ely wrote his *Social Aspects of Christianity* the same year Kellar attended his lectures and took his program. In it, Ely sounded themes that later became staples for Kellor. For example, he promoted "preventative philanthropy." Rather than sporadic gifts, this preventative philanthropy argued for state programs to help the poor even before they needed it. Ely contrasted this with "positive philanthropy" which only cured existing evils. Perhaps being a little too flippant, Ely wrote, "It is all very well to hang anarchists. It is better to educate the young, so to purify politics, so to build up the home, so to reform our business methods as to take the standing-ground out from under the anarchists."[54]

"Preventative philanthropy" would become a recurrent cry of Kellor's life work. Later, in *Social Aspects of Christianity*, Ely wrote that the servant girl question is answered when the employer seeks to do their duty towards their servant. Kellar followed this tact exactly. Kellor seems to have gone to more than the one Ely Chautauqua. In one visit to a Chautauqua, she took a course on political economy with Ely. Collin and the Eddy sisters taught Kellar in classes and took her into their home, and to the lectures of one of the leading Social Gospel leaders. Kellar's activist career paid tribute to the design of Coldwater's leading activists.

Religion, Morality, and Kellar's Trajectory

Kellor participated in the transition of reform from having a religious basis to more secular suppositions. Her early writing included Protestant style judgments of moral failings. Her later writing only suggested bureaucratic solutions to problems all men faced. She dropped pronouncements of her lingering strains of individual Protestant morality for systemic analysis. Ely and the WCTU were seriously religious. Rev. Collin eschewed doctrinal certainty for sociological analysis. His example prepared young Alice to lead us from the age of Christian social analysis to that of sociological analysis.

Ely could have easily written Collin's plea to Coldwater's 1894 graduating class, "You must be American and Christian enough to consider it your chief object in life to live for the enlightenment and welfare of your community and your country."[55] Whereas Ely would have, however, gone on to quote scripture, Collin never did. Collin used the church to "talk over sociological questions." He especially welcomed workingmen "of any church or no church" to come and discuss the improvement of "not only society generally but government as well, local government especially."[56] This secular bent stands out even more when you compare Collin's writing on social purity to that of other preachers in Coldwater. To him, social purity meant improving society rather than expunging human sin.

In 1896 Collin and the church collided. After seventeen years of service to the community, ministers of the Presbytery began pestering him about his literal agreement with Presbyterian doctrines. Confident that he could not convince them of his ways, stunned by their unwillingness to accept interpretation, and very much unwilling to preach "what was not his own conviction," Kellar's reverend quit the denomination and resigned his pastorate.[57]

Dramatically, Collin then told his parish members that he did not want to split the community. He told them that he would establish a new unaffiliated church if every parishioner in the congregation agreed to join. If a single parishioner disagreed, if it would cause any level of division in the community, he would peacefully leave the city to let them go on as a unified community under a new leader. In an act of incredible solidarity, all the parishioners joined him in his defection from Presbyterian control. Collin continued as Kellar's pastor.

In his first sermon to his reconstituted parish, Collin explained that the bases of his philosophical system were found "in nature, in the bible, and in history." He told his parishioners that in addition to the Bible, his views relied on "the assistance of the best thinkers accessible to me." And his study led him to believe that the highest goal of the Church was to create "fellowship of man with man."[58] That sentence very exactly presaged Kellor's highest goals, Collin prized unity. And this necessitated that he spoke for a universalized ideal of man without regard to doctrinal splits.

Collin certainly influenced Kellar with his classes on sociology, immigration, prison reform, methods of relieving the unemployed and the situation of African-Americans.[59] As with Ely, Collin's list of topics closely approximated Kellar's later agenda.

But more subtly, as Collin, Kellor highly valued unity; her Americanization program was one long extended war on exclusion. And she fulfilled Collin's trajectory towards secular thought. As she evolved, her work increasingly ignored history, tradition, and culture and she developed a philosophy that saw all workers as members of an undifferentiated human community. Our present view of citizenship stemming from political, rather than moral or cultural considerations, echoes this split from religion to a social science model that Rev. Collin modeled.

Kellar's Launch

Finally in our catalogue of lessons, we can learn about Americanization by looking at Alice Kellor's hometown, we should note the obvious: Coldwater introduced Kellar to media. As a reporter for the *Coldwater Republican*, Kellar attended conferences of the Woman's Press Association.[60] Towards the end of her Americanization work, Kellor headed the American Association of Foreign Language Newspapers (AAFLN). As such, she controlled the majority of foreign language advertising in America. Young Alice began her ascent to media power through her Coldwater gossip column.

Nobody who read Alice's columns "Tinkles from the Telephone" or "The Telegraph" could have known that this proud close-knit town was raising a woman who would have pretentions of reshaping the world and succeed. But it is a mistake to say Kellor just happened to come from Coldwater. The strong-knit community, replete with women activists, served as a model for

Chapter One

Kellor's brand of Americanization. And, as Kellor's rejected the cultural or religious sense of citizenship for a political vision of connection, this bent towards sociology pervades the way we discuss citizenship today. In a real sense, even when Kellor worked to unite the entire world, she aimed at expanding the sense of human connection she experienced in Coldwater, via techniques she learned in Coldwater.

Coldwater took pride in its schools. When few towns actually had high schools, a four-year diploma from Coldwater's high school earned you automatic entrance into the University of Michigan. Again, Alice dropped out of high school to help her mother earn a living by doing domestic work for Coldwater's wealthier residents. In 1892, when she would have graduated, she instead reported on the proceedings for the *Coldwater Republican*. But where the school system stopped teaching young Alice, the community started.

- CHAPTER TWO -

CORNELL, BASKETBALL, and WOMEN'S AMERICANIZATION

Cornell, Segregation, and Gender

Frances Kellor might have chosen Cornell because Rev. Collin's brother was a professor there. It might have been because, unlike other universities, if you passed the entrance exam you could enroll without having graduated from high school. She might have chosen Cornell because it was a working class university. At any rate, Kellor began working towards her law degree at Cornell, at the age of twenty-two, in 1895.

The entrance exam was not easy. The test included sections on United States history, government, German language, arithmetic, and plane geometry. Young Alice had obviously learned a lot in Mary Eddy's library and Rev. Collin's classes. But Kellor left Coldwater with more than information. She carried memories of Mary Eddy as a strong female activist role model. The vibrant Women's Christian Temperance Union

Chapter Two
---

modeled public female activism for her. Via experience, she found out about wealthy donors' ability to uplift the less fortunate. She learned to network. She discovered her ability to write. And she came to bond in friendship with women. Indeed she returned to Coldwater to visit many times in the coming years.

Leaving Coldwater also had an impact on Kellor. In Coldwater, young Frances Alice Kellor went by the name "Alice" and spelled her last name "Kellar." Upon entering Cornell she dropped her middle name in name in favor of her first, Frances. According to one source, this was done to show appreciation for the older Eddy sister. Inexplicably, she also changed the spelling of her last name. In contradistinction to the vision of an Americanizer bent on foisting her ethnicity on others, this change hints at self-invention – looking forward, not backwards. From this time forward she signed her work "FAK" and would be widely known as Frances Kellor.

Cornell really only went fully co-ed with the opening of their Sage dormitory in 1875. In going coed the university was forward-thinking. We must remember that at that time many people still believed intellectual exertion harmed women. In 1870 only one-third of American colleges and universities were co-ed.[61] By admitting women, Cornell risked its prestige. It coveted having a reputation equal to that of Harvard or Yale. But the acceptance of women threatened to make them sink to the level, "of an Oberlin or a high school."[62]

Though many previously lived off-campus, in 1884 Cornell decided that all women students had to live in the new dormitory under the supervision of a female chaperone. The women protested to no avail. Though Cornell had been a leader in granting women access to higher education, by the time Kellor got there in 1895, it had tied the vision of women's liberty to an insistence on propriety, supervision, and regulation.[63] Carol Smith Rosenberg argued that "late eighteenth and most nineteenth-century Americans assumed the existence of a world composed of distinctly male and female spheres."[64] Cornell's actions provide solid evidence of Rosenberg's claim. The women were literally cloistered into what has been recently labeled a "female dominion."[65]

It is hard to gauge whether Cornell's segregation enhanced or hindered women's experience of Cornell. Female students there were targets of popular ridicule. Males in fraternities pledged not to speak to Cornell women and excluded them from all social events. Women were barred from the editorial boards of publications.[66] This hostility, though, likely brought the women closer to each other. In Coldwater, Kellor had lived exclusively with women; she had gone from her mother's home to that of the Eddy sisters. And after leaving Cornell, she often lived and worked in the female dominated world of settlement houses. Solely living with women might not have seemed like a great sacrifice to her.

Kellor became president of the female debate club.[67] Had the clubs been co-ed, this executive experience might not have been available to her. Trisha Franzen wrote, "woman-centered institutions and organizations . . . not only provided power bases for political work, they were also sites where women were mentored and promoted into social welfare and other reform-related employment."[68] This living situation further embedded Kellor into what was then called the "girls' network."[69] Thus, being cloistered in a female dominion could have inadvertent advantages. One of the women who went to school with Kellor claimed to have "danced out of Cornell" with her "heart whole, and marvelous memories behind."[70] Cornell's sexism would strike many as odious. Yet years later, Kellor kept a Cornell banner on her office wall.

Truth and Fiction

The wall at Cornell that separated women from men was porous and Kellor fought with the help of a female-run network to dismantle it. Cornell women were not totally isolated in their dormitories. Sage, the female students' dormitory, had mixed boating parties in the summer. Further evidence of sex mixing comes from the fact that fifty-five percent of female attendees who married chose Cornell men.[71] But in athletics, discrimination teetered on near exclusion. And, even within their own sphere, women were not allowed to engage in competitive sports.

Kellor's life partner, Mary Dreier, thought the creation of the Cornell rowing team came quickly in a showdown between Kellor and Cornell's president. This exciting story has the twenty-two-year-old Kellor organizing the women's rowing team at

Cornell soon after her arrival. When she asked the school to set up formal rowing courses, she got, instead, a summons to the president's office. He threatened to dismiss her. "However," Mary recalled, "she argued her case so well that he agreed not to dismiss her and decided to allow her and the other girls who wanted to learn how to manage boats, to continue."[72] Thus the Cornell Athletic Council was formed.[73] How brave and heroic for a new student with no social background! This tale, like the one wherein Coldwater's Eddy sisters found Kellor after she accidentally shot herself in the hand, is likely apocryphal.

The evidence actually indicates that a long collective battle, rather than a heated individual confrontation, established the rowing team. Other than Mary's telling of the story, we have no corroborating evidence about her confronting the university president and single-handedly winning the right to establish a team. The real story is actually more mundane, more typical of Kellor, and more praiseworthy. Kellor was role player in the battle to establish the women's rowing team at Cornell. This seems more characteristic of Kellor's overall career. She constantly formed organizations and worked within their constraints. In politics, as well as in sports, Kellor's greatest strength lay in coordinating and working within teams.

The Battle Begins

An article in the *Cornell Daily Sun* from January of 1896 tells us that the women of Cornell University petitioned the athletic council to have a male coach, Mr. Courtney, instruct them in rowing. This would have granted some official recognition to the female team. The article also stated that the agitation for this arrangement had been going on for two years. That means that it predated Kellor. The article explained that, though they had tried for the prior two years, "the obstacles seemed too great."[74] Now Cornell's president seemed to support them and they had the success of Wellesley's female rowing program with which to argue their case.

Thus, the evidence points to a change of situation, not the arrival of a single heroine who dominated the situation; change must sometimes await opportunity. But the day after petitioning the Athletic Council, because the men's coach already had enough work leading the men's team, the members voted down the women's request.[75] The political and attitudinal situation had not changed as much as the female athletes had hoped.

Just two days after their rejection by the Athletic Council, the women went outside of the campus for help. They called on the coach of the Wellesley women's boating team, Coach Lucile Eaton Hill. She sent a very interesting letter to the young athletes. Coach Hill's entire letter being printed in the school paper indicates that they had sympathizers on the editorial board. Coach Hill wrote, "Of course we do not race; we row for form, technique and pleasure, and hygienic results are prime factors."[76] This quote helps us understand some of the concerns of those thwarting the program. These shall be rehearsed in more depth later on, but competitive sports were thought unsuitable to the dainty and refined nature of women. March 1st, 1896 the eager young co-eds had Coach Hill come lecture at the university.[77] Coach Hill's public lecture outlined plans she thought Cornell should undertake for women's athletics. She also met informally with the women of the Sage dormitory.

At this point, we have our first solid evidence of Kellor's involvement in the fight for women's sports as well as many other firsts in her career. That March, the young women formed the Sports and Pastimes Association (SPA) as a blanket organization to oversee all women's athletics. Likely due to her studying law, Kellor helped form a committee to write a constitution for the group.[78] This was the first of many constitutions and organizational rules she drew up over her career. It was quickly adopted. It specified the qualifications for every elected position. Kellor took part in the government of the PSA under the meager category, "general student."[79] This is the first political organization we have a record of Kellor joining. In addition to these tasks, the women then had to raise money to buy a boat. Thus, we have the earliest evidence of Kellor's use of philanthropists to fund her projects. This extracurricular work tutored her in skills she would use as often as her law degree.

The athletes' actions resulted in a boat made of California redwood that had strips of tan and nickel trimmings. The female students' struggles and practical obstacles did not end there. They had to stop practicing for the winter because they did not have a rowing machine. The SPA voted money for one, but they had no place to store the rowing machine. The female athletes

Chapter Two

had a subscription drive to get the money to build the boathouse. They got architectural designs and land donated. The girls built the boathouse and housed the rowing machine. And by the time spring was over, they had a team that was able to row fairly well. Showing great legal savvy, in 1898 they incorporated in order to be able to own property such as sporting equipment. As a law student, Kellor might have aided in this effort.

The story of Kellor confronting Cornell's president titillates. But the strategizing, organization, and struggle this group of young women put into creating the rowing team better anticipates the Kellor's characteristic of fostering reform by fomenting group activism. The second earliest photo of Kellor actually shows her with her fellow rowers, not alone. But, unfortunately, it was not until June of 1898, two and a half years after Kellor began working to get the rowing team, and after Kellor had left the school, that the team finally officially debuted their dark blue flannel gymnasium suits and blue duck sailor hats.[80] Alas, in this early struggle, Kellor was ahead of her time.

The tedium of this tale got included for context's sake. As we will read, Kellor wrote articles and a book about sports and gender; ultimately, she argued that sports would help women become public activists. When reading her sports related work we should remember how much public fortitude was required for there to be women's sports about which to write at all. Many historians claim that the Americanization movement Kellor led only sought to oppress immigrants and rob them of their voice. But this interpretation loses viability when we learn how hard she had to fight to get her own rights vindicated. Cornell's women's rowing team started practice as early as 6:30 am. The men's team also started this early. But the men's team did not have to battle to obtain equipment.

Sports and Gender

In choosing the name "the Sports and Pastimes Association" the young women carefully avoided using the word "athletic" because it would hint at "competition, specialization, [and] a desire to be superior."[81] Needing to compromise and strategize, they sold their group as a recreation organization and thus ended up with what one student described as an "unfortunate name."[82] The struggle of Kellor and her comrades should remind us that Kellor not only wrote academic tomes that proffered pristine ideals; she engaged in activism and so often had to do battle with the popular beliefs of her time.

In the 1880s the female collegiate population routinely got calisthenics-based exercise programs to develop their form and grace.[83] YMCA instructor James Naismith invented basketball in 1891. Female coaches, such as the heavily documented and celebrated Senda Berenson Abbott, soon realized basketball's potential as a woman's sport.[84] As men kept playing football and baseball, women initially dominated basketball.[85] In North Carolina, for example, the women's intercollegiate basketball competition preceded that of the men's by a decade.[86]

But women's basketball engendered a lot of controversy. In the name of decency, men were sometimes barred from watching women play. The same Coach Hill who supported the Cornell women's rowing team argued that basketball "should be stopped absolutely so far as girls under the college age is concerned, and it should be admitted only tentatively" for older women.[87] Beyond physical damage, Coach Hill worried about, "excitement upon the emotional and nervous feminine nature, and the tendency to unsex the player."[88] Worries about women losing their femininity dominated the concerns about female sports. The cultural milieu necessitated that Kellor make her sports career, articles, and book on athletics about gender.

Did Coach Hill believe what she said about women's sports? How deep did these prejudices cut? We must remember Coach Hill worked as an advocate *for* women's athletics. But she consistently argued that it was inappropriate for women to engage in competition. We could easily excuse Hill's statements as strategic. She could have been comforting the many parents, school boards, and others in positions of power who worried about the impact of basketball on femininity. Coach Hill might have felt it necessary to distance her rowing program from basketball and competitive sports in order to save it. But she expressed the same concerns in an introduction to a book she edited that, it could safely be assumed, targeted those already practicing women's sports. People took the concerns Coach Hill expressed seriously.

Coach Berenson Abbott and Kellor made similar statements about competition. Kellor, more than any other early female author on the subject, really interrogated the meaning of competitive sports for women. Without evidence, it would be patronizing to assume these women did not believe that which they wrote. Yet for Kellor, as we shall see, we have evidence that she was being strategic. Kellor consciously managed her presentation of gender throughout her career. Her reasoning changed as circumstances allowed. Her rapid rise in the world shows that she positioned herself well.

Gendered Basketball

One historian concluded that Kellor's writing "foreshadowed the philosophy of Title IX by the better part of a century."[89] The literature on the history of women's sports largely overlooks Kellor. But, she was a seminal theorist of sports psychology.[90] Kellor published her first article on women's athletics: "A Psychological Basis for Physical Culture," in 1898. Written just after earning her law degree at Cornell and just before her entry into the University of Chicago, the article's heading simply listed her as "Frances Alice Kellor, Coldwater, Mich."

In her 1898 article, Kellor wrote that, "It is assumed in this discussion that women and men are attempting to do an equal amount and equal variety of brain work, and this being true, there should be an equal amount of energy."[91] In the first hands-on social science research we know of Kellor undertaking, she conducted interviews that revealed that women doing calisthenics continued thinking about their schoolwork. Kellor concluded that calisthenics without the playfulness that

Chapter Two

competition engendered did not fully relieve the mind of anxiety and thus did not free up energy. Sports with play were necessary because mental rest and stimulation were "indispensable to the best and most original intellectual work."[92] Thus, Kellor began her work as a hands-on social scientist and announced that she herself aspired to the title of intellectual.

In her 1898 article on physical culture, Kellor praised and quoted Coach Hill's program at Wellesley. She noted the ongoing success of the organization Coach Hill helped found at Cornell. People, Kellor acknowledged, worried that with competitive sports women might develop "a spirit of rivalry similar to that existing among men."[93] Perhaps strategically, she offered a solution: not keeping records of victories or defeats would prevent this nasty potential side effect.

Kellor's final sentence in the article showed both subtle defiance and Kellor consciously positioning herself within the public opinion. It seemed "far from probable," Kellor reassured us, "that women will acquire the same spirit of contest as has man." If it did, she hoped it would happen "with the sanction of public opinion." In the meantime, her "womanliness and conservative tendencies will operate so that she will not act otherwise than in accord with the prevailing opinion and democratic wish."[94] While she conformed, Kellor herein identified public opinion as the real obstacle and hinted at progress.

In 1900, Kellor published an overview of women's basketball. At this point she no longer needed to argue for playing because both high school and college women played the sport. But gender issues still pervaded the discourse. She explained that while men only had one set of basketball rules, women had three. These three variations descended in roughness from the men's rules to the women's. At Hyde Park High School and the University of Chicago, for both of which Kellor coached, they played the first and second most "male" types of basketball. The aforementioned Senda Berenson Abbott invented the third and most feminine type of basketball. Berenson's rules restricted women to zones and forbade "snatching" the ball when others were holding it. Kellor did not discuss Berenson's type of basketball being played in Illinois. Thus, by omission, Kellor let the reader know that her region had rejected these feminized rules.

Kellor told her readers that the University of Chicago had only had one injury requiring substitution in two years, due to good supervision. Girls got hurt at the high school level, she asserted, not because they play the roughest style of basketball, but due to a lack of supervision. In terms of prescription, Kellor advocated more training followed by the constant application of normal men's rules by officials.[95] Thus, the very mode of playing basketball displayed a gendered spectrum. Kellor coached a male style of basketball while arguing for the adoption and consistent application of male rules.

35

Chapter Two

Sports and the Female Mind

In 1906, an Illinois conference is said to have supported the coming 1907 ban on girls' basketball teams playing other schools' teams.[96] At this meeting of the Public School Physical Training Society, Kellor read and then published an eleven-page article entitled "Ethical Value of Sports for Women." One modern writer specifically implicated Kellor's article in the premature downfall of Illinois' intercollegiate women's basketball.[97] A contemporaneous reviewer of Kellor, however, criticized her for never mentioning that when women play "basket-ball as men play it is likely to prove harmful."[98] So while the modern writer blames Kellor for not going far enough, her contemporary complained that she went too far.

"The Ethical Value of Sports for Women" detailed themes Coach Kellor had developed during her five years as a basketball coach at settlement houses and high schools, as well in her position as an "Instructor in Physical Culture" at the University of Chicago.[99] We do not always primarily consider sports a vehicle for ethics, but that is the theme of this seasoned coach's paper. And, Kellor showed astonishment and disappointment that many other coaches did not recognize the ethical dimensions of sports.

Kellor spent much of her paper criticizing the typical female mindset. She told of one girl who, off a good hit in baseball, nearly got to second base and then returned to first base! When asked why, she replied, "I noticed the first baseman was a friend of mine and I came back to tell her something."[100]

Kellor was flabbergasted. She described another girl who chased a ball into centerfield that went under the scoreboard. When the player ran up, two men were standing near. The female player asked, "Would one of you men mind getting that ball for me?" This pose of helplessness in front of men infuriated Kellor. Coach Kellor also claimed that "some women are abnormally sensitive and introspective or morbid, and live too much on the subjective side of life." Boldly, she asserted these tendencies drew them into "religious cults which appeal primarily to the subjective self." Sports, she claimed were "objective" and prioritized action over feeling. Thus, competitive sports could help to remake females' psyches.[101]

Defensively, Kellor reassured the reader, "I have yet to see a group of girls made masculine by holding these ideals before them." But in a bold cultural summary she claimed, "Every woman's club which makes it possible to have games is erecting a barrier against nervousness and too much introspection."[102] Women needed to cultivate "observation, attention, concentration, memory, imagination, initiation, reason, and will power."[103] By cultivating these attributes in women, basketball could increase their power. And, Kellor insisted that these were "not essentially masculine qualities, they are but human qualities."[104] Women's deficiency in these qualities meant that they needed athletic programs even more than men.

In addition to "individual" characteristics, Kellor described the potential "social" lessons in sports, such as their "democratic" nature. In her words, "A game is a well nigh perfect democracy.

Nothing is so good for the girl as to find that money, clothes, family, prestige, or 'pull' are as nothing, - that they do not help her to play good ball or make a team." As a person without any heritage, Kellor was predisposed to appreciate that in sports a girl "stands or falls absolutely by what she is and can do, and realizes that the game makes all equal."[105] In praising this component of sports, Kellor praised the very attribute that allowed this child of poverty to befriend the powerful Astor, Vanderbilt, and Roosevelt families. In terms of social lessons, sports taught teamwork, the need for social cooperation, equality, and meritocracy.

But perhaps the most personally revealing gender concept to emerge in Kellor's 1906 "The Ethical value of Sports for Women" concerned her aesthetic ideal of gendered decorum. Her ideal women were to combine assertiveness with poise. She would not allow women who "persisted in poor dress" off the court to play with the team. Slang was forbidden on the court. She asserted that "Disagreeable expressions, uncouth language, squealing and yelling, crying, lying about the floor, eating between halves of games, [and] masculinity" undermined the aesthetic she sought.[106] This last attribute is especially interesting considering the fact that she herself regularly donned male attire. In a delicate balance, women presenting themselves as controlled and aware of decorum would allow them to challenge gender boundaries, to compete in male arenas.

Athletic Games Introduced

Kellor's efforts as a sports theorist culminated in her 1909 *Athletic Games in the Education of Women*. This book introduced new sports philosophy stances as it developed older ones. *Athletic Games* was co-written with the director of the University of Chicago's Woman's Department of Physical Education, Gertrude Dudley. Kellor worked in Dudley's athletic department at the University of Chicago. But at the time of publication, Kellor was working full-time with immigrants; their professional relationship had long passed.

In this work, the two examples of ditzy female behavior that appeared in Kellor's 1906 paper reappeared. And Kellor's arguments for women using men's rules also got repeated herein. But that does not mean that Dudley only lent her name to the book. Dudley had a long history of sports activism that paralleled Kellor's. As early as 1901, Dudley created intercollegiate basketball games at the University of Chicago. In 1904, she helped establish the Women's Athletic Association (WAA). Perhaps significantly, Dudley's group embraced the word "athletic" that Kellor's Cornell group had avoided in order to distance themselves from the implication of competition. Yet simultaneously, the motto of Dudley's WAA, "Play for Play's Sake," seems to have been chosen specifically to denounce the idea of victory as a goal.[107] Regardless, Dudley was a strong presence in female athletics. And although Dudley never wrote anything about sports apart from this book she co-authored with

Kellor, it does not mean that Kellor only used her old colleague's name for credibility.

In addition to personal experience, *Athletic Games* rested upon quite a bit of national research. Via survey, the authors determined what varieties of basketball were played at what level of schools. They also looked for the prevalence of intra-mural play. Less than one-third of the eighty-three settlement houses they examined included any athletics. And some responded that they avoided competition because sports "make the girls rough."[108] Their survey found that fifty-seven percent of athletic instructors had attended schools of physical training, thirteen percent went to schools of elocution, etc. Only twenty-one percent of instructors taught athletics alone. The authors vainly scoured college course catalogues to look for signs of ethical or sociological theory in the physical training courses the instructors took.

The effort to gather objective facts did not preclude the authors from having strong sociological and theoretical points of view and agendas. They thought the physical benefits of sports too well known to require elaboration. Instead they focused on the moral aspects of sports. Kellor still dwelt, as she had in 1906, on sports' ability to shape personal characteristics. But *Athletic Games* greatly increased attention to the social implications of these personal characteristics and their importance for society.

Women to Become Political

In *Athletic Games* the authors argued that we needed to start paying attention to women's sports education because women's roles in society were rapidly changing. The authors told us that in 1900 more than 5 million women had gainful employment. The extension of property rights had made women "investors, capitalists, and employers." Women now also entered into the political arena more frequently. Some states had let women have the franchise, and in others "they vote upon educational questions and other public matters such as taxation."[109] The authors repeatedly announced "the demands now made upon women are different from those of fifty or twenty-five years ago, when the home and social duties constituted the chief claim."[110] As women became public actors, their old modes of socialization needed modern supplements.

Increasing the parameters of Kellor's 1906 article, the authors emphasized the social goals of changing women's psyches. They claimed that traditional women's "sense of morality is personal rather than social and passive rather than active."[111] When women "condemn murderers but not adulterators of food or officials of a trust who put up the price of ice so that babies in tenements die for lack of it, they fail to see that they are condemning the lesser rather than the greater offender, simply because the connection of cause and effect is not so apparent in the latter cases."[112] Rather than gossip about infidelity, they wanted American – born women to "lend a hand to their immigrant sisters" and to "protest against adulterated foods and medicines" even if they do not use them.[113] In a statement both slightly misogynistic and hopeful, they declared that women as a rule are "indifferent to any form of morality other than the virtue of their own sex."[114] As public actors, women had to start to look outside of their homes for morality.

Social Consciousness Detailed

Athletic Games retains a sense of Coldwater's small-town Protestant morals. In it, the authors quoted the famous female reformer Jane Addams as denouncing "The dance halls filled with frivolous and vapid young people in a feverish search for pleasure." In an overt ode to the past, Addams called the dance halls "a sorry substitute for the immemorial dances on the village green in which all of the older people of the village participated."[115] In choosing this quote Kellor and her partner indicated some level of nostalgia for the past and dislike for the modern urban predicament. Victorian overtones lingered in their damnation of dance halls.

Even so, *Athletic Games* looked beyond dogmatic Protestant morality. The continuing influence of H. P. Collin's practical Christianity appeared when Kellor suggested that basketball can provide a healthy alternative to dance halls. In this section she and Dudley addressed the objections of Christians who would not want such activities on Sunday by noting that many working women only had this day off. Furthermore, "The dance hall, the picnic, the excursion all run on this day. Why not be practical Christians and understand the methods of business competitors and counteract them at every vulnerable spot?"[116] Christianity had to give way to modern situations. Kellor already grounded her philosophy in pragmatism rather than dogmatism.

Christianity only gets mentioned twice in this book. In the other reference the authors claim social ethics get retarded via women's "interpretation of Christian teaching along the narrow path of individual salvation rather than as an injunction to lose one's life in order to find it more abundantly through effort in behalf of the community."[117] Collin taught her well - perhaps too well. Kellor almost never again mentions Christianity after this 1909 writing. The ethic that shines through here worships at an altar of social improvement via community awareness and activism. It is within the sacrifice to the group that one finds salvation.

An overemphasis on individualism could, in fact, harm social causes. The authors asserted that women change occupations more rapidly than men. This meant that they might "first consider whether they as individuals need the union, not whether the movement for bettering conditions needs them." Focusing on individual needs undercut the social understanding required for unions: "At the very basis of their struggle for better conditions, higher wages, more leisure and better citizenship lies the necessity for team work and group loyalty." Dudley and Kellor also hoped that trade unions would use sports to give the female workers "consciousness of a common cause."[118] Sports taught a social, and thus pro-social, outlook.

Chapter Two

And this social team consciousness needed moral underpinnings. In a section entitled, "Social Qualities and Efficiency" the authors warned that "One may have coolness, accuracy, judgment and many other qualities, but unless these are brought into an ethical adjustment team work and social consciousness do not result."[119] Kellor retroactively sided with her activist mentor, Mary Eddy, when she denounced "non-ethical" organizations that "exist solely for the entertainment of their members."[120] Sports with ethics in mind instilled an ability to work without ego on a team for the benefit of the group. It was hoped that such a posture would transfer to the desire to work in groups for social causes.

There is also a Victorian small-town morality in these sports theorists' appreciation of the public gaze. They linger on the importance of public decorum. These concerned women wrote that audiences would only provide moral uplift if jeering did not happen. More personally, the authors claimed that "Players in perfect physical condition are a delight. With gathered-up strength and a fair amount of muscle, good mind, elastic step, good clear skin and bright eyes, they are in good spirits and good humor and not too confident." *Athletic Games* compared this to a team that "looks dull, languid and listless, with slouching demeanor, a sour or bored expression and a take-it-for-granted air!"[121] Herein we find the ideals and morals that Kellor sought to promote via her own presentation.

The descriptions of poised feminine aggressive women that *Athletic Games* fleshes out present a nearly spiritual version of activist ideals. They often echo Christian missionary sensibilities. The code of social ethics sports impart, we are told, should have "no more sense of giving than of receiving, no admission of superiority, no attitude of judgment, no consciousness of magnanimity, no reliance on patronage."[122] In a fine distinction the authors cut, they concluded that philanthropist were personally motivated while true social ethics should command purely altruistic efforts. In a nearly spiritual manner, the individual needed to lose herself in her social task.

But Kellor did not only prize self-abnegation. She and Dudley wrote that "the dominating note in women's sports should always be the joy and exhilaration and fun of playing, not the grim determination to win at any cost." She did not want her athletes to become "too hard and business-like."[123] The phrase "play spirit" appears from her earliest writing on sports to her last. Kellor claimed that the routine of reformatories killed the "play spirit" and thus turned out "a machine, which without its operator either runs amuck or becomes a mere automaton."[124] Kellor found the discipline and team work of progressive reform fun.

Athletic Games provides a prescription for social activism and the remaking of women's postures and attitudes towards the world. Yet these are also perhaps the most personal of any of Kellor's writings. To understand these writings is to understand her ideals, her sense of decorum, and her sense of the importance of fun as well as discipline. Coach Kellor embodied these attributes.

Chapter Two

Athletic Scholarship

Kellor has been nearly excluded from intellectual history. Yet *Athletic Games* attempted to capture and guide the ethical changes necessitated by women's changing place in society. The proposed use of sports to remake women's ethics also points to a couple of possible reason for her exclusion. One reason, of course, is that she is not a male. Only a couple of feminist historians recognize any women among the pantheon of progressive intellectuals. In addition, while *Athletic Games* contains some social theorizing, it largely provides a nuts and bolts look at practice and how changing practice could change our thoughts. In Kellor's time, the work's association with practical reform and action would have lowered its esteem in the eyes of the male-dominated academic world.[125]

Yet, Kellor and Dudley's awareness of the divide between intellectual and active learning put her in the middle of their contemporary progressive intellectuals' discussions. Progressive intellectuals such as John Dewey often discussed their frustration with the conceptual divide between thought and action.[126] Dudley and Kellor echoed this sentiment when they wrote, "The demand for social education is met now, so far as it is met at all, by instruction along purely intellectual lines, by courses in economics, sociology, politics, etc., in what one might call the technique rather than in the spirit."[127] Athletics taught the spirit. When students engaged in sports they did not receive university credits. These physical culturists lamented that this new model of learning through action had yet to cut its way through "custom, prejudice and tradition."[128]

Not only did we need instruction that departed from the purely intellectual, we needed to recognize the intellectual content in sports. More athletic educators needed to consider "their place in the social structure." Kellor and Dudley expressed disappointment that in the training of athletic instructors, "sociology was in no case included among the subjects of training." As a result, these instructors had "a narrow horizon and lose their perspective and the relation of their work to citizenship and progress."[129] If we define intellectuals as persons that put their actions into a conceptual framework, Kellor qualifies.

Lessons for Americanization

Kellor sought to Americanize via engaging citizens in participatory democracy. Evidence for this claim appears in *Athletic Games* when the authors laud the fact that one or two settlement houses had now "provided athletic classes for various local unions and that the unions themselves were increasingly taking "an interest in games as a means of making a more efficient democracy."[130] Along these lines, the book provided an interesting justification for sports leagues. The authors wrote that the "formation of athletic associations . . . encourage student self-government." These associations also bring "people together in pleasant democratic association."[131]

While emphasizing teamwork, sports would empower individuals. These democratic enthusiasts argued that the reasoning behind sports rules or rulings needed to be explained because, "Nothing is more detrimental to the spirit and democracy of games than the superior cock-sureness of the instructor" who will provide no reasons.[132] Furthermore, in *Athletic Games* Kellor argued that coaches should remain inconspicuous because, "As a rule, players do better work and develop initiative, self-reliance and other qualities more rapidly when they are not dominated by her presence and personality."[133] Rather than coerce people into passive conformity, Kellor sought to empower the very minority group to which she belonged: women.

Also significant, in terms of Americanization, this 1909 read claimed, "Folk dances appeal to the various nationalities and some may understand the purposes of the union better through its simple appeal to their love of their home country and its associations."[134] This book will argue that Kellor, at times, seemed to embrace what might be called "Multicultural Nationalism." And though referring to labor unions, this 1909 statement seemed unaware of xenophobia and indicates a sort of thinking compatible with someone having some level of regard for the nationalist potential inherent in cultural pluralism.

Americanization versus Multiculturalism

And herein a nuance concerning Kellor's tolerance merits attention. *Athletic Games* assumes, celebrates, and tries to guide women's emergence from the domestic sphere into the public sphere. As a progressive, Kellor celebrated such progress. Susan Okin has recently argued that a tension exists between multiculturalism and women's rights. Okin asserts, "most cultures have as one of their principal aims the control of women by men."[135] Kellor denounced traditional practices where girls were being pressured to leave school to enter arranged marriages with cousins. It is instructive to note that Kellor did not single out any particular immigrant groups for condemnation. Kellor held a progressive view of history. She only denounced the generic preindustrial confinement of women.

A gendered lens sensitizes us to the potential for emancipation for half of the immigrant population in Kellor's progressive Americanization program. Kellor's vision herein was not purely negative. She fought *for* women's empowerment. In this respect her values were decidedly progressive and not Victorian. While potentially in conflict with traditional immigrant gender roles, her progressive argument for feminism did not aim to limit women's choices or diminish liberty. Kellor, in fact, rarely judged immigrant cultures. Yet she is clearly fighting for a feminist agenda. And as such one could argue that she disrespected traditional cultures. But the more appreciative reading would notice how Kellor presaged, formed and promoted the modern view of women as public political actors. To the extent that females play sports or engage politically, they embody Kellor's modernist ideals.

Radically, when her contemporaries worked to convince Americans to put aside their fears that sports would make women too masculine, Kellor argued that women needed sports

Chapter Two

precisely because they needed to become more masculine. Kellor wanted women to become active shapers of the modern world into which they were emerging. She wished other women to take on the public reform roles to which her Coldwater, Michigan mentors, the Eddy sisters, had dedicated their lives. Whereas Kellor does not totally disparage families, she does not want them to continue to occupy a central place in women's mental landscape.

Not only was the demand for women's "development of group consciousness beyond the family circle" theoretical and political, it was personal.[136] Neither Kellor nor Dudley married men or had children. Both led very public lives. And Kellor's urging of women to take on public political roles did not only apply to other women. After completing her law degree at Cornell, rather than settling down, Kellor spent the next two years in prisons helping the world to see the potential in incarcerated African – American women in the South.

– CHAPTER THREE –

SOUTHERN FEMALE AFRICAN – AMERICAN PRISONERS AND WHITE WOMEN

Kellor Attacks Biological Racism and Sexism

After graduating from Cornell and before heading to the University of Chicago, Kellor returned to visit Coldwater. Celia Parker Woolley wrote about meeting Kellor there in her book, *The Western Slope*. Kellor made Woolley think of gender issues: "A self-made woman! We worship the self-made man, base and pinnacle of the republic, but imagination quails a little before the self made woman, who has 'carved her own career.'" Yet Woolley then assured the readers that "Frances has done this, without injury, as I see, to that precious thing we call womanliness."[137]

Chapter Three

Kellor had indeed taken the path less traveled. She was just the third woman to graduate from Cornell with a law degree. This accomplished, Kellor now enthusiastically effused about her plan to enroll in the University of Chicago's criminology program. This ruffled Woolley's feminine sensibilities. Woolley advised her to "rest . . . stop stinting yourself of every reasonable comfort, eat more food, wear better clothes, live and enjoy yourself like other girls."[138] Kellor, instead, sought to spend the summer in prisons gathering data to challenge the world's leading criminal sociologist. While she never graduated from the University of Chicago program, her achievements reveal an astounding ability for comprehensive thought and a deep attachment to helping women.

In academia, the biological explanation for crime had credence during the transition into the twentieth century. Kellor has been credited with leading the transition to environmental explanations in the academic field of criminology.[139] Whereas classical theories of criminology considered crime a rational individual choice, the new school of biological positivism measured the inherent tendency towards criminality in groups. Rather than crime being an individual choice or a result of bad genes, Kellor led a generation toward the view that environmental conditions fostered criminality.[140] As in sports theory, Kellor made seminal contributions to academic criminology.

Kellor's work at the University of Chicago resulted in the book, *Experimental Sociology: Descriptive and Analytic*. The book, as well as the many articles and considerable research that supported it, specifically aimed to challenge Cesare Lombroso and the Italian school of criminology he led. It seems hard to believe that Lombroso was once taken seriously, but he was one of the leading criminal sociologists in the world. And, as ripe for an obvious challenge as Lombroso seems to us today, directly challenging him, when just a female graduate student, demonstrated a great deal of confidence and nerve in Kellor.

Lombroso practiced anthropometrics, the measurement of people. Seeking to prove the existence of the biological disposition for crime by noting bodily commonalities in female criminals, he made completely outrageous statements. For example, in his book, *The Female Offender*, he wrote, "She has very strong jaws and cheek-bones, sessile ears, hypertrophy of the incisors, atrophy of the lateral teeth, and dullness of the sense of touch. She is, in short, the complete type, not of a born criminal, but of a prostitute."[141] Since Kellor lived with other women her entire life, more than a dislike of absurdity might have occurred to her as she read Lombroso's claim that "among lesbian couples who live together as heterosexuals, at least one is usually a prostitute."[142] Regardless of Kellor's motivation, Lombroso became her academic target. She became the first person to refute Lombroso by replicating his studies.[143]

Lombroso categorized female criminals by their weight, cranium shapes, height, and hairiness, as well as dullness of vision, hearing, smell, and taste.[144] Despite what she deemed their "weirdness," Kellor also engaged in anthropometric measurements by employing an early precursor to the lie-detector, the kymograph. One reporter claimed that this strange precursor to the lie detector could "know positively whether that person is criminal or honest." He even told readers, "It will also tell the extent of vanity or modesty." The Kymograph measured respiration and heart rate during electric shock and questioning. Providing evidence that Kellor might have an odd place in the history of science, the newspaperman concluded, "It is only recently that its [the Kymograph] possibilities came to be recognized through Miss Kellor's investigation."[145]

To demolish Lombroso's sexist theories, Kellor first measured and compared White women in college to White women in Northern prisons. She found no significant differences between their features and sensitivity to pain. Then, to systematically attack racism, in 1900, she received funding from a woman's group and traveled 3,277 miles through eight states in the South to test African-American women in Southern penitentiaries.[146] With this evidence she hoped to show that environmental factors, not biology, accounted for differences between criminal and non-criminal women.

All totaled, our fledgling sociologist spent nearly two years in prisons. By the end of this research, she had enough evidence to assert, "It is of no practical significance if an individual possesses asymmetries, high cheek-bones, or heavy jaw."[147] She sought to cast Lombroso out of sociology. "Many Americans know criminal sociology only through Lombroso and his popular articles, and these are not representative of the serious subject of the study." After her monumental study she was able to brag that "European investigators have devoted more attention to the theoretical work. The Unites States has emphasized the practical side, because its best investigators have been practical, experienced men."[148] With one tour and book, this graduate student seemingly defeated Lombroso, vindicated the criminal sociology of Chicago and the U.S. and put a serious dent in the growing scientific justifications of racism and sexism.

Kellor's Egalitarianism

Kellor's first article on crime and first academic article had the sensational title, "Sex in Crime." Her first article on sports claimed that, though needing the same mental breaks to do the same sort of intellectual work as men, women were naturally "less active and more phlegmatic" than men.[149] It admitted differences between men and women. Though published the very same month, "Sex in Crime" argued for total equality between sexes. The article contended that women were not "made of finer clay." It announced that such thinking has made women's lives "one of restricted activity and slavery rather than one of freedom of activity and independence." Such sexist thought portrayed women as "midway between a child and a man."[150]

Specifically, "Sex in Crime" argued that women were just as criminally inclined as men. Women only appeared less criminal due to being spared punishment, biased statistics, and

Chapter Three

overlooking women's crimes of prostitution, abortion, and infanticide due to their private nature. Differences in gendered crime statistics resulted from "opportunity" not "inclination."[151] Yes, women's size also limited their ability to commit some crimes. But the main limitation on women's equality in this arena came from men. Men protecting women from the struggle for existence had diminished the aggressive tendencies that fostered crime. She illustrated this point by noting women cannot commit many crimes because they are barred from power in government and business. Given the opportunity, more would get arrested for graft and embezzlement. One wonders if any other social scientists have used this tactic to argue for equality previously or since.

"Sex in Crime" held women as biologically equal, but still gave a lot of power to the environment. Her book on African-American women prisoners sought to defeat the biological argument. But before launching into the evidence she mustered on behalf of these downtrodden women, we shall look at a personal interaction with a prisoner she included in the book. The selection has been included due to the rarity of documented personal dialogue between Kellor and others. In addition this interaction speaks to the charge that Kellor, like other progressives, had an elitist attitude towards those she sought to help.

In the vignette the African – American inmate does not want to have her photograph taken. Kellor is authoritative.

"I hears you want to take my picture."

"Who told you so?"

"Well, look heah. They tells me downstairs as how you've been down takin' pictures of our houses [which was true], and now you wants mine, and I want you to dun understan' I won't have it." [Admission Kellor's]

"Didn't I tell you what I wanted it for?"

"Yes."

"Have you got any reason not to believe me?"

"No."

"Then I'll tell you what you can do. You can come in here immediately and have your respiration taken, or you can go downstairs, for I have no use for you."

The woman didn't like being turned out, so she came in."[152]

One scholar profiling Kellor argued that she had an "antidemocratic impulse implicit in her conception of reform."[153] Another scholar noted that progressive intellectuals had to contend with the irony of wanting to serve "the whole of the people" as "an elitist whose own mores and life situation would prove somewhat alienating from the very public he or she had chosen to serve."[154] In his charge of elitism, this scholar leveled the accusation that many progressives "could not imagine democratic change arising spontaneously from the people."[155] Kellor's harshness with this African – American lends credence to the accusations that Kellor and thus her Americanization movement might have been harsh and domineering towards the poor, immigrants, and the powerless.

One could also argue that Kellor included this conversation in her book to convey a tone that showed her ability to command in field where professionalism meant being "more like a man."[156] She likely understood that readers might question the authority of a young woman taking on the world's leading criminal sociologist. But Kellor did not seem prone to insecurity.

Overall, the evidence indicates that Kellor's tone reflected her taking herself seriously as a scientist with a task to perform. When Celia Parker Woolley encountered Kellor before she left Coldwater for the University of Chicago, she asked Kellor about the humanity of the kymograph's using reactions to pain to measure the subjects. With a dollop of hauteur Kellor replied, "Our studies are pursued in the interest of science. The sentimental aspect does not interest us."[157] Even when speaking with college-educated White women such as Celia Parker, confident haughtiness suffused her discussions of scientific research. Young Kellor, twenty-five years of age, took on airs with all.

The Elitist Charge Returns

In *Experimental Sociology* as well as the many articles that accompanied it, Kellor demeaned African – American culture.[158] We cannot but cringe at one of her harshest statements: "No race outside of barbarism had so low a grade of domestic life. In none other the child received so little training."[159]

And yet such a description, though with less tact, parallels many conservative estimations of the inner-city gangster culture we hear today. Her accord with today's liberals, on this front, would come with her blaming environmental factors for the barbarism she saw.

Published in 1901, *Experimental Sociology* remains cognizant of the lingering effects of slavery and poverty, "Negroes have not had quite forty years in which to *create* and establish all the sound principles of domestic life. Only in a small degree have they been taught the need of morality, sobriety, and fidelity, and in matters of cleanliness, sanitation, prevention of disease, etc., they have been left to look out for themselves. Where from five to ten persons cook, eat, sleep, and die in one or two rooms, what can the family morality be?"[160] [Italic in original] Despite a lack of appreciation for diversity, herein Kellor's attention to environmental factors helped launch our modern sensitivity to situation.

Also arguing on her side, Kellor pulls no punches when describing the racist horrors of the South. She reported that women put in fourteen-hour days manufacturing shoes in Southern penitentiaries. To keep aged female inmates working long hours, they were sometimes given stimulants.[161] And, "Flogging with a heavy strap is the universal method of punishment. The men are flogged upon the bare back, while the women are sometimes allowed to retain their clothing."[162] She brought discriminatory practices to America's attention such as this one noted by a Southern man, "if a white man murders a negro, we *let him off;* if a negro murders a white man, we *lynch him.*"[163] [italics hers]. Kellor's displeasure at African-American culture did not aim at justifying the status quo.

Furthermore, Kellor's analysis routinely blamed the mainstream culture's attitudes for minorities' failures. In the South she opined that, "Until there is greater respect for the negro home, the morals in that home will be lax."[164] Employing a humanistic analysis, she noted that people often behave well in order to be seen by others as upstanding. Therefore African – American crime could be explained by the fact that "If they [African-Americans] are honest, they obtain little credit for it. It is difficult for them to reach an ideal of self respect when no one has faith in that ideal for them."[165] As Kellor argued concerning immigrants, the majority populations' cultural attitudes and exploitation created poor attitudes in Southern African-Americans.

Intimate Sociology

It has been argued that women developed a more personal, empathetic brand of sociology than the one men championed.[166] While *Experimental Sociology* contained rigorous analysis and historical frameworks, suggested complex legal reforms, and used the probing kymograph, Kellor's approach revealed a belief that getting to understand the cause of criminality ultimately required getting to know the incarcerated women personally.

In reading *Experimental Sociology* we learn about the lives and mindsets of African-American inmates at the turn of the prior century. Much of it is charming. For example, Kellor asks about the women's reading habits. Forty-five percent had only read the Bible. She finds that their favorite dime novels were "Jesse James and Diamond Dick."[167] And, while fifty-seven percent had seen no plays whatever, two of the plays they had seen were "Ten Nights in a Bar-room," and "The White Slaves."[168] As children, in order of popularity, the female African-American inmates played: dolls, hide and seek, ball, jump the rope, see-saw, jackstones, and marbles.

Sometimes morality creeps into Kellor's intimate descriptions of these women. She editorialized, "While outdoor games are physically more healthful, the freedom from supervision makes possible the acquirement of bad habits and the formation of doubtful associates."[169] Still, she sounds very enthusiastic when she describes two games peculiar to the South: hide-switches and poison.

Kellor sometimes tells her readers good things about African – Americans. She found the wishes of both Whites and African-Americans fell into the categories of physical needs, domestic and economic conditions, sentiment or sociability, and ideas of religion and ethics. The stress on economics, Kellor tells us, reflected women's economic dependence. In one of several favorable comparisons, she then noted that though their desires were the same overall, in African-Americans she found "less cynicism and stronger family ties than among whites."[170]

Chapter Three

In *Experimental Sociology* we hear the voices of the women themselves. In a section on religion one woman says she, "Tried, but never did get religion."[171] In a statistical analysis African – American and Whites' letters home, Kellor details how many ask for support, concern affection and children, tell of loneliness, etc. But she also illustrates these categories with page after page of long letter excerpts. Empathy can be seen in Kellor's introduction to one group of letters: "This shows the feeling of many of these women toward policemen, and sometimes justly." One of the letters reads:

> "I was going home when a policeman runned after me and took me to the station-house and told the Captain that he knew me and that I had no home. The next morning he told the Judge that I was under the influence of liquor. If this be let run no one can go out on the streets: but he got the wrong pig by the ear this time. I didna have any money about me to buy me any drink."[172]

Kellor's Comprehensive Vision

For all of *Experimental Sociology*'s inclusion of personal vignettes, it is a thorough work of social analysis. In an analysis that foreshadows the philosopher Michel Foucault, she situates her reform within the evolution of "the *idea* of crime."[173] [italic in original] The idea progresses through four historical stages and points to the environmental view of crime and criminal reform which Kellor helped pioneer.

In primitive society, revenge was administered by individuals or via "private warfare and blood feuds."[174] As society developed, the state took over punishment. But vengeance and retribution still motivated reactions to crime. During the Middle Ages, the royal idea of the protection of society began to emerge. Still, in this stage the system employed death, torture and mutilation. And while still violent, by the eighteenth century the concept of due process had started to emerge.

Kellor announced that "the fourth period – that of prevention – is just dawning."[175] With such a perspective, we could aright society in order that people might not commit crimes. And if people did commit crimes, rather than vengeance, science would study the person and their social situation in order to readjust them to society. She said the punitive method was centuries old and "conservative;" her preventative tact was modern and "revolutionary."[176]

Kellor was a progressive. She believed that society was improving and the past was barbaric. Our society tends to eschew words such as "primitive" and judgments of culture. Yet, it was from this vantage point that Kellor could declare that, "The South is still in the age of revenge and punishment. Its system is neither systematic nor scientific."[177] Sharper yet she declared, "With reference to Virginia almost nothing need be said. Her system dates back to the days when mutilation was a common penalty."[178] In one article heading, Kellor overtly told us that the "South is Backward."[179] If we eschew the right to judge African-American culture or any others, we must also give up the right to judge the South.

And Kellor applies some of the same solutions she has for others to African-American culture. In Kellor's 1909 book *Athletic Games in the Education of Women,* Kellor argued that sports could make women more aggressive and active politically. In *Experimental Sociology,* Kellor argued that sports could help African-Americans overcome the "spirit of imitation and dependence" and foster "independence."[180] The same wording describing this athletic benefit appeared in Kellor's 1909 book. Thus, she provides the exact same solution for White women as she does for African - American culture.

Again, from a perspective of progress, Kellor felt free to judge and make recommendations for the indigenous culture. As her mentor Rev. H. P. Collin would have it, she not only hoped that the quality of Southern African – American preachers would improve, but that they would study sociology. Collin's voice likely echoed in hers as she said sociological sermons could improve the parishioner, "not by characterizing him as a transgressor, but by enabling him to reason out his own position" on social problems.[181] Here again, we see Kellor wishing to empower those in society with the least power. As we saw with the basketball example, cultural improvement herein was not only for African-Americans.

Controversially, our protagonist accepted segregation. She wrote, "There is a misapprehension in the South of the idea of 'social equality.' They [Whites] believe it implies marriage, entrance to homes, etc. The use of that term in the North does not mean mingling at the white's social functions, or entering the home, but economic, financial, cultural and educational conditions that will enable them to maintain similar grades in their own race and to have literature and recreations of equal standards."[182] Thus, Kellor aimed at equality, while assuring her Southern readers that they could keep their separation.

With reason, this Washingtonian compromise of racial separation would infuriate many. But, as she did with women and sports, Kellor understood the limits of the social milieu in which she worked and hinted at different social arrangements in the future. On the edge, she prognosticated, "The free intermingling of the two [races] is impossible, at least for many generations, because a deeply-rooted social and racial prejudice and undesirable because it is not the best way to help the negroes." The clause concerning generations was radical in its time. But for the moment, she concluded that "The negro is practically disfranchised, and so revolutionary is the feeling of the whites that any attempt to force a change is useless."[183]

Kellor's discussion of segregation only lasts a couple of pages. But this female lawyer advocated page after page of technical legal reform. She attacked the corruption of judges who get paid by the conviction. Many of her suggestions concerned technical issues such as rules of evidence and burden of proof.

Chapter Three

She looked at the corruption of the jury system resulting from people paying jurors to replace them, the point being that her sociology was not purely sentiment and broad observation; it engaged in the details of the legal system.

Two of the eight chapters of *Experimental Sociology* lay out detailed reforms and proposals for further research. But nearly every page follows Kellor's characteristic theme of blaming the social attitudes of majority culture for the degradation of the poor. This becomes more remarkable when we recall that her overall project is not saving incarcerated African-American women from their plight, but attacking the very basis of scientific racism and sexism. In a sense, it was just an added bonus that Kellor's voluminous work touched upon the overall plight of the African-American women themselves.

When judging our intrepid sociologist, we should recall that she maintained a basic "social justice" orientation throughout her career. At no point in her career did Kellor put the lion's share of blame on the "under-class" (a term she likely introduced to America in *Experimental Sociology*).[184] She judged African-American morality from a Victorian middle-class vantage point. She believed in progress and so saw some cultural attributes as better than others. And with this judgmental stance, she ultimately hoped to bring the South into the modern age. In condemning society this revolutionary sociologist not only delivered a blow to ascendant racist thinking, but launched currently common modern idea that a poor environment can contribute to individuals' criminality.

Kellor Drops Out

Beyond situating Kellor's ideas in her world, our account should also consider her personal place in the world. Kellor left the University of Chicago after publishing *Experimental Sociology,* but before obtaining her doctorate. The great irony is that she set out to discredit and expel a sexist academic, Lombroso, and it is likely that the sexism of the academy led to her being expelled. And residual sexism might now make some think of her merely as an activist rather than a true intellectual.

While she attended the University of Chicago, it had one of the leading – and for a time only – graduate programs in sociology in the country. Between her enrollment in the fall of 1898 and her final quarter in the spring of 1902, Kellor took and passed 45 academic courses. And among her professors were the most famous sociologists and economists in the world: Albion Small, Thorstein Veblen, and George Herbert Mead.[185] During her years there, she also published articles in the academic *American Journal of Sociology*. And if that were not enough, she successfully challenged the world's leading school of criminology with the heavily researched *Experimental Sociology*.

Mary Jo Deegan wrote about the University of Chicago during the years of Kellor's attendance and found it highly bifurcated by gender. She argued that "male sociologists were expected to be abstract thinkers."[186] In contrast, women were considered practical thinkers who were more amenable to research and social work concerning homes, family, and housing. Making this distinction real, the university created a School of Civics and Philanthropy for women. The work herein had a "second class status compared to 'theoretical' sociology."[187] One historian supported this point by noting that Kellor's own academic advisor, Charles Henderson, addressed his social work textbook to a female audience.[188] Echoes of the discounting of women's abilities perhaps explain her near total exclusion from intellectual history today.

Truthfully, we do not know why Kellor left the University of Chicago. The decision might have reflected the fact that even with doctorates, women had great difficulty getting hired as professors.[189] And even if she could have gotten employment in a university, it would have been within the women's social work department and thus held low esteem. Her restless desire to engage in further sociological activism could also explain her decision to leave. And just as it had forced her to leave high school, a lack of funds might also have forced her to leave graduate school. We simply do not know why she dropped out. But her move to New York City proved necessary for her rise to fame and power.

– CHAPTER FOUR –

FOR THE LOVE OF WOMEN

Lesbian

Some scholars have called Frances Kellor a lesbian.[190] Others would consider the label anachronistic. The characterization depends partially on how you define the term and read the evidence. If one uses the definition that only refers to "intense woman-to-woman relating and commitment," Kellor qualifies as a lesbian.[191] She spent nearly fifty years, off and on, living with Mary Elizabeth Dreier. When Kellor died, Mary received many letters of condolence for the loss. One well-wisher wrote that she "knew of your close and affectionate friendship."[192] Mary herself wrote of pain after "47 years of fellowship and friendship."[193] If a primary emotional bond with another woman makes one a "lesbian," Kellor qualifies.

If one adopts a definition that defines a lesbian as someone who has sex with other women, extant letters suggest that Kellor still qualifies. In 1904 Kellor wrote Mary, "The colors and sunlight make me hungry for you."[194] In 1905 she teased, "I have this whole car to myself and if you were here I could put my arm around you and hunt out one of those tiny curls – and embarrass your shy little girl. You are such a dear blessed little girl. You will not get lonely cause I'll have a little good night with you and Thursday isn't far away. There love burns thru beautiful nights you dear sweetheart – Seven"[195] Though Victorian and coy, Kellor's letters surreptitiously hint at sexual intimacy.

On the other hand, it was uncovered that Mary had a secret crush on her brother-in-law, Raymond Robins.[196] Furthermore, in old age Mary reminisced about a time they lived in someone else's home, "At night we went into our rooms and worked very hard continuing our work which was always unfinished at the end of the day. Then we would meet in the kitchen to have corn flakes and cream."[197] On the other hand, the Dreier family likely kept the Mary Dreier's letters private until the 1970s due to their revealing Mary Dreier's sexuality.[198] Mary and Frances' love, sexual or not, shone through in their pet names that always ended their letters to each other. Mary was "Six" or "Sixy" and Frances was always "Seven" or "7."

In understanding Kellor's character and maneuvering in the male-dominated world of politics, Kellor's gender identification provides more interest than her sexuality. We have all seen the black and white photos of Hester Street. While many associate these photos with a romanticized vision of immigration, few associate the Lower East Side with homosexuality. But the Hester Street area, as we entered the twentieth century, had a large and vibrant homosexual community.

Scholars have concluded that homosexuality did not then bother people as much as those who adopted the characteristics of the opposite sex. The term coined for such people was "inverts."[199] Evidence indicates that Kellor merits classification as an invert. Kellor's early life as a tomboy has already been described. Some evidence of gender specialization appears in Kellor often calling Mary, "my dear little girl."[200] A paternalistic attitude shines through as Kellor reassures Mary, "I don't expect love to make a sociologist or any other ologist out of you."[201] And if Frances took the role of the man her relationship with Mary, she also took a masculine, curt, businesslike personality when running political organizations.

In nearly all of the photographs of Kellor, before and after retirement, Kellor sported male attire. In one photograph in which Frances and Mary are greeting Eleanor Roosevelt, Kellor has her arm around Mary in a typically masculine posture of ownership or protection. Interestingly, in the second photo we have of Kellor, she is wearing a rowing team uniform and another woman is dressed in full drag. Since people are fluid and the definition of invert has no absolute objective basis, classification cannot be absolute. And a strong counterpoint to Kellor's publicly brusque and businesslike persona exists in overly gushy private letters to Mary. Yet, as we saw in her athletic writing, Kellor considered masculine personality characteristics more conducive to public activism than female attributes.

Chapter Four

Romantic Activism

Rather quickly after their 1903 meeting, when Kellor was thirty years old, she started living with Mary Dreier and her sister Margaret. Interestingly, by moving in with the Dreiers as she had with Mary and Frances Eddy, our young heroine once again moved in with older sisters. And, in both cases the sisters were much better off financially than Kellor (though nearly everyone was). Each pair had inherited money. Though the Eddys apparently did not fund all of Kellor's education, their providing a home and encouragement transformed Kellor's life. In addition to living in the Dreiers' Brooklyn home, Kellor spent many vacations in their second homes in Connecticut and Florida.

The second pair of sisters may have funded Kellor's career. Mary Dreier gave a salary for life to another woman activist.[202] In order to make her organizations economically feasible, as early as 1910, Kellor stopped taking any money for her work.[203] She returned her first recorded salary of $2,500 back to the state.[204] In fact, Kellor never took more than one dollar for any positions she held during the progressive era. As Kellor had no personal wealth, it stands to reason that the Dreier's supported her financially.

In any case, Kellor could have survived without the Dreiers' help. By the time she met Mary, Kellor was already somewhat established and, as a workaholic, she would never lack for a position or work. And from an early age Kellor showed great pride in being self-sufficient. As Kellor left for the University of Chicago, Celia Parker Woolley asked her about money.

Kellor's umbrage came through when she replied, "I have always been able to earn my living."[205] The Eddy sisters were part-time activists. But the Dreier sisters used their wealth to pursue full-time activist careers. Rather than financial support, intense dedication to politics bonded Kellor to these pairs of sisters.

Margaret Dreier was instrumental in the rise of the Women's Trade Union League (WTUL). Mary and Frances likely met when Kellor worked with Margaret for the WTUL.[206] But this would have been only one of many opportunities for them to meet. Mary eventually became president of the New York WTUL and she gained notoriety as the investigator of the 1911 Triangle Waist Company fire.[207] But Margaret led the way into politics for both siblings. Frances actually dedicated her 1904 book, *Out of Work: A Study of Employment Agencies: Their Treatment of the Unemployed, and Their Influence Upon Homes and Business* to Margaret Dreier.

In their nearly fifty years together, Mary and Frances frequently showed up together on stationary of political organizations. Mary was originally described as much more reserved than Margaret. Yet people were struck by how much, under Frances' tutelage, Mary had "come out."[208] Mary even once got arrested trying to stop a scab from crossing picket lines. The newspaper expressed shock that authorities would "lock up a woman like Miss Dreier . . . LIKE A COMMON CRIMINAL!"[209] [capitals in original]. Margaret's husband, Raymond Robbins, was one of the most powerful men in the Progressive party. A real claim could be made that theirs was the "First-Family"' of the progressive movement.

Kellor's Place in Academia

Our subject's last book before solely dedicating her professional activities to the plight of immigrants, culminated in her aforementioned 1904 book, *Out of Work*. On the book's title page, Kellor's listed her position as "Fellow, College Settlement Association." Kellor originally moved to New York in 1902 to be a fellow at the New York Summer School of Philanthropy (NYSSP). While a fellow at the NYSSP she lived at the College Settlement Association's Lower East Side settlement.[210]

The NYSSP was an experiment in which Columbia University tried to reach out to and educate broader segments of society. This outreach specifically targeted the female social workers who ran the settlement houses of New York City's Lower East Side. Thus, this institution created a bridge between social workers and a proper academic university. This biography argues that Kellor's status as a female social worker has kept her from being taken seriously as an intellectual. The NYSSP reaching out to settlement house workers physically illustrates this divide. Kellor's involvement with the NYSSP institutionally situated her between academia and the female-dominated world of settlement workers.

Out of Work has the distinction of being the first book to call for the regulation of employment agencies.[211] It also called for their national coordination. Thus, if nothing else, *Out of Work* mattered for its contribution to the formation of the modern Federal unemployment management system. Still, apparently, not all academics today are convinced that a work of hands-on research such as Kellor's, which manifests in practical remedies, merits a space in intellectual history. To see where it would fit into such histories we need to look below the surface of the text; as Kellor implemented her ideas, in addition to writing about them, her ideas can be found in the consistency of her program themes and structures.

The modern intellectual historian Kevin Mattson has explained that progressive intellectuals' main quest was to "understand how a democratic public could form under the conditions of modern industrialism."[212] In the prototypical small nineteenth century town Kellor grew up in, Coldwater, Michigan, groups argued for and got a racetrack built. As a Protestant town, racetracks were morally questionable. Together, residents decided rules for running the racetrack that town residents themselves could live with. And they worked out how to pay for the racetrack locally in what amounted to town hall meetings. Such intimate governance would not work in the emerging urban - industrial age in which large impersonal forces ran the unwieldy economic and political systems. Rather than town hall meetings, to curb urban plight and worker exploitation, a strong Federal government was needed.

The strong Federal government would necessarily be distant from everyday citizens' lives and input. Bureaucrats and experts familiar with laws, economic systems, and forms of regulation would curb abuses. This rule by experts had anti-democratic characteristics. Kellor's desired revamping of the Southern penal system, for example, would not take place via voting. The incarcerated women could not redesign the system themselves. Nor, for that matter, would the everyday White citizens with their busy lives. And those inside of the system assumed its forms rather than progressively looking to redesign it. A strong Federal government would employ experts who would tame the abuses of the industrial – urban age. Progressive intellectuals wondered what the place of voters would be in this rule by experts.

To respond to this challenge, Kellor developed a hierarchical networking approach to governance. Kellor's many organizations did not so much create and run programs as coordinate disparate pre-existing local efforts. This was how she involved local activists in national organizations. This was how she carved out a place for local individuals in national governance. Hers was a pyramid structure wherein local activist groups would tackle local programs; systematize their efforts for coordination; and ultimately, have input into the design and implementation of Federal policy. By coordinating local activist groups she gave them the power to matter in the industrial – urban era.

One would be mistaken to think of this as an unreflectively chosen methodology. First of all, her work on athletics demonstrates that she was very aware of the potential for structures to foster change in cultural attitudes. Secondly, the fact that this coordinating structure consistently reappeared in her work shows that it did not simply result from happenstance. Third, as we shall see later, Kellor overtly attempted to redesign society based on the importance of coordinated reform efforts that involve citizens in national politics. If Kellor's writing did not always speak of theory, she expressed one consistently in the structure of her organizations.

Kellor Attacks Again

For *Out of Work*, Kellor and nine other women went undercover as workers and employers to 732 employment agencies in New York, Boston, Chicago, and Philadelphia. For credibility as workers, they had learned to "talk in up-to-date slang about places and mistresses." After some time, they could "pass for either the better class of employees or the poorer class of employers."[213] In an investigative journalism mode, they adopted different names and personalities. Though the book purported to be a work generally concerning unemployment and the use of employment agencies, it largely focused on the plight of women applying for domestic service jobs.

We should take notice that Kellor's first three books, *Experimental Sociology*, *Out of Work*, and *Athletic Games*, focus on limitations and injustices women face. In 1904 domestic service was the single most important class of women's gainful employment.[214] That means that, with the possible exception of those in prison, domestic workers were society's most vulnerable and widely exploited group of women. Whether or not this trend of working for poor women, and specifically her focus on domestic workers, resulted from her mother being a relatively poor domestic worker, we cannot know. But her overriding concern with women's issues cannot be denied.

Kellor's investigation found that domestic workers were routinely scammed by employment agencies. Nearly all of the agencies demanded a fee upfront to secure work. Sometimes they purposely sent domestic workers to horrible places and then refused to further employ them or return their fee when they quit. The women had no recourse against employers who did not pay them. For better jobs, a "gift" would often be required. Kellor told us that many an heirloom was lost this way. And when the women finally obtained domestic work, they often had to sleep in closets and endure abuse from their employers. Sometimes the agencies would act as banks and charged high fees for holding the women's money. Many of these agencies provided boarding and charged excessive housing and transportation costs. They would hold the women's belongings until they had worked off their debt. In such situations the agencies reduced the women to peonage.

Morality and White Slavery

Just as *Experimental Sociology, Out of Work* had a moralistic edge. An entire chapter uncovered the world of prostitution under the sensational name of "white slavery." Via threats or promises, applicants for domestic work were sent into houses of ill repute. Kellor's team reported that some of the whorehouses were surrounded by high walls and imprisoned the women. One woman who tried to escape was so brutally beaten that she died in the hospital as a result. As evidenced by the ease with which the investigators penetrated these operations, these brothels largely worked in the open. Out of town men could go to these "employment agencies" and buy girls for the night. If made pregnant, the employers sent the girls to the hospital or the country and quickly replaced them. At this point these girls would have lost so much self-respect that, according to Kellor, they would have become permanent victims.

There has been some recent retelling of the history of so-called "white slavery." One article noted that the settlement house worker "displayed puritanical zealousness in her desire to protect the alien woman against sexual pitfalls as well as against unsubstantiated charges of prostitution."[215] Hence the charge of elitism from the last chapter emerges again. And there are moments at which Kellor's account can sound sensational and lurid. This evidence gives credence to the charge that moral reformers got work by denouncing alternative lifestyles.

But the reformers who worked on these issues lived in these neighborhoods and did not invent these stories. One government commission reported 3,600 court convictions for running brothels and solicitation occurred in four months during the time Kellor was investigating. One of the Commission's female investigators was beaten and another killed when it was discovered that they were agents.[216] The dangerous underworld Kellor uncovered seems to have actually existed.

Still, Kellor's early work does exude normative moral judgments. She thought that employment agencies based in saloons were designed to rob the clients of their money, hope, and sense of direction. Kellor reluctantly admitted that some women seemed to go to the brothels willingly. Modern audiences might laugh with jaded cynicism at the condemnation of prostitution Kellor wrote in an article that accompanied *Out of Work*. It pleaded that we must reach the African – American woman migrating North for work, before she "has become incompetent, immoral, intemperate, and imbued with the idea that in this great city she need not work."[217] Kellor did not consider sex work a respectable, positive option for women.

Just as Rev. Collin represented a transition from fundamentalist Christianity to a sociological vision, this moralistic edge in Kellor declined over time. This transition is interesting, again, as it parallels the increasingly secular nature of our society and institutions. Whereas, again, Protestant moralizing used to greet anti-social behavior, we now instinctively look for the economic or environmental conditions that led the person astray. In fact, as in our response to urban unrest, we often condemn the system that caused it and not the behavior. Moreover, we have become sensitive about morally charged words like "prostitute" and prefer the judgment neutral "sex worker." Kellor's transition from Protestant moralizer to social analysts has particular interest as she headed the very

Americanization movement that was charged with molding character of immigrants during this transition.

The Mind of Society

While moral judgment lingered, Kellor blamed white slavery on environmental factors. Poverty, a network of pimps, and a lack of social support increased the vulnerability of the female immigrants from overseas and rural communities. Yet Kellor was not simply a crude environmentalist. In *Experimental Sociology* she not only laid the misdeeds of African – Americans on economics mechanistically; she blamed their misdeeds on the majority White culture's prejudices. Similarly, Kellor's analysis of the woes of domestic workers laid blame for their exploitation on the cultural attitudes of their employers.

When investigating undercover, Kellor reported, "It is no exaggeration to say that, almost without exception, the kind of treatment we received depended primarily and almost entirely upon whether we were 'ladies' or 'servants.'" As if studying the basis of social constructs as much as employment, Kellor would sometimes leave the "servants" waiting room and enter the "ladies" room, allowing the women to talk her for some time before announcing that she was a servant. With a "note of wrath," women would tell her to "know your place."[218] Kellor did this to highlight the artificiality of social distinctions that separate people. Her work displays a prescient eye for noticing the artificial class distinctions and snobbery that eased exploitation.

Chapter Four

The ultimate solution to domestic exploitation required dissolving the artificial distinctions between women. In articles written for *Harper's Bazaar* and *The Ladies' Home Journal*, our sociological investigator claimed that the root of the so-called "servant problem" existed in calling it the "servant problem." To the employer-class readers of those magazines, this phrase referred to the inability to get dependable workers. But Kellor insisted that getting an employed woman to continue as a domestic worker often depended upon whether she was treated as a "human or slave."[219] She proposed eliminating the terms "*Mistress* and *servant*" to give "the business dignity."[220] [Italics in original] If you call a person a servant, you demean them to the point where they will not stay in your employ. Kellor repeatedly attacked the socially constructed divisions between people.

In place of "servant," Kellor recommended "*employee, household worker, maid, cook*, etc, and where they have specialized, *houseworker* or *household aid* or *helper*."[221] [Italics in original] She said the use of first names "more than any other one thing helped us to feel like servants." When undercover, she resented that potential employers "looked us over, point for point, exactly as one estimates animals at a stock show."[222] As she would repeatedly do with immigrants, Kellor asked her readers to "put ourselves in the maids' place and treat them as we should like to be treated."[223] With such sensitivity, simply by recognizing the humanity in those whom you employ, she told her employer-class readers, communication would flow and the 'servant problem' would dissipate.

Although at one point Kellor claimed that the "servant problem" was "primarily an employer's responsibility" and she consistently sought to protect the poor, she nearly always aimed at solutions that all sides wanted.[224] Rather than demonizing, she conceded that, "notwithstanding the many humiliating interviews, there have been many employers who have been considerate and even courteous to us."[225] Yet she condemned the work of the Woman's Education Union (WEU) because "They are one-sided, and can only see the problem from the employer's standpoint."[226] One agency would not hire immigrants, which Kellor said prevented "co-operative and educational work."[227] In her analysis, cooperation, not competition, made the business sector possible.

A decade prior, one of Kellor's mentors, Rev. H. P. Collin, had taken her to Chatauquas. At one, she took a course taught by one of the leading Social Gospel proponents of the day, Richard T. Ely. At this time Ely spoke of calling people "servants" as being the source of the "servant problem." He and Rev. Collin, as Social Gospel advocates, argued that all sectors of society should understand their mutual dependence and help each other. They preached social unity. Kellor developed techniques to manifest these ideals.

Coordinating Solutions

In both her Americanization work and her attempts to aid domestic workers, Kellor cultivated inclusive activist networks. Several groups in separate cities had already begun investigating conditions affecting domestic workers. Rather than start a competing organization, Kellor started a group to coordinate the efforts of the pre-existing organizations. She called this umbrella organization the Inter-Municipal Committee on Household Research (IMCHR). Our coordinator announced, "Organizations, employers and employees, and all interested will be asked to co-operate, by sending to this bureau experiences, opinions, criticisms, suggestions, experiments, opinions, criticisms, suggestions, experiments, and proposed solutions."[228] Thus while the IMCHR had a leadership structure, it recognized that "each city has its own large local committee which caries out the details."[229] Kellor's organizations all sought to coordinate, rather than replace, pre-existing activist groups.

Ultimately, Kellor proposed that existing good employment agencies unite and form a system of "model agencies."[230] The IMCHR drew up standards by which to certify them. Permanent standardized records as well as a complaint and inspection department would provide agencies, no matter how small, with the ability to get on the IMCHR approved list.[231] Their seal of approval would assure potential employers that the women working therein were not being treated poorly. The listing of reliable local employment agencies, approved boarding houses for employees, and training schools would aid both employers and domestic workers in their choices. Characteristically, this reform structure sought cooperation for the betterment of all.[232]

Standardization facilitated coordination. The worker's need for letters of recommendation led to forgeries, corruption, and exploitation. The IMCHR standardized such letters. The IMCHR also created standard forms for inspecting complaints against agencies, employers, and workers. With this data the IMCHR could generate agency comparisons and statistical reports. The gathered information was reviewed nationally and disseminated locally. Local press departments furnished "a monthly bulletin; material furnished to newspapers and periodical; and statistics, papers, lecturers, and references to clubs and other organizations."[233] These organizational structures turned reform organizations into sociological investigation bureaus that could inform the public.

Interestingly, Kellor wrote that she looked forward to the "placing of college women in related lines of research and practical work; assistance to legislative and educational work."[234] Eventually, Kellor aimed to run all of society on a sociological basis. Even in this early work, we see the idea of reforming society via employing an army of sociologists. With our gendered lens, we should notice that she specifies herein that a cadre of female activists is the goal. Perhaps this represented an acceptance of the idea of women as social workers. However, it also presented the idea of replicating the communities of female activists she had heretofore surrounded herself with.

Out of Work compared seventeen state laws and three city ordinances. In an accompanying discussion, our analyst

Chapter Four

explained that she preferred ordinances to statutes, "since they are based on the needs of a particular community, which knows something of its own conditions."[235] Yet she noted that when the state enacts a law, it is uniform and graft is less likely. Furthermore, city laws "are less permanent, are likely to change with the party in power, and depend much upon the administration for proper enforcement."[236] But ultimately she held that "the guarantee of real and permanent reform is voluntary action by those involved."[237] Thus, her discussion argued for democratic participation as the best guarantor of successful reform.

Out of Work included a generic employment agency law that reformers could fight for and legislatures could consider. In addition, the book detailed and compared the processes by which some of the laws were stalled and passed. Kellor hoped activists would use this book as a resource for effecting legal change. The year *Out of Work* was published "due to Frances Kellor's revelations and influence," the New York Legislature enacted the "Employment Association act into law."[238] *Out of Work* served as a practical guide to hands-on reform. We could simply read it as a training manual. Knowing Kellor had such a strong academic background, we can assert that writing a practical manual, as opposed to florid academic generalities and abstractions, reflected an informed choice.

Out of Work hoped to turn all of its readers into budding activists. In the first paragraph of *Out of Work*, Kellor wrote, "The author has omitted tables and statistical details, at the risk of being called unscientific."[239] She did so to "address her work to the general readers."[240] Here we see an attempt to be popular and practical that would not endear her to the abstract male thinkers of the academy. Characteristically, Kellor worked to get all of society involved in investigating social problems and implementing solutions. Herein we see a profound vision in which professional sociologists, the State, and an active public would work together to help women.

Academics then and now might also discount Kellor's intellectual contributions, due to her publicizing her efforts and ideas in *Harper's Bazaar* and *The Ladies' Home Journal*. Indeed, neither publication has a reputation for hosting esoteric academic discourses. Yet this forum allowed her to speak directly to the women who were treating their servants poorly. This forum could make the average woman aware of activist networks, enlightened hiring options, and proposals for regulatory laws. By 1904 Kellor had published in academic journals. Her relentless newspaper articles and use of women's magazines reflected a conscious decision to involve the wider public in her reforms. Using popular women's magazines shows her to be a public intellectual and demonstrated an astute understanding of media.

Topics

Out of Work focused on three categories of women: "Immigrants, negroes and country girls who have come to our cities."[241] Importantly, in light of her Americanization work,

Chapter Four

immigrants did not constitute a special cultural problem herein. In this work Kellor lumped long-term Americans and immigrants together; "There is another class of girls, chiefly American and Irish, which is aggressively opposed to training."[242] Kellor's portrayal of resistance to training is neither menacing nor relegated to immigrants. At this point economic plight, not cultural threats, concerned her.

Kellor never again wrote about migrating long-term Americans. She overtly fought for African – American women until about 1910. And she focused on the needs of immigrants from 1906 to 1921. Again, rather than moral reform, African – Americans needed protection from exploitation. The overlap between working for African-Americans and immigrants that we see in *Out of Work* establishes continuity between her early social justice work and her Americanization work.

Experimental Sociology was published in 1901. *Out of Work* came out in 1904 and *Athletic Games* became available in 1909. Neither *Experimental Sociology* nor *Athletic Games* pays any attention to men. *Out of Work,* by contrast, has one chapter solely dedicated to men. As Kellor shifted towards working on immigrants nationally, the generic immigrant in her work became male. Still, these later works often contained a section specially dedicated to women. Seeing her early focus on women primes us to not take the gendered nature of her Americanization work for granted.

– CHAPTER FIVE –

KELLOR CROSSES THE COLOR LINE

Intimate Americanization

The Dreier family, Kellor's family by "marriage," made immigration issues personal. Mary and Margaret Dreier were first-generation Americans. Mary Dreier, Kellor's partner, continued communicating with her family in Germany into old age. Their father, Theodore Dreier, immigrated to the United States at the age of twenty-one. Four years later he returned to Germany and found his bride, Dorothea Dreier. The Dreier family spent several months each year in Germany, visiting family. Mrs. Dreier did not have perfect English and Mr. Dreier wrote the majority of his personal letters in German.[243] Mr. Dreier participated avidly in the German society. And his children admired him greatly. Though he died before Kellor could have met him, Kellor could not have been totally insensitive to immigrants without some sort of personal rebuke from the Dreier family.

Chapter Five

While living with the Dreier sisters, Kellor also intermittently lived at the College Settlement House until 1905, when she would have been 32 years of age. During this time, when in Chicago, she also lived at Jane Addams' Hull House.[244] Both of these institutions sat in the heart of immigrant neighborhoods. And it was in these immigrant neighborhoods that Kellor began her Americanization work.[245] So Kellor not only spent her life as a part of an immigrant family, she stared her Americanization work while living in immigrant communities.

Our young shaper of our modern world got her first government position concerning immigrants when New York Governor, Charles Evans Hughes, visited Lillian Wald's famed Henry Street Settlement house. Wald invited Governor Hughes because she said understanding "can best be accomplished through an intercourse with the immigrant in which the dignity of the individual and of the family is recognized."[246]

Ultimately, the Americanization services provided for immigrants required immigrant participation. And, beyond nice sentiment, obtaining immigrant participation in Americanization efforts required understanding the needs of immigrants. All charges to the contrary, Kellor was not a distant figure who looked down on immigrants from afar. Her connection to immigrant communities was real and intimate.

Immigrants Invented Americanization

The term "Americanization" seems to have come from immigrants themselves. Still in existence today, the Educational

Alliance was a leading early organization serving immigrants in Manhattan's Lower East Side. In 1895 the Educational Alliance held a street fair, the program of which stated, "The scope of the work of the Educational Alliance shall be of an Americanizing educational, social and humanizing character."[247] In a 1905 report the Educational Alliance listed its first goal as helping the Jewish immigrants "comprehend the spirit of the American Institutions and adapt himself to the conditions which surround him here."[248] In sum, the report announced that the "first aim and object of the Alliance is to Americanize the recently arrived immigrant."[249]

Although deeply involved with immigrants beforehand, Kellor did not herself use the term "Americanization" earlier than 1906. Furthermore, she did not use the term regularly until 1915. And the Educational Alliance had direct connections to Kellor's organizations. Felix Warburg and Jacob Schiff, for example, sat on the board of directors for the Educational Alliance in 1898, and had positions of governance in Kellor's Committee for Immigrants in America in 1915. These immigrant leaders guided Kellor's policy throughout her career as an Americanizer. Kellor also coached basketball at the Educational Alliance. It seems reasonable to assume that Kellor adopted some of her Americanization platform from the Educational Alliance.

Distribution and Assimilation

The charge has been levied that immigrant leaders undertook their Americanization efforts out of an embarrassment

Chapter Five

over the unassimilated cultural state of their brethren. This charge contains some merit. Yet, the Education Alliance had over four hundred paid and volunteer teachers.[250] In 1906 the Educational Alliance's "English and Civics" class had, "a daily attendance of over five hundred, with a waiting list of over one thousand."[251] Every Friday night, "moral lectures in Yiddish, in which the special aspects of American life confronting the immigrant, drew 900 audience members," to the Educational Alliance.[252] Across New York City, in 1905, there were 75 evening schools offering elementary courses for adults. Nearly 36,000 foreigners were taught in 553 special classes.[253]

In recent decades, historians have been nearly unanimous and constant in their condemnation of Americanization as an imposition forced on immigrants by intolerant Americans. But in the 1940s, Americanization Historian Edward Hartmann concluded that, in reference to English and civics courses, "In practically every case, these classes were organized upon the request of the immigrants themselves."[254] It seems improbable that this widespread participation by the immigrants only stemmed from the cultural embarrassment of community leaders; at some level these newcomers themselves appreciated Americanization activities.

One such wealthy leader of the Educational Alliance, Jacob Schiff, created the Industrial Removal Office (IRO) to relocate immigrants out of New York City and onto farms. He was a wealthy German Jew who immigrated to America as a young man. His removal program targeting newly arrived Jews could be used to bolster the view of Americanization as a cultural imposition born of the embarrassment of assimilated German Jews by their newly arrived Russian kin. Though he must have had a German accent, Schiff was urbane and not of peasantry. Kellor later made Schiff's national distribution of immigrants a central part of her Americanization program. One could also use the Orwellian nature of the IRO's name to argue that Americanization sought to assimilate unwashed immigrants.

But material reasons for wanting to work on the distribution of immigrants existed as well. The "padroni" or "padrone" was an Italian contractor who supplied worksites with Italian workers. While Kellor admitted that some of these men could provide a useful service, the majority were immigrants who abused fellow immigrants. Padrones controlled the room and board of immigrants at worksites. Kellor found during her extensive travels through worksites some railroad camps that "If the food is unfit to use or they [the workmen] do not receive all they order, no refund or adjustment is ever made."[255] For a mandatory fee, the padrone housed their ethnic kinsmen in "an old shack, or a dismounted or ditched box car alongside the track."[256] And many of these housing accommodations "were so crowded and unventilated that they soon become infected and full of vermin."[257]

The padrone also scammed the workers on transportation. Rounding off the abuse, the rate of pay was often falsely advertised. Often, upon arrival at the remote job site, the worker would find no work available. When the work existed, the employment often lasted a shorter amount of time than had been promised. This meant that after great travels and expense, after earning little or no money, the workers would find themselves broke, ill-clad and fed, and far from home. Kellor thought that a rational national bureaucratic system of employee distribution would prove more immigrant-friendly than the "system" run by the Italian-speaking padrones.

Our social engineer proposed a national employment agency. "When there is demand for labor in one of the commercial centers, its branch will communicate directly with the bureau at Washington. This bureau will then communicate with the labor exchange at the most convenient distribution center, and order the necessary labor."[258] The sending bureau would inspect the workers to make sure they had the necessary skills. And, mirroring Kellor's system for domestic workers, this national employment agency would be able to select industries to which they would send workers and thereby apply pressure for industrial reform. Finally, the national distribution bureau would arrange for transportation. Inclusively, both workers and industry would be better served by this national coordination.

This system would make the padrone superfluous. Herein, we see great overlap between Kellor's agenda and the leader of the Educational Alliance, Schiff. But Schiff sent workers to remote farms in order that they might assimilate culturally.[259] For Kellor, organized distribution was to replace a system where immigrants "enter into a fierce and demoralizing competition with each other for starvation wages."[260] Her distribution advocacy never mentions assimilation. Even at this early point in her career, Kellor had less of a cultural agenda than the leader of the Educational Alliance.

Some of Kellor's distribution program and nearly all of Schiff's aimed at getting immigrants to the farm. Participation provides the ultimate test of whether or not the Americanization efforts were a form of top-down coercion that aimed at conformity. A study of the Yiddish press found newspapers "repeatedly urge Jews to return to the soil." And, by 1922, 75,000 Jews found the arguments persuasive enough that they utilized relocation agencies and moved to farms.[261] Many immigrants considered this Americanization program a boon.

Americanization from the Bottom-Up
Even if the embarrassment of culturally assimilated descendants of immigrants did kindle the Americanization movement, a large number of newer immigrants did not dread adopting American customs. A study of the Yiddish press during the era in which Kellor worked in immigrant neighborhoods, found the foreign press to be an agency of Americanization. The author of the study, Dr. Mordecai Soltes, found the Yiddish press' "main editorial function to be to interpret American events, ideals, and institutions to its immigrant Jewish readers." A numerical analysis found, "The proportion of editorials devoted to general American issues is about twice as large as all others combined." The Yiddish press sought to bring immigrants "nearer to America

in sentiment, thought and action."²⁶² It aimed to "stimulate national pride in their adopted country."²⁶³

Granted, Soltes' study took place under the threat of immigration restriction; thus, it overtly worked to vindicate the foreign press and immigrants. But Lillian Wald, herself a second-generation Jew, noted that the Yiddish press carried biographies, in Yiddish, of "George Washington, Abraham Lincoln, and other distinguished Americans." Furthermore, she reported that an Italian daily ran discussions of the Constitution serially.²⁶⁴ Soltes had a reason for bias, but Wald and others confirmed his statistical analysis. And had these newspapers that taught American identity not pleased the immigrant communities they served, they would have gone out of business.

While thus far we have focused on the largely Jewish Educational Alliance and Yiddish press, other ethnic groups also participated in Americanization efforts. In 1901 Italian-Americans and Americans of foreign origin created the Society for Italian Immigrants (SII). To help their brethren, they hired the experienced teacher and social worker, Sarah Wool Moore.²⁶⁵ Moore got her start working with a widow of an Italian immigrant in far away construction project labor camps near her home. In her schools the immigrants themselves "gave as their chief reason for wanting to learn English 'to become citizens.'"²⁶⁶ In 1902 she published an illustrated English-Italian textbook. At the end of each of Moore's lessons the immigrants chanted "America" and sang the Garibaldi hymn.

Later, one of Kellor's Americanization groups became the conduit for Moore to obtain state funding for her worksite schools in remote locations.[267] The SII also anticipated Kellor's efforts by greeting Italian immigrants at the docks and helping them secure work and housing, education, and general assistance. They even engaged in a limited amount of distribution work amongst Italians.[268] The Society for the Protection of Italian Immigrants (SPII) did similar work.[269] By 1903 the SPII even falsely claimed to have fulfilled Kellor's goal of breaking up the padrones' runner system.[270] The fact that different groups of immigrants in disparate places launched parallel programs suggests that these Americanization efforts had an underlying grounding in common and widespread immigrant needs.

African – Americans and Immigrants

African – American women largely faced the same situation as immigrants. White agents in the South promised African-American females great lives in the North. These agents arranged for transportation and told the women they could work the costs off later. Upon arrival in the North, these eager workers' possessions were taken as collateral. The agents tripled the cost of transportation, charged the women more than the normal rate for housing, and provided them work at wages below the market rate. Being "Alone, friendless, penniless, $18.50 in debt, and her trunk in the agent's basement" made the new arrivals "ripe for exploitation."[271] Provocatively, Kellor asked

Chapter Five

of African – American women in such situations, "Can she be said to be anything but a slave?"[272]

Just as she had worried about "white slavery," Kellor worried about the immoral temptations that faced African – American sojourners. Race only factored in as prejudice made African – American women especially vulnerable. Noting that immigration made more European domestics available, she informed her readers that this was leading to "the gradual closing of the doors of the best homes and hotels and restaurants, which are coming to prefer whites, and the negro woman is forced into less desirable places and lines of work."[273] Economic systems, unscrupulous agents, and societal prejudices, created moral peril for the African – American women that exceeded that placed before White immigrants.

Though last to be hired at good places, Kellor largely considered African – American women who came north looking for work to be the same as European immigrants. She wrote, "Ellis Island has its missionaries who guide and direct the immigrant women: . . . but there is no one to extend a helping hand to the country girl from the Southern port."[274] That was, Kellor continued, "the only difference between the problem of these girls and the problem of the white girls."[275] As such, to help them, she recommended using the "system of missionary agencies and homes, which has been put into operation during the last year for young Jewish immigrant women."[276] Kellor's article entitled, "Assisted Emigration from the South" advocated a system of distribution for African – American women that paralleled the one she advocated for immigrant men.[277]

Immigrants were also like African – Americans. When trying to convince a person working with African – Americans to also work with immigrants, she argued, "The work in so many of its phases is so closely allied to the work among colored that I do not believe you would be dividing your interest if you join forces with us."[278] One of Kellor's organizations offered Robert E. Park, later a famous sociologist, the position of Education Secretary for her immigration work. This offer for immigration work was made on the basis of Park's work at the African – American school at Tuskegee.[279]

Creating a League

When Kellor studied incarcerated Southern African - American women in order to defeat racism and sexism, her efforts culminated in her 1901 book, *Experimental Sociology: Descriptive and Analytic*. Kellor's 1904 book, *Out of Work*, paid quite a bit of attention to Southern African – American women coming north for employment as domestic servants. Seeing African-American women's struggles in the South and the North, likely contributed to her recognizing the need for national coordination. Kellor consistently based her programs in pre-existing local efforts while striving for national coordination.

In 1897 Victoria Earle Matthews, who was born into slavery just one month into the Civil War, started the "White Rose Working Girls' Home."[280] Prior to Kellor, "Mathews saw the

Chapter Five

viciousness of the employment agency racket early and in the mid-nineties acted against it."[281] Matthews' organization "provided travelers' aid, employment advice, and temporary lodgings for working girls new to the city."[282] Like the Jewish and Italian agencies, by 1905, the Matthews' White Rose Girls' Home met new arrivals at the docks.[283] They then escorted the women to their places of employment or to the White Rose Home for shelter.

Matthews organized volunteers, but her inability to keep up with the numbers led Kellor to enroll the help of her Inter-Municipal Committee on Household Research (IMCHR). Kellor had launched the IMCHR in 1905 to help domestic workers. In 1906 Kellor founded the National League for the Protection of Colored Women (NLPCW).[284] Kellor's "new League sought to do on a national scale what Victoria Matthews had begun in New York."[285] Again, in this effort, rather than take over work herself, Kellor characteristically aimed to coordinate pre-existing organizations.

With an increasingly characteristic eye towards national solutions, Kellor explained, "A national organization can control the seaports and establish close relations between rescue agencies in the South and those in the North."[286] Three years after being established, Kellor's National League had affiliates in New York, Philadelphia, Memphis, Baltimore, Norfolk, and Memphis. The NLPCW cooperated with "the Colored Mission, the White Rose Home, the Brooklyn YMCA, and other shelters."[287] In 1910 Kellor's NLPCW merged with two other groups to form the National Urban League.[288] Typical for Kellor, even the forming of the National Urban League involved Kellor's NLPCW networking with two other pre-existing groups.

Complicity and Exclusivity

As we saw in *Experimental Sociology*, Kellor's work with African – Americans could be criticized for accepting too much of the racial status quo. The Hampton Institute held that African – Americans should be educated for their station in life rather than their potential. Kellor and Matthews carried out their work with the help of the Hampton institute. Mrs. Matthews led the charge via carrying the message of the "exploitation and degradation facing colored girls in the northern cities" to the Hampton Negro Conference in 1898.[289] Accepting that going north involved African – Americans in crime, the Hampton Institute's magazine proclaimed, "Certainly we ought to be thankful for every influence that tends to keep . . . the colored woman, in the South."[290] Matthews even edited a book of speeches by the segregationist Hampton school icon Booker T. Washington.

Herein we see complicity in the status quo, yet the White Rose broke the Hampton guidelines by having courses on "race history."[291] Kellor echoed the Hampton philosophy, when she asserted, "History, geography, languages are much less calculated to adapt the mass of negroes to their present, and likely to be, future environment, than are physiology, hygiene, domestic and manual training, civic government, and some knowledge of industrial and financial principles."[292] Yet, just a

Chapter Five

couple of years later she advocated "educational opportunity for training of Negro social workers, and social science education for Negro leaders in other walks of life to prepare them for leadership in urban centers."[293] This change may have reflected philosophical change or strategic public positioning. Regardless, Kellor advocated that African – Americans be trained to lead social service reform efforts.[294] And Kellor publicly praised Matthews, an African-American, throughout her New York City work with African-Americans.

African – Americans and European – Americans worked together in Kellor's organization more generally. One modern author noted that with the NLPCW "for the first time, Negroes in any appreciable numbers shared responsibility for the operation of charitable agencies."[295] Kellor wrote, "The colored people are really doing his work of helping their unemployed women themselves."[296] But she also reassured her readers that "The white people can help them."[297] And support from the African – American community seems confirmed by the American Methodist Episcopal Church magazine praising "the great services rendered by Mrs. [sic] Frances A. Kellor."[298]

Kellor's Americanization work and her work leading to the formation of the National Urban League both built upon previously existing indigenous efforts. Ultimately, Kellor saw Americanization as a program meant to involve America's residents in participatory democracy. Her coordinating local activists rather than replacing them, advocated this strategy in action. Yet another exemplary characteristic in Kellor's networking style appeared in stationery which revealed Mary Dreier's appearance on the governing board of the NLPCW and the National Urban League's early executive committees.[299] From hereon out, Kellor stopped emphasizing women and her targets became more purely male.

– CHAPTER SIX –

AMERICANIZATION FROM THE TRENCHES

Leaving Home

Next to Jane Addams, Lillian Wald is America's most famous Settlement House founder. Modeled on homes, the settlement houses provided community services such as childcare and some educational courses. And these settlement houses were strategically located in immigrant neighborhoods. Whereas Addams held court in Chicago, Wald's Henry Street Settlement sat on New York City's Lower East Side. Kellor stayed in and worked out of both houses.

Many female settlement house leaders had women for life partners and Wald did not have children. Ironically, the public images of their hosts often stressed their maternal characteristics. And, despite being Jewish, Wald's image was that of a motherly Protestant woman raising immigrants. And though Jane Addams fought for garbage collection in her settlement house neighborhood and worked on national campaigns, she also had a maternal image. Kellor never associated herself with these homes and roles. Instead, Kellor dragged Wald into the depths of men's filthy industrial sites.

Wald and Kellor spoke about labor issues on panels together as early as 1906.[300] In 1908 Lillian Wald asked New York Governor Charles Evans Hughes to come dine with her and Kellor in her famous Henry Street settlement house. In writing about her conviction upon the eve of inviting Governor Hughes, Wald praised the distribution plans being bandied about. These distribution plans largely concerned men going to labor camps. As Kellor began to focus on immigrants in general, she began to give the majority of her attention to men.

Kellor's Alphabet Soup

Governor Hughes left the meeting in Wald's settlement house "armed with maps and documentary evidence." And shortly thereafter he created the Immigration Commission (IC) in order to investigate the "condition, welfare, and industrial opportunities" for immigrants in New York State.[301] Wald and Kellor were the only two females on this eight person investigatory body.[302] The work of the IC officially ended in April of 1909 when it turned in its final report. The report recommended the creation of the Bureau of Industries and Immigration (BII).

Chapter Six

In October of 1910, around her thirty-seventh birthday, the BII was created and Kellor became its head and the first woman to head a New York State bureau.[303] During the period Kellor also created the private New York – New Jersey branch of the North American Civic League for Immigrants (NACL). This group served as the root of the many private organizations she would lead as an Americanizer. Thus, Kellor ran the government's CI, BII and the private NACL at the same time.

Before moving on, the name of the Bureau of Industries and Immigration merits comment. Note that the name of the bureau, as Kellor's IC recommended, considered industry, not cultural conformity, the corollary to immigrant issues. In fact, the primary emphasis on industries in the name recognized immigrants' contributions as workers. It is worth noting that the name of Kellor's first major group concerning immigrants said nothing about culture or Americanization. The name correctly conveyed that reforming industries, in which immigrants worked, was the BII's first order of business.

The division between Kellor's CI, BII and the NACL was not always clear. One article accurately noted the NACL got formed due to "the need felt for a body of private citizens to carry into effect the many suggestions made by Gov. Hughes's Immigration Commission."[304] And Kellor presented BII plans to the NACL.[305] So the groups worked independently, but also cooperated. In many respects, they were one group with Kellor as the common element.

In Rochester, the BII took over the NACL's "survey of the foreign districts" while they were still in progress.[306] The BII shared membership other than Kellor. The Constitutional and corporate lawyer, Louis Marshall, sat on the IC.[307] He and the powerful banker Felix Warburg both backed Kellor for her BII position and took an active part in the NACL. The aforementioned Jacob Schiff of the Educational Alliance and the Industrial Removal Office also helped Kellor get her BII position and served on boards of successor organizations to the NACL.[308] On a visit to education facilities built at labor camps, Kellor arrived representing the BII and Warburg represented the NACL. This was recorded in minutes despite the fact that Kellor headed, and so could have represented, both.[309] When people could not fill a role from one organization, someone would temporarily fill in from another.[310] And the NACL printed and distributed BII reports when the legislature furnished no money.[311]

The overlapping membership of Kellor's groups highlights Kellor's intense propensity for networking. Throughout her career she would surround herself with wealthy and powerful men. These networks also connected her with immigrants and local activists. This cooperation also illustrates her consistent integration of private organizations and governmental bodies. Kellor unfolded a vision of Americanization wherein governmental bodies and private organizations, immigrants, activists, and citizens would cooperate, and thus find unity, via participation in progressive causes.

Chapter Six

As the agendas, membership and projects of the groups Kellor headed overlapped, this discussion will largely treat them as a single conglomeration.

Exploitation

By the time of its April 5, 1909 report, the IC had held forty-two meetings, nine conferences, thirty-seven hearings, and examined one hundred and ninety three witnesses.[312] Yet, characteristically, Kellor and Wald first went amongst the immigrants themselves. They, Mary Dreier and a photographer, got an automobile and toured state and city worksites across New York.[313] The state sites included the enlargement of the Barge Canal and the extension of the Erie Canal. The city-sponsored work camps they investigated surrounded the extension of an aqueduct from the Catskills to New York's water supply.

Kellor and Wald co-wrote an article that began with an emphasis of the importance of these projects to America. They wrote, "[the Barge Canal] is planned as a connecting link between the ore and grain producing states and the markets of Europe through the great port of New York."[314] Showing immigrants' importance to America set the reader up to understand the unfair bargain we were giving immigrants. To this end, the article went on to detail the failure of the state and city laws that were meant to protect them.

The state contracts said nothing about the men, and thus left them open to abuse. The state, Kellor and Wald reported, "takes great care to prevent the freezing of cement, but permits any kind of houses to be used for its laborers."[315] The city contracts, the authors noted, "require a standard of sanitation, of housing, of medical care." Unfortunately, the city's enforcement was "handicapped because it has no authority beyond the city limits."[316] None of the provisions were systematically enforced. Thus, Kellor and Wald argued that the immigrants helped America, but none of America's institutions helped the immigrant.

When the BII and NACL took over the IC's work, they extended the investigations to include factory work camps, railroads, road projects, and disparate immigrant communities. In detail, they investigated thirty communities, sixty-seven transportation projects, ninety-nine private industries (including mines, quarries, canneries and fertilizer plants), in addition to one hundred and sixteen government projects.[317] Kellor investigated African – American women in Southern penitentiaries alone. In *Out of Work*, Kellor employed a small group of women to investigate work conditions undercover. She, Wald, and Dreier initially studied industrial sites together. Now Kellor had created larger organizations to undertake her thorough sociological surveys of social problems.

Inclusion and Exclusion

Significantly, Kellor's organizations found that horrible working conditions did not prevail for long-term Americans. Within the same camps, the contractor usually puts up a house for long-term Americans of "good tarred paper" and had it

Chapter Six

repaired often. The BII found that "The contractor has no interest in supervision of any kind over the alien, but he assumes this for the American." Not under the control of the padrone, American workers could "buy [food] where they please."[318] But the problem went beyond the abhorred "cupidity of the bosses" to active prejudicial "discrimination."[319] Employers considered long-term American workers human and immigrant workers expendable.

But just as the government and industry had abandoned the immigrant workers, so had the local towns. The camps were often as big as small towns. Had immigrants been included in the adjoining community's politics they would have comprised a significant voting block. Private factory workers' camps were "located within some township, but they are so largely composed of aliens that they are . . . ignored by the American community. The people who comprise them, therefore, have neither civic nor political existence."[320] They were "entirely ignored by the American part of the community."[321]

Though larger cities addressed such issues, "small towns are not alive to their responsibility, and look bewildered when any interest is shown in the 'foreign section'."[322] As a result, the immigrant sections had no fire protection, garbage removal, police protection, educational or medical services. At the work sites, "The owner and his representatives set the standard of living, sanitation, law and order, and outside authority, like health and police officers, are only called in emergencies." As a rule, "whatever the town has of good housing, recreation, play grounds, night schools and kindergartens is not very generously, if at all, extended to the 'outsiders'."[323]

In an interpretation that foreshadowed much of Kellor's later work, the last sentence of a fourteen-page NACL report read, "The prejudice existing in many such towns against foreigners is due in no small measure to lack of understanding and inability to get each other's point of view."[324] Succinctly, an article concluded, "Miss Kellor's hope is that patriotic societies and similar organizations will turn their attention to the problem of foreigners who live on the borders of so many townships throughout the state; that they will invite them into the civic life of the community and try to make them understand that they are going to be really a part of the United States."[325] Extending the standard infrastructure and political power long-term Americans enjoyed to immigrants comprised much of Kellor's definition of Americanization.

Morality

The common references in Kellor's work to the material interpretation of the "American standard of living" greatly overshadow her extremely rare references to foreign cultural traditions. Kellor worried about the rowdiness of the camps. Kellor judged, "The general characteristic of these camps are that they are wholly un-American, being devoid of Americanizing influence." She explained, "With rare exceptions, there are no amusements or recreation other than the saloon, and no educational facilities, and no religious influences. Most of these

Chapter Six

camps are remote from the town authorities and are a law unto themselves."[326] In these selections we do hear Victorian moralistic cultural judgments.

Yet whereas railing against poor working conditions for immigrants fills nearly every page of every article, these statements about saloons are early and also relatively rare. Even then, Kellor's morality may be typified by her arguing blue laws be amended to allow the sale of alcohol on Sunday from 10 to 11 pm because "It is better to have a law you can enforce than to have one that is not enforced."[327] A sentiment of protection dominated the implied small-town Protestant morality when Kellor denounced the practice wherein, "Just before pay day from 25 to 100 women from New York City come to camp and stay until the men have spent their money."[328] But again, she wants the immigrants to have economic independence, not stop folk dances or change their clothes or language.

In the few statements wherein Kellor mentioned normative behavior, the following formulation dominates; The "State is responsible for maintaining American standards of living, not a foreign one, and once admitted to this country, equal rights are guaranteed. Nowhere are aliens more discriminated against than on the public works of the state."[329] In Kellor's work, attaining the "American standard of living" nearly always came from access to government services as well as proper housing and working conditions. Though morality blended in, here we find a material, more than a cultural definition of being American.

Swindles and Cheats

Outside of researching labor camp facilities, the IC focused on scams perpetrated upon immigrants, such as the selling of forged steamship tickets. In fact, the immigrants would sometimes buy tickets via installments, pay much more than necessary and then find that the tickets were invalid. But fraudulent tickets were just the beginning of the victimization of immigrants. The purchaser would often arrive at the dock and be told that their boat was not leaving and be forced to incur usurious hotel and baggage storage fees while waiting.

The most tragic abuses happened to those buying tickets for their family overseas to come to America. When their families overseas heard that their tickets were ready, they would sell their belongings, leave their homes, and go to the city of embarkation. When families found out that the tickets were fraudulent, they "find themselves destitute in a foreign city. Some return home, although they have sold off all they possessed, others starve among strangers." They would often remain homeless while their American relative tried to scrounge up enough money for replacement tickets. Sometimes waiting family members were even arrested for begging.[330]

At the time of Kellor's investigation, convicting swindlers required proof a ticket was refused from the European port. This made getting a conviction practically impossible.[331] This widespread abuse of this mobile population needed regulation. Fraudulent ticket sales comprised just one example of threats to unwary immigrants. Fraudulent banks proliferated. Many used pilfered stationery to establish credibility. Kellor went undercover and found obtaining well-known bank's stationery easy. Even if the bank had stationery from a mainstream bank, "neither the stub nor the order given to the purchaser contained any name of the firm issuing it."[332] Kellor's Commission on Immigration found in one year "there were twenty-five failures of these [private immigrant] banks, in which $1,459,296 was lost to the depositors."[333]

Real estate agents sold land to immigrants that had been overpriced, paid for on a nearly permanent lay away system, and was often nonexistent or useless. In one exemplary real estate case, the NACL found a family exploited and starving. They took the real estate company to court and gave the immigrant family money for food.[334] "Runners" were those who met immigrants on the docks in order to scam them. They took people to overpriced hotels, kept immigrant's luggage, sold them on non-existent jobs for a fee, introduced them to other scammers, shortchanged them and used counterfeit money in currency exchanges. The NACL busted at least one counterfeit ring and got the involved runner put in jail. Kellor's group took pride in being "much more active than they [other groups] in running down these swindlers."[335]

Personal Protection

Kellor's NACL was actually the New Jersey – New York offshoot of a larger, more conservative, organization centered in

Boston. But her organization's work almost immediately overshadowed the Boston branch.[336] At the creation of her NACL, Kellor announced, "The first thing we intend to do is to establish an agent at Ellis Island." Despite the existing protective agencies, "there is no Hungarian society at Ellis Island; neither is there a society to look after the Poles. As for Italians and Hebrews, it is for the most part only special cases that are taken care of."[337] Though the Education Alliance sent quite a few, the need for immigrant guides went well beyond what they could supply. It was for these efforts that Kellor got dubbed the "chaperone of the immigrants."[338]

While the head of a state government bureau, Kellor set up and worked from an office adjacent to the docks where immigrants arrived. The NACL "Immigrant Guide and Transfer" department handled 24,410 immigrants in the 1910 – 1911 year and 39,892 in 1911 – 1912.[339] Kellor also formed a "conciliation" department that "heard, investigated and sought to obtain settlement of all complaints brought by aliens."[340] "In 1912 no fewer than 1,140 persons appeared at the NACL office with complaints concerning non-payment of wages, fraudulent representations made by employment agents and labor contractors regarding terms and conditions of work, overcharges for food and supplies and ill-treatment at labor camps, and other illegal practices."[341] Between 1912 and 1913 they handled nearly 2,500 complaints.[342] The next year Kellor's groups adjudicated nearly double the number of problems.[343]

Chapter Six

Even as a government leader, Kellor personally manned the offices on the docks. A puff – piece on Kellor described these interactions as hurried but never ignored. She also advertised her services and warnings of scams in Italian, Polish, German, Yiddish, French and Hungarian newspapers. Furthermore, to increase awareness among those embarking for America, she published these materials in fifty-seven dialects in European media.[344] Typically, her program linked intimate local efforts to broader networks. For the first time this work showed the incorporation of the international angle that eventually drove her from Americanization.

The Legal Branch

Kellor's legal training proved essential to her success. She analyzed possible legal remedies for the southern penal exploitation in 1901. *Out of Work,* her investigation of domestic workers, ended with a comparison of state laws and how they were implemented. In 1904 New York enacted the Employment Association Act, due to Kellor's efforts. It was said to be the "model statute of the kind in the United States."[345] In 1905 she and Margaret Dreier suggested "a national committee to draft a uniform employment agency law, to be submitted to various States for their adoption."[346] And, in 1906 her Intermunicipal Committee on Household Research (ICHR) presented two Bills to regulate employment agencies.[347] The employment Bills passed.[348] The BII alone got sixteen "important immigrant protective or welfare laws passed" during its first three years.[349]

The NACL featured a legal branch and an education branch. This divided structure became Kellor's typical organizational structure. Characteristically, rather than invent their own organization, the NACL formed a working relationship with a pre-existing organization, the Legal Aid Society (LAS). Her group chose the LAS because it had "for its purposes the rendering of legal aid, gratuitously, if necessary, to all persons, regardless of race, color or creed." Also, their dedication to "righting the wrongs of the poor." The NACL gave the LAS office space and a contribution of $2,500 a year "to cover the expenses of this branch office." And they called the resulting group the "Immigration Branch of the Legal Aid Society."[350] The LAS selected the attorneys involved and the NACL approved them.

The immigration branch of the LAS wrote many laws. For example, In 1911 a NACL investigation into Greek neighborhoods caused the LAS of the NACL to advocate a law to forbid shoe shining on Sundays as the children were being worked from "7 a.m. until about 9 or 10 p.m. seven days a week."[351] Still another law made it illegal for porters and hotels to hold tickets for clients. Banks, according to one of their laws, had to have a ten thousand dollar bond in order to do business. Other laws regulated steamship ticket salesman and allowed for the inspection of labor camps.

Some of these laws seemed overbearing. They gave the government power that could be said to violate civil liberties. In Massachusetts, the NACL pushed a law to compel those

Chapter Six

between the ages of fourteen and eighteen who could not "read and write legible simple sentences in the English language" to be a "regular attendant" at school.[352] One law mandated that records be kept on who was employed and where. Others seemed perfectly reasonable. Employment contracts had to be "in a language which he [the immigrant] is able to understand, the name address, the work to be performed, the hours of labor, wages offered."[353]

In order to work up public support Kellor often used newspapers and spoke publicly. In reference to the regulation of bankers and steamship ticket sellers, the *New – York Tribune* claimed, "The public demand for state regulation of bankers for immigrants and steamship ticket agents arose from the series of articles printed in the *Tribune* airing the gross abuses which the state commission found."[354] In 1906, "Standing in an automobile, Kellor conducted street meetings" to back a candidate, William Jerome, who, in turn, backed her laws.[355] One article had her traveling to New York's capital, Albany, twice in one week to get assurances of a signature from the Governor.[356] Kellor's legal efforts required both public and behind-the-scenes politicking.

The NACL legal department also worked on incredibly intimate projects. In the weekly report of July 12th, 1911 we find the case of Anna Smallen vs. Mrs. J. Saltzman. The notes on it read, "Wage Claim. Referred by the Brooklyn office. The defendant called at the office on receipt of my letter and after a brief interview signified her willingness to pay the complaintant wages in full and also return the clothes . . . Complaintant has received her salary and clothing." In the list of cases, many of the entries resemble number one hundred and eighty-one which reads, "Loss of baggage. Interviewed Mr. Kellerman of the Cunard S. S. Co., who is willing to settle the matter for $15."[357]

All totaled, during the week of July 12, 1912, the LAS of the NACL settled two hundred and twenty three intimate cases. These intimate records sit strangely next to discussions of state legislation and the "briefs on jurisdiction and power of foreign consulars" being compiled for Kellor. The networking strategy Kellor created had advantages. While the NACL's legal team pushed state laws to rectify systemic abuses, they also handled individuals' cases.

The Educational Branch

In addition to the legal committee, the NACL had a very creative Educational Extension that engaged in research and activism. They set up a commission to investigate the educational needs of labor camps and established or cooperated with local school authorities to create schools. They also sought to promote education in at worksites "by means of libraries, lectures, industrial and domestic training."[358] In Brooklyn the National White Land Company employed "250 and 300 Poles and Italians" and the company asked if "the League would be willing to supervise an educational and welfare experimental" program at the factory.[359] The Educational Extension of the NACL undertook this effort.

Chapter Six

Sometimes the legal and educational wings coordinated. In 1911, the Educational Extension met with the Legal Commission and the Italian Immigrant Society (IIS) to discuss "The Italian Society Camp School Bill."[360] The bill had passed the House and Senate but the governor refused to sign it. The educational and legal branches met to address the Bill's weakness in the hopes of gain approval upon resubmission. The wording of the bill got amended so as to make the organization less permanent-sounding. The NACL agreed to enlist the backing of the influential New York City school superintendant Julia Richman, and other groups to pass the law. And before submitting the changes to the legislature, the NACL Education Extension asked for time to have its members approve the changes.

The time the NACL Education Extension asked for to get member approval reflected the NACL's balance between centralization and democracy. Throughout her career, Kellor sought to further the well-being of the vulnerable by coordinating the efforts of pre-existing groups. The Educational Committee attempted to "supervise all educational experiments, organization of local committees, and work in isolated camps and communities."[361] But the committee's plan specified that it "Shall take no steps interfering in any way with the autonomy of any organizations represented upon it."[362] In the NACL constitution, item two conveyed that "the League . . . seeks to strengthen existing organizations."[363] Kellor had a commitment to supporting, rather than replacing, local activists. In this structure, ultimately, the local, state, and national efforts did not have to cancel each other out – they supported each other.

One justification for coordinating, rather than replacing, local groups was that it allowed the intimate contact evidenced in the previously discussed legal cases. The NACL successfully invited the Society of Jewish Social Workers and other groups to its conferences in order to "have the benefit of the point of view of the various associations representing particular immigrant races, and having at heart the welfare of these races in America."[364] A NACL survey provided blank space on the survey for groups to provide "Any suggestions for cooperation."[365] The networking structure facilitated understanding immigrants' needs and keeping in touch with those who worked with them in diverse settings.

Acting as the head of the BII, Kellor explained that great practicality resulted from coordinating pre-existing groups. She told her group that "Something like fifty or one hundred different organizations are doing work with reference to naturalization, but there is no connection between these different organizations, no standard of work, and no method by which one organization may know what the other is doing."[366] Arguing that power would come from combining efforts, she lamented, "in the matter of legislation, there has been practically no cooperation, so far as I know, between the different societies. There is no method at the present time [to inform groups of] bills which would work to the advantage of the immigrant and bills to be opposed." And Kellor's

Chapter Six

work kept "various societies informed . . . with all studies and experiments made of immigrant matters."[367] Combining efforts created power and efficiency.

This coordinating structure allowed the Education Extension to undertake both investigations of city-based immigrant communities and help isolated immigrant communities.[368] Working closely with the Italian Immigrant Society (IIS), the NACL Educational Committee attempted to "supervise all educational experiments, organization of Local committees, and work in isolated camps and communities."[369] They then got the city "to approve the item of $25,000.00 for twenty-five visiting teachers."[370] Teachers such as these were to be deployed "Wherever a sufficient number of minors are temporarily congregated or segregated where no instruction is provided."[371] The NACL funded teachers at obscure worksites throughout the state.

In the Polish section of Rochester, the school district refused to start classes because they thought that the public school classes a mile away were close enough. Fomenting activism, the NACL circulated petitions to show interest in English classes to authorities.[372] They also obtained the names of 2,783 children's names "representing 31 different nationalities and reported them to local school authorities in 103 cities and towns." As a result 1,148 students were placed in schools." Rochester school authorities expressed gratitude because their truant officers could not have located the children without the lists of names of entering foreign-born children.[373] Without empowering locals, the New York based NACL could not have successfully helped efforts in other cities, as they did in Rochester.

Women Linger

As Kellor turned all of her attention to immigrants, she focused more on male workers. Still, she maintained some attention to women. The NACL continued investigating domestic employment agencies. In their first year, they investigated twenty-two, reported one for association with prostitution, and got the proprietors of another arrested for arranging prostitution.[374] In one labor camp "single women were found cooking for squads of men who had no dressing rooms, no bathing place, no sanitary conveniences, and no privacy whatever."[375] As late as 1910, in her capacity as director of the Inter-municipal Research Committee, Kellor unsuccessfully attempted to establish a "national commission on immigrant women." Among other concerns, Kellor said she hoped it would aid female traveling alone and provide emergency housing for domestic workers who lost their jobs "at a moment's notice."[376] The inaugural document of the NACL declared, "unmarried immigrant girls will be watched to see they reach their destination."[377]

Beyond specific items, Kellor's very presence in the male-dominated world of state government represented a victory for women. She and Wald had been the lone females on the IC. When she took charge of the IB, she became the first woman to head a state bureau. One newspaper expressed surprise exclaiming, you would guess that "the head of the New York State Bureau of Industries and Immigration would be some big strong man."[378] In her work with the NACL she worked with very powerful men. Mary Dreier claimed Kellor had "so forceful and brilliant a mind that she appealed particularly to men who had reached maturity and were known in the community, such as distinguished lawyers, bankers and industrialists."[379] No other woman sat on the fifteen-member Legal Affairs Committee of the NACL. As a woman, Kellor's very presence aided women's advancement.

In making the claim that Kellor had a legacy, a 1952 eulogy showed that the then existing Wage Claims Unit of the State of New York had an unbroken, "lineal descendant" from her Bureau of Industries and Immigration. This governmental department helped workers alleging non-payment or underpayment of wages. In stressing the legacy of the BII on the Wage Claims Unit, the article noted that "since its establishment in 1919, the Division with which this Unit is now consolidated has always had a woman director."[380] Just as Kellor had dragged Lillian Wald out of her feminine settlement house milieu and into working men's spaces, her rise in government brought women into the male bastion of political power.

Americanization, as the Educational Alliance and other immigrant groups conceived of it, meant creating educational programs and distribution strategies, while sending social workers to docks for the newly arrived. Rising from the neighborhood to the state perspective, Kellor created systemic educational and legal umbrella groups that followed the immigrant from the dock to the worksite. She thereby attempted to address both the individual and the state government he worked under. Now the nation began to fear immigrants. To allay these concerns, Kellor would both build upon the social justice efforts she had already developed and attempt to transform America by implementing a whole new type of national government.

The earliest photo of Kellor

(The Schlesinger Library, Radcliffe College)

FRANCES A. KELLOR.

Kellor's graduation photo from Cornell

(Cornell University)

Kellor (center) with Mary Dreier (left) and Margaret Dreier Robbins (right)

(The Schlesinger Library, Radcliffe College)

Kellor in regalia during the 1912 Progressive Party presidential run

(*The New York Times*)

Kellor, the young professional, goes to work with a Cornell banner behind her in 1913.

(*The New York Times*)

Kellor (left) motoring with Mary (right), 1920

(The Schlesinger Library, Radcliffe College)

Kellor, playful in an intimate moment

(The Schlesinger Library, Radcliffe College)

Kellor in a 1916

(*The New York Times*)

Kellor (right) on porch with tie and hair up, and a butch young woman
(The Schlesinger Library, Radcliffe College)

Enjoying leisure at the Dreiers' vacation home

(The Schlesinger Library, Radcliffe College)

– CHAPTER SEVEN –

THE NATION SOURS AND NEW NATIONALISM IS BORN

The Dillingham Commission Raises Tensions

In 1907 America's concern over immigration became so strong that Congress authorized a commission to study the immigration situation: The Dillingham Commission. Their charge was to statistically document all things concerning immigrants. The forty-two-volume report looked at crime, schooling, settlement, employment, and many other factors. The Commission's most lasting intellectual contribution was popularizing the distinction between the "old immigrants" from northwest Europe and the "new immigrants" from southern and eastern portions of Europe in the popular mind.

The Dillingham Commission found that the inferior racial stock from "new immigrant" areas was diluting America's Anglo-Saxon blood and that, therefore, immigration should be restricted. In defiance of the Dillingham report, the American

Jewish Committee entered one of Kellor's articles into the official report to suggest that America should support and protect immigrants against the many abuses they face rather than limit immigration.[381]

The Dillingham Commission released its volumes in 1911. Kellor responded with the position paper "Needed – A Domestic Immigration Policy." The title referred to the Dillingham report not containing any domestic immigration policy. Invoking sarcastic understatement that could remind one of her wry Coldwater writing, Kellor said she counted herself among "that small group of dreamers who had expected the promulgation of a domestic policy, who had waited for a constructive note, who had hoped that the government might be urged to accept some of the responsibilities which it now leaves to benevolence." Kellor noted that seven of the commission's eight recommendations concerned "restrictive machinery" and "exclusion." In response, she offered a whole new paradigm. Rather than "the negative note of increased deportation," Kellor argued that we needed a national system of aid to immigrants, a positive domestic policy.[382]

Education constituted a strong part of Kellor's positive multifaceted program. Immigrants needed schools. Currently, she noted "the Bureau of Naturalization requires a knowledge of English and of American institutions, but in no way provides any such instruction."[383] But herein she also specified that the government should "prepare, in languages which he can understand, information which will be of service to the alien."[384] Following her adopted Coldwater guardian Mary Eddy's lead, she called for "library facilities for aliens."[385] And most radically, she suggested teaching political advocacy because "there are children to enter our schools and women entitled to rights and privileges as yet unknown to them."[386] These were but some of the features a positive domestic policy towards immigration could include.

Kellor's positive program also continued to focus on the material needs of immigrants. Education was important, but that would not be enough because no policy could be good that sent them to worksites where "they live like animals."[387] Kellor argued that language differences and transience meant immigrants needed special accommodations in the judicial system. When cheated by their employers, they "literally run the risk of staving while they are trying to collect wages due."[388] She recommended a string of protections, starting with social workers at docks, that her Bureau of Industries and Immigrants had provided. Kellor's programs had always emphasized the material over the educative.

Americanization Considers Fear

However, Kellor now announced that the material protections themselves could have an educative component. She wanted the immigrant to know that the American nation stood behind him. She forthrightly conceded that providing immigrants materials in their own language might not improve their situation.

But she still thought it intrinsically valuable, as it would convey the notion that "the new country is interested in him as an individual."[389] And, in her response to the Dillingham Commission she opined, "How can we possibly expect an alien to be law-abiding, properly respecting and honest, when his first experiences in this country are robbery, overcharging, neglect and frequently instructions to evade the law?"[390]

This formula, wherein social justice helps assure good behavior on the part of immigrants, acknowledged the growing fear of disruption by immigrants in America. But, unlike others who addressed this potential, Kellor laid the blame for such potential at the feet of long-term Americans. She argued that we must replace the hatred found in the Dillingham report with positive protections that would make the immigrant feel attached to this country. Many of Kellor's Americanization programs employed the homily that people have favorable attitudes towards those who treat them well.

Scholars not only miss how much Americanization sought to aid immigrants, they fail to notice the program's heavy and relentless criticism of long-term Americans. In her reply to the Dillingham report, Kellor inveighed against long-term Americans' "unreasonable prejudice, amounting to the feeling and belief that foreigners are a different kind of people from 'our people.'" Due to the prevalence of prejudice, Kellor stated, "No process of assimilation will, therefore, be successful which does not educate and amalgamate the native-born American as well as the alien."[391] Kellor worked towards unity between all residents of America. And, as long as the long-term Americans hated immigrants, divisions would appear in the national social fabric.

Kellor declared that we need policy aimed at "the assimilation of the immigrant after arriving – constituting our domestic policy."[392] Important to understanding Americanization, herein Kellor's use of the word "assimilation" resembled our current use of the word "integration," especially economic integration. As she explained, "Assuming that our domestic policy is assimilation . . . the essentials of such a policy obviously do not lie in regulations, repression and negation." Instead, she recommended "fair industrial opportunity, distribution, protection, education and equal protection of the laws."[393] This was necessary because immigrants "are strangers and must find homes; they are unemployed and must find work."[394] For Kellor, assimilation meant economic integration. Economic inclusion was a pillar of Americanization.

Kellor Joins the *New Republic* Intellectuals

In the 1960s, and in some quarters today, historians started denouncing progressives as political reactionaries. Progressives' reform programs have been castigated for actually seeking to placate workers and forestall radical reforms. Since the late 1990s the progressives' reputation has been improved. Historians' revitalization of progressivism has stressed its intellectuals, such as John Dewey, Herbert Croly, Walter Weyl, and Walter Lippmann.[395] Historians have argued that a failure to be radical does not make one a proponent of the status quo. In addition, there has been an increased appreciation for just how radical their programs were. Since all four of these central intellectuals worked on the *New Republic* magazine, this book refers to them as the "*New Republic* intellectuals."

Croly gave the name "New Nationalism" to Theodore Roosevelt's 1912 election platform. This platform sought to have the Federal government given the power to create social justice. This philosophy noted that the age of small towns, like Kellor's Coldwater, Michigan, had passed. As discussed in Chapter Four, whereas men previously guided their destiny via individual initiative, now large impersonal economic forces ruled man's fate. The era of small towns like Coldwater, Michigan was over. Individuals holding town hall meetings could not bend the new industrial forces to the service of man. This philosophy birthed the notion of the strong Federal government that bloomed under the New Deal and continues to this day.

Rather than a free market or locals, progressive intellectuals would tame the economy by Federal regulations. This strong government run by sociological experts would, naturally, lessen the import of elections. The average citizen knows very little about topics such as economic theory, city planning, and industrial regulation. And, once Federal regulatory mechanisms were put into place, average citizens would not need to vote on them. Our votes, to this day, affect very little in specific Federal policy. Experts with power, rather than individual voters, would humanize industrial forces.

The *New Republic* intellectuals who designed New Nationalism obsessed over how to maintain the relevance of individual voters and political participation in this government by experts. This question seemed especially vexing in light of the centrality of democracy to America's national identity. Historians today consider the question of how to maintain the relevance of democracy to the industrial era's newly strengthened Federal government by experts, to be the main conundrum considered by progressive intellectuals.[396] Kellor's work directly addressed this very question.

Beyond the fact that each of the *New Republic* intellectuals worked for her, Kellor's overlapping agenda, including that of her Americanization work, shows that her projects should be evaluated in the context of the *New Republic* Intellectuals. Our protagonist's exclusion from nearly all analyses of the *New Republic* crowd, likely stems from her implementing policy rather than working in pure theory. And, when books on the topic merely refer to Kellor as a "reformer," as opposed to a leader or theorist, we understand the sexist undertones.[397] Whereas male intellectuals wrote books filled with abstractions and suggestions, Kellor actually implemented New Nationalist ideas. Her distinctions should argue for her inclusion, not her exclusion.

The Nation Sours and New Nationalism is Born

We need to write Kellor back into this story. By examining the ways in which Kellor's programs, including Americanization, succeeded and failed, we can better understand the strengths and weaknesses of the *New Republic* intellectuals' ideas. Reciprocally, understanding their quest helps us understand the theory behind Kellor's Americanization project. After all, Kellor's brand of Americanization was an implementation of the *New Republic* intellectuals' New Nationalism agenda. In doing so we will also put Kellor's Americanization movement back in the context of the Progressive movement that informed its ideals.

In 1912 Kellor resigned from her post as the head of the Bureaus of Industries and Immigration, and deemphasized work with immigrants as she developed and implemented a comprehensive national reform program called "the Service." This program tackled nearly all known social issues using a sociological structure she created. As Walter Lippmann and John Dewey had wanted, the Service united America's population and political system via participation in activism aimed at national progressive reforms. Previously, Kellor's Americanization included substantial, yet piecemeal, protections for immigrants. But now, as tensions fomented by the Dillingham Commission grew, Kellor temporarily left Americanization and immigration work to redesign the American system of government and the nature of being an American.

Chapter Seven

The Service's Background

In 1912, ex-President Theodore Roosevelt ran for the Office of the President of the United States on the Progressive Party ticket. If, as the leading *New Republic* intellectual Herbert Croly argued, Roosevelt embodied the nation's aspirations, he had a great deal of help discovering them. Rather than a traditional party, social workers and reformers such as Kellor made up the bulk of the Progressive Party insiders who advised Roosevelt. While they thought such participation improper for women, *The New York Times* admitted, "Miss Addams, Miss Kellor, Mrs. Raymond Robins [Margaret Dreier], and people like them, practically dictated to him [Roosevelt] the social and industrial welfare planks of the Bull Moose platform."[398]

And while Croly came up with the campaign's "New Nationalism" slogan, Kellor took a leading role in the "Female Brain Trust" that wrote Roosevelt's platform.[399] Thus, two sources of Kellor's inspiration, academic progressive intellectuals and female settlement house reformers, came together to guide Roosevelt's 1912 campaign.

One of Kellor's contributions to Roosevelt's campaign was the Progressive Party's immigration plank, which announced the goal of promoting immigrants' "assimilation, education, and advancement."[400] Significantly, the Progressive Party's immigration plank stressed economic means of achieving this tripartite goal. The first part of the plank called for "the establishment of industrial standards" to get both immigrants and long-term Americans "a larger share of American opportunity."

The second part of the plank generically denounced indifference to immigrants. The last section suggested distribution of immigrants. Distribution, again, referred to Kellor's plan for connecting the unemployed to employment opportunities around the nation.

Echoes of the numerous protective measures Kellor created to protect the immigrants from banking, ticketing, and lodging scams also appeared in the Progressive Party's immigration plank. The plank announced a determination to "rigidly supervise all private agencies dealing with them [immigrants]." With a heavy industrial emphasis, this plank contained no hint of the need for attending to culture or ideas. Its contents confirmed that Kellor's basic definition of assimilation referred to the immigrant's material well-being and economic integration. Concomitantly, this plank also confirmed that protecting and providing for immigrants comprised much of what Kellor initially meant by Americanization.

Kellor's fantastic sociological vision, the Service, began when Roosevelt lost the 1912 election. From the outset, people understood that Roosevelt probably would not win the Presidency. Though possibly quixotic, Kellor considered the campaign effort "an unparalleled training school for women who have not participated in political affairs . . . before they have the ballot."[401] Progressives generally saw the campaign as an opportunity to publicize their platform and thereby educate America. After Roosevelt lost the election, the Service served as an organizational structure that embodied the progressives' activist agenda by keeping citizens aware of and involved in progressive causes between elections.

Incidentally, the organization under discussion was known under different names during its tenure: the Progressive National Service; the National Progressive Service; and the Service Wing of the Progressive Party. In addition to these designations, official branches went by the names of states and municipalities. The Wisconsin Progressive Service provides one such example. Since the word *service* appears in each of these titles, in this writing Kellor's sociological scheme for running American politics will simply be referred to as "the Service." From the end of 1912 until the end of 1914, the Progressive party officially bifurcated. The political machinery limped along. And Kellor's Service constituted the activist half of the national Progressive Party.

Suffrage First

Before moving past the Presidential campaign and onto the Service, we must momentarily appreciate the gendered significance of Kellor's activism for Roosevelt. *The New York Times* noted that if anyone would have guessed a year prior to the Progressive Party's 1912 Presidential campaign that women would take almost as prominent a campaign role as men, that they would have organized women's bureaus, and have put women on its National and State Committees, they would have been "thought mad."[402] Women's very participation itself rewrote gender roles.

During the Presidential campaign, with three other women, Kellor served as a member of the National Committee of the Progressive Party. She was the lone female on the Party's six-member Executive Committee Administrative Board.[403] Her long and close association with Roosevelt helped her get these positions of trust. After reading her book *Out of Work* in 1906,[404] Roosevelt instructed his Cabinet members to pay attention to what Kellor had to say.[405] During the campaign he boasted, "It's been a great thing to see how women like Miss Addams and Miss Kellor, and women like that, have gone into the campaign. You can't estimate the effect they have had in boosting it to a high level."[406] Kellor's executive level participation in a Presidential campaign represented a milestone in the empowerment of women.

As a Presidential candidate, Roosevelt exclaimed, "I always favored woman's suffrage, but only tepidly, until my association with women like Jane Addams and Frances Kellor, who desired it as one means of enabling them to render better and more efficient service, changed me into a zealous instead of a lukewarm adherent of the cause."[407] Though he relied more on Kellor, this second instance of pairing of Addams and Kellor's names by Roosevelt shows that the public held them in near equal esteem at this time. It also points to their both being very significant contributors to women obtaining suffrage in America.

As a result of convincing Roosevelt, the Progressive Party became the first major political party to advocate female suffrage. This first put other parties on the defensive; they too had to take a stand. The Progressive's position cleared the way for the Republican Party's controversial 1916 advocacy of female suffrage. Kellor also played a leading role in getting suffrage on that platform. On a national level, very few women have had as much influence on advancing female political participation and women's suffrage as Kellor.

The Service's Purview

Kellor shared the *New Republic* intellectuals' conviction that the political system of the 1800s was not fit to govern a modern industrial state. Kellor's policy article, "A New Spirit in Party Organization," began with the observation that "Politics in American had become a question of nominations and elections."[408] Kellor considered elections to be circuses that rarely resulted in practical results. Lippmann perhaps more eloquently summarized the *New Republic* intellectuals' very same view of candidate-based government, when saying in elections, "if one half of the people is bent upon proving how wicked a man is and the other half is determined to show how good he is, neither will think very much about the nation."[409] To America's detriment, political parties only thought of elections.

To start her "New Spirit" policy paper, Kellor bemoaned the fact that political parties did not listen to social scientists or social workers. Kellor came up with a plan to supplement, if not

The Nation Sours and New Nationalism is Born

replace, electoral politics. The Progressive Party bifurcated just after the Progressive's 1912 electoral defeat. The political portion of the Progressive party kept its focus on elections; the Progressive Service of the National Progressive Party founded, created, and directed grassroots political participation to chase the Progressive Party platform between elections.

Succinctly said to have "directed its attention primarily to the development of a laboratory of investigation and recommendation," the Service used experts, along with their research, to systematically address all of the nation's social problems.[410] As with several of her other organizations, Kellor drew a flow chart to outline the structure of the Service. This chart gave responsibility for four broad areas of social ills: Social and Industrial Justice, Conservation, Popular Government and, finally, the Cost of Living and Corporation Control. The Service organized people to fight these four categories of ills at the State and local level.

Excited at its prospects for "pioneering of the human spirit" and exploring "the moral resources of our fellow citizens," Jane Addams ran the Bureau of Social and Industrial Justice.[411] And, as the flowchart mapped out, the subcategories under her department's purview included Men's Labor, Women's Labor, Immigration, Social Insurance, and Child Welfare.[412] While head of the entire Service, Kellor also ran the immigration branch Jane Addams supervised. The Immigration department wanted a national organization of labor distribution and the founding of more immigrants clubs.

Significantly, the flowchart conveyed that immigration belonged under the category of Social and Industrial Justice. The visual also conveyed that Kellor saw immigration as one part in a comprehensive attack on all social problems. The adjustments that society needed to make regarding immigrants constituted one part of a comprehensive plan for a better society. The flowchart represented the nation as an activist organization that addressed social ills comprehensively in coordination with the State. The flowchart institutionalized the New Nationalism ideal of collective national cooperation.

Addams' "Social and Industrial Justice" department had the most activity.[413] Its advocacy of "Sickness Insurance and Service Pensions; Unemployment and Old Age Insurance," foreshadowed the New Deal.[414] The famous progressive naturalist, Gifford Pinochet ran the Service's "Conservation" department. And the "Direct Legislation" department focused on suffrage. And while it seems to have covered currency and markets, the name of the final group, "Cost of Living & Corporation Control" speaks to Kellor's goal of total national coordination of the economy.

How the Service Governed

As Kellor's previously formed group, the North American Civic League for Immigrants, the Service had an educational branch and a legal branch. Connecting her to the *New Republic* intellectuals, John Dewey worked for the Service's educational branch and Walter Weyl, an editor of the *New Republic* magazine, worked for the legal branch of the Service.

The structure of the organization conveyed a crucial part of Kellor's ultimate vision. Sociological findings from each of the bureaus in charge of a category of social problems were to be translated into curriculum by the education branch and legislation by the legal branch. The curriculum would explain the legislation and the need for the legislation to the public. The hope was that when the populace came to understand the problems and solutions via the educational branch, they would demand that politicians enact the progressive legislation that the Service's legal branch recommended. Pressed by popular sentiment, the legislators would have to enact this legislation that the sociologists had recommended. In this way, the Service's combination of research, education, and bill writing would intelligently guide politics.

With the above structure, the Service aimed at creating a fundamentally different form of government in America. Sociologists would design the legislation that the people would press the legislators to enact. Legislators would just be bureaucrats in implementing the sociologists' popularly supported findings. Misappropriating a word from Lester Frank Ward, this would be a "sociocracy."[415] The real leaders of this brand of New Nationalism would be the sociologists. And Kellor would be the head of all the sociologists. And, Kellor nearly got this vision off the ground without Roosevelt winning the 1912 election.

As an intriguing counterfactual, if Roosevelt had won the 1912 election, Kellor, as the head of the Service, would have had official backing to implement this new form of government. It is not simply hyperbole to say that with this victory she could have fundamentally rewritten the way our government works. Kellor could have also come close to running the society via running the Service if the political half of the Progressive party been more successful in subsequent elections. Had Roosevelt won, this campaign might be remembered as much more than just another Presidential election.

The Service's Achievements

At the base of the Service sat local progressive clubs. The Service by-laws stipulated that upon securing ten or more members, an official local club would be established. The local clubs would elect members of the state service committees.[416] These were, in turn to be federated into a state league of clubs.[417] The national and state Service branches also sent organizers to confer with and rally the locals.[418] And once a year each State Service Committee was to host a conference, during which all progressive participants would "discuss the measures before the people, social and economic problems and all matters which come within the terms of the Progressive platforms, national, state, and local."[419] Thus the communication flowed both up towards the national level and back down to the local level.

In 1914 Kellor wrote that, "twenty –one States have State services which do for each State what the National Service does for the country in acting as their clearing-house between States."[420] Rather than create the agendas and dictate them, the Service's Federal structure sought to foster and guide state and local participation. Thus the Service's structure united the nation in political participation. The structure of the Service, as the *New Republic* intellectuals dreamed, brought the national perspective to the people and let the people inform the national agenda. An appropriate, if paradoxical, name for the Service's vision would be "Local Nationalism."

The state committees also had educational and legislative branches, as well as committees dedicated to specific causes. The education branches of the Service were particularly strong. Between January 1 and August 31 of 1913, the Education Branch of the Service distributed 86,534 pieces of literature[421] and then created the Progressive National Lyceum Service (PNLS) "to carry the message of good government through the Chautauquas and Lyceums of America."[422]

By August of 1913, the PNLS had "some 1,000 speakers for Progressive meetings of which about 500 are available for meetings outside of their own states."[423] In the first half of 1913, the PNLS had facilitated 574 speakers who made 896 speeches.[424] The Service produced six progressive Stereopticon lectures, containing 50 slides each, on topics such as popular government, trusts, as well as women and child in toil.[425] The PNLS repeatedly sought deals with Thomas Edison to make Progressive Service films. The Service had a very aggressive public education branch that instituted forms of mass media.

The Service also had many successes in the legislative field. Here again, we see communication, cooperation, and mutual aid uniting the national and the local. The national legislative committee kept in contact with State Progressive legislative committees. The national legislative committee collected and analyzed laws. And then they fed versions of laws to different states. Conventions were held where progressive legislators and lawyers came together and conferred in large numbers.

By 1913, the Service had been instrumental in creating and passing at least 18 State laws;[426] 13 more had been championed and defeated, and 15 Federal bills had also been prepared.[427] The third woman to graduate from Cornell with a law degree, Kellor implemented a social structure in order to maximize progressive legal coordination. And while the legislative branch got laws to legislators, the educators taught the public about them. This structure thereby constituted a mechanism for the sociological rule of society by the Service in the name of the people. This structure would turn all Americans into progressive activists who were interested in law, as Kellor herself was.

One PNLS pamphlet explained that the Service was "to make political responsibility an acknowledged factor in the life of all the people, all the time."[428] The pamphlet further enthused that "its work is to secure a larger understanding of what *every* citizen must do to assure self-government."[429] [Italics in original] One meeting's minutes reported Kellor arguing that "the various clubs over the country, of which there were about one hundred and ninety in New York State, claimed that they had nothing to do."[430] While the vision of the Service did engage quite a few activists, it ultimately failed to turn into a movement.

Out of Service

A rift between the industrial leadership of the political wing of the Progressive Party and the activist leadership of the Progressive Service caused the final ending of Kellor's experiment in 1914.[431] But the failure to ignite excitement at the local level seems to have ultimately doomed the Service. Local club dues were to pay for the Service. Although some reports show that it had the means to expand, Kellor admitted to Jane Addams that, "the difficulty of getting money has been a serious one."[432] The citizens did not rise to the occasion en masse when Kellor built the structure to involve them in popular political action.

New Nationalists generally struggled with how to integrate Federal expert leadership and popular input. Perhaps the subtle condescension in Kellor's claim to have "136 experts serving upon its National Committees and 278 experts serving in

Chapter Seven

its local Service branches" undermined the Service.[433] Kellor's brother-in-law Raymond Robins said the Service had too much of a top-down stance and claimed it lacked "organization from the precincts up."[434] But Kellor understood the need for local activism coming from local understanding of local problems. She told the Service's executive committee that local participation had to be fostered, as "no New York committee could possibly do the work of a Buffalo committee."[435] The failure to engage the public happened despite her best efforts. She could not bridge the geographical gap implied in the term Local Nationalism.

Understanding why the Service did not garner enough participation has important implications for the viability of democracy today. Kellor's immigration work focused on a single issue. Groups specific to those problems were willing to coordinate on solving them. One possible reason the Service failed to garner support could be that the local groups it rested on were not pre-existing. Another would be that its wide focus did not pique peoples' specific interests. The legislators and educators did their part. But the people did not become the all around sociological investigators and contributors that Kellor had hoped. She had much more success getting groups already working with immigrants to pitch in.

New Nationalists sought to unite the nation in reform. They largely sought to do this via embodying the popular political will in the national government. Progressive intellectuals never clearly formulated or agreed upon mechanism for reading or utilizing the popular political will for reform. Croly, it is interesting to note, goes from championing Roosevelt intuiting the popular will to schools teaching activism around the time Kellor institutes such schools, without any credit going to her. Lippmann had dreamed of such schools early on, but became more cynical. Both figures worked with Kellor in some capacity later on. Both John Dewey and Walter Weyl participated actively in the Service. Kellor's being influenced by the *New Republic* intellectuals was likely reciprocal.

From the New Nationalist perspective, a person could be said to have become Americanized when they adopted a national political perspective. America, the nation, could only fully be called Americanized when all of its sectors and inhabitants signed onto a national progressive reform agenda. In contrast to the Dillingham commission's focus on immigrant crime and exclusion, Kellor promulgated the ultimate positive inclusive domestic policy. Her Americanization program did not only, or even primarily, seek to Americanize immigrants. When excluding the Service from discussions of Kellor's Americanization program, we fail to understand its nature and scope. Americanization was her version of the New Nationalist agenda.

– CHAPTER EIGHT –

MULTICULTURAL NATIONALISM

Return to Grassroots

As the Service fell, Kellor went on a binge of activism that affected both the immigrant and non-immigrant poor. A month after it ended she took Theodore Roosevelt, unannounced, to several homeless shelters.[436] He raised $14,000 for these shelters at a benefit by telling the audience of the outing he had taken "in company with Miss Kellor."[437] In her capacity as the leader of the Committee for Immigrants in America (CIA), Kellor fought against the Commissioner of Charities in order to utilize churches as homeless shelters. This activism binge by this proponent of nationalism aimed to help America's poorest.

In a public confrontation, our street fighter said that before closing churches to the homeless, her opponents should visit the saloons and employment agencies that were being used as lodging houses. Sounding radical in the face of those who worried that relief would lead to dependence, Kellor proclaimed,

"It is not jobs, but relief, that will solve the problem to-day. There are no jobs, and we can't make them." *The New-York Tribune* reported that Kellor "pried loose a mass of philosophy" in her speech. In it she showed great faith in a the power of education in a democracy when she announced, "I believe there is a great need of stimulating the people of this city to a realization of conditions."[438]

In a 1915 letter to the editor, Frances Kellor argued that America should expand the use of Ellis Island as a homeless shelter. She told readers that the current vacancy rate at homeless shelters reflected poor policies, not a lack of need. Eighty percent of the shelter users were immigrants. The fact that those who became public charges could be deported kept them out of proper shelters. If they had twenty-five cents they were excluded. Furthermore the men could only spend seven days a month at the shelters. Calculating for her audience she announced, " . . . there are twenty-three other nights he needs shelter."[439] As a result of these policies these unemployed immigrants slept under the Brooklyn Bridge, on the streets and in the backs of saloons.

Kellor noted the injustice of the fact that "In summer they do the work for this country . . . but in the winter the city says to them: 'You do not belong to us.'"[440] But Kellor did more than just publicly advocate for homeless shelters. During the month in which Kellor wrote her editorial concerning Ellis Island, her Americanization group, the Committee for Immigrants in America

Chapter Eight

(CIA), provided "6,855 baths, 1,839 shaves and 123 haircuts" at Ellis Island. The CIA also served tens of thousands of breakfasts, lunches, and dinners at their headquarters.[441]

As a nationalist, Kellor's work often aimed at national responsibility. In recognition of our debt and responsibility to the immigrants, she said "the Federal government should open Ellis Island wide for the unemployed aliens."[442] Yet, as usual, her group worked within a network of reform agencies. In fact, Kellor's organization was not the main one working towards opening Ellis Island as a homeless shelter. Still, her activism had enough credibility with those on the streets that eight hundred homeless men threw her a party in recognition of her contributions.[443]

America Bundled

Kellor blended ideals and activism incredibly well. In February of 1915, Kellor organized a project called "Bundle Day," which asked citizens and organizations to donate unused clothes for the poor. Kellor used her media savvy to create interest. An article noted that, "Advertising placards and newspapers and hundreds of thousands of seductive tags raised awareness of the event."[444] These tags in new clothes being sold asked the buyers to donate their old clothes. All totaled, Bundle Day distributed 500,000 bundles of clothes to the needy.[445]

For Bundle Day, Kellor coordinated the efforts of pre-existing organizations that were not usually involved in reform. Railroads, police stations, and hotels were among the clothes collection sites. Department stores provided racks and collected and transported the clothes. The Bundle Day headquarters filled five floors of a Fifth Avenue loft. The "Lackawanna Railroad" donated the coal to heat the building. Volunteers cleaned, folded, and distributed the clothes. One newspaper called it a "sociological phenomenon."[446]

Roosevelt visited the Bundle Day headquarter during distribution, and Kellor escorted Roosevelt up and down the six-floor building via stairs.[447] When asked, he would not pose for photographs alone, "insisting that Miss Kellor stand with him."[448]

Roosevelt also exclaimed, "It is really all so wonderful to think of how the people of New York responded to the appeal for clothing . . . Half of those who observed it liked the passing sensation of being generous; the other half liked the lasting sensation of being clothed."[449] He was perceptive, for a goal from the beginning was "reaching the average man and woman in a simple way who had not thought about the subject [poverty]."[450] Kellor agreed. She beamed, "The biggest thing about Bundle Day is it is socializing the city – everybody is lending a hand."[451]

Multicultural Nationalism

Following upon the heels of Bundle Day, Kellor organized the most high profile of all Americanization efforts, Americanization Day. Held on the Fourth of July, it provided a chance for long-term Americans to welcome immigrants to America and for immigrants to introduce themselves to long-term

Americans. Whereas Bundle Day socialized the city, Americanization Day would socialize the nation.

A bit of administrative jumbling occurred beforehand. Kellor changed the North American Civic League for Immigrants (NACL) into the Committee *for* Immigrants in America (CIA). [Italic added] The *New Republic* magazine editor, Herbert Croly, served as one of its directors. To organize Americanization Day, the CIA then created the National Americanization Day Committee (NADC), which quickly became the National Americanization Committee (NAC). Again, as the names changed with a blur, we shall refer to these Kellor's organizations interchangeably.

And, again illustrating consistency in order to establish it as a theme, one of Kellor's new organizations acted as a clearinghouse that coordinated pre-existing groups. The CIA's first report explained that the group sought to assist reform efforts by providing "information, advice, assistance suggestions, recommendations, analyses, surveys, speakers and materials upon every phase of domestic immigration, without cost, without favor, and without prejudice."[452]

In addition to maintaining a supportive methodology, the CIA retained the Service's goal of national integration. In fact, the CIA was formed to spread the successes of the New Jersey and New York branches of the NACL nationwide.[453] New Nationalism's emphasis on coordinating disparate sectors of society in reform also appeared in the report of the CIA's first report, which explained, "The government may accomplish things which the philanthropy cannot and vice versa; industry can institute experiments and make progress along lines where the others would fail. There can be no successful policy of intelligent and effective assimilation until there is a 'get-together' movement."[454] Kellor consistently worked to unify all sectors of society and all of its members.

The amount of get-together Kellor mustered amazes. Presidents Wilson and Roosevelt endorsed Americanization Day. Cities and states endorsed it. Cornelius Vanderbilt had Tiffany and Company design four buttons promoting the event. Julius Rosenwald, the Sears magnate, contributed to the project. Sixty-two railroads put up posters and 7,612 were posted by various industries.[455] The YMCA, YMHA, DAR, churches, and the Chambers of Commerce participated. Through the government's naturalization clerks, the names and addresses of aliens admitted to citizenship during the preceding year were gathered and invitations were sent. The Federal government chipped in by helping distribute the 179,250 units of information concerning the event.[456] Americanization Day coordinated the public and private sectors.

And Kellor stressed the importance of citizen participation in helping immigrants. In a quote showing activism would change people, at the CIA's first meeting Kellor said in their work, "Necessary to strengthen the hearts and to uphold the efforts of trained men and women in the field is the cooperation of average

Chapter Eight

American citizens." Of the citizen, the group enthused, "He and he alone can eliminate race prejudice and class distinctions and hold out the hand of friendship and personal service which will disarm the exploiter and enable the immigrant to express his best self."[457] Kellor saw citizen participation as a prerequisite to her vision's implementation.

Americanization Day Goals

Americanization Day organizers sought to extend a welcoming hand to immigrants. One poster advertised the event with the CIA motto, "Many Peoples, But One Nation." From there it read, "Make it a day of welcome to all foreign born citizens and an invitation to all residents to become citizens. Make our 13,000,000 immigrants feel that they are a part of and have a share in American institutions." Another poster asked, "What can we do to help them become *Americans first?*" [Italics in original] It answered, "We must do something as a nation to make them feel at home – feel that their interests and their affections are deeply rooted in America." It concluded, "We must do something to make them feel that they are part of, and have a share in, American institutions."[458]

Although Kellor released another copy of her industrial justice program at the same time as the Americanization Day event, the Day did not aim at material comfort.[459] Rather, it supplemented her social justice program with personal contact intended to bond the population. It Americanized via friendly interactions in the street. Assessing the effort, Kellor noted that it had made "city officials extend recognition and welcome to thousands of new citizens and make them feel for the first time the friendly arm of the government in place of the repression, discriminations and injustices hitherto dealt out to them." As a compliment to programs aimed at improving immigrants' material well-being, Americanization Day attempted to make the welcoming of immigrants to America overt.

Americanization Day Mixer

Americanization has been characterized as hostile to immigrants. But Americanization Day could not have been so successful without enthusiastic immigrant involvement. Referring to the city's Jewish participation, a *New York Times* reporter noted that "the celebration is no formally arranged, extraneously imposed State ritual. It is a neighborhood festival. Houses are gay with flags hung by the people who live in the houses. . . . . [It featured] red-white-and-blue electric lights paid for by the fathers of the children who dance under them."[460] As per usual, rather than dominate the civic proceedings, Kellor wrote to the immigrant communities themselves that "we need your ideas, your advice, and your active co-operation."[461]

Across the nation Americanization Day successfully brought immigrants and long-term Americans together. With just six weeks of organizing time, the NAC sparked enormous and peaceful symbolic events in over 150 cities.[462] Importantly, immigrant participation ran high. Between 10,000 and 15,000 Pittsburgh residents, predominantly foreign-born, heard 1,000

Chapter Eight

children sing patriotic songs.[463] A newspaper in Erie, Pennsylvania, reported, "The spectacle of some thousands of new and prospective new citizens marching in parade yesterday was truly inspiring."[464] In Detroit, over half of the 20,000 participants were reported to have come from other nations.[465] In Los Angeles, for Americanization Day, many new citizens were welcomed at high schools. In Kansas City, Missouri, "222 new citizens representing 19 nationalities were guests, one being a woman."[466]

And we should know that the Americanization Day movement targeted the attitudes of long-term Americans as much as those of immigrants. In Hibbing, Montana, 10,000 long-term Americans watched 150 immigrants take the oath of naturalization. As they said, "I do," a large American flag was raised and the band played the national anthem to "cheers and applause from the onlooking thousands."[467] A mile-long parade followed. The event celebrated inclusive civic pride. Despite the weather, in front of 7,000 people, a speaker "congratulated those of foreign birth that they had chosen Missouri for their home and congratulated them again on choosing St. Louis."[468] This celebration fostered civic and national pride as it reinforced the view of America as welcoming to immigrants.

Americanization Day peaked, as World War I peaked, on July 4th, 1918.[469] And the largest celebration happened in New York City. On that day 70,000 people, representing 40 nationalities, paraded up Fifth Avenue. One newspaper reported that great floats were expected from the huge immigrant groups, but praised "the remarkable exhibitions put forward by Armenia, Syria, Switzerland, Spain, Venezuela, and other nations whose floats and marchers were on a plane of artistic effect that is not often found in a street parade." Native Americans and several hundred Filipinos had floats. The Bolivian float had llamas.

The intended new bonds forged between long-term Americans and immigrants remind us of the personal bonds Kellor might have felt in her small hometown of Coldwater, Michigan. She delighted in Americanization Day reports wherein immigrants claimed that though "they had been here many years it was the first time they had shaken hands with an American."[470] Rather than a jingoistic litmus test, Kellor sought intimate connections. Her beaming assessment of Americanization Day expresses her goals: "In many communities this has changed for all time the relationship of American-born and foreign-born men and women in America for, the barriers once down, Americans have found immigrants much like themselves, with the same sorrows, aspirations, hopes, and joys, and the same patriotism and loyalty to America."[471]

Multicultural Nationalism

Kellor sought a loyalty and love of America. Again, her CIA's slogan was, "Many Peoples, But One Nation." And yet her literature also asked that people become "Americans First." Under the increasing pressures and paranoia of World War I, in addition to intimate bonding, Kellor hoped that parading immigrants in their traditional garb under the flag would show

Chapter Eight

that all sorts were loyal to America. We normally do not mix multiculturalism and nationalism. Kellor did. We can call this combination of diversity and nationalism, "Multicultural Nationalism." Recognizing the extent to which Multicultural Nationalism seems oxymoronic can increase our awareness of how historically conditioned our assumptions are.

A lack of historical imagination could make us assume intolerance in Theodore Roosevelt's Americanization Day speech in which he advocated banishing hyphens and demanded that naturalized citizens be taught to "become Americans and nothing but Americans."[472] Yet, later in the very same Americanization Day speech, Roosevelt stated, "There can be no objection to, on the contrary in many cases good will come from, preserving other languages, and above all by spreading among all our people the best old-country traditions and customs."[473] Later still in the speech, he noted that "the man or woman who speaks of foreign-born citizens with habitual contempt or hostility, using offensive nicknames about them, is doing all that can be done to perpetuate hyphenated Americanism in its worst form."[474] Roosevelt's Americanization Day denunciation of hyphens denounced intolerance.

We also see equating equality with the denunciation of hyphens in the Americanization Day speech of an official NAC representative. He argued that, "There should be no distinction recognized or exercised between native and foreign-born citizens. All should have equal opportunity."[475] He capped that statement by exclaiming, "We do not want any hyphenated citizens."[476] Herein the hyphen was equated with injustice. Kellor herself was proud that during Americanization Day, "in many cities the national colors and songs of various nationalities were used."[477] Celebrating America and advocating the end of the hyphen did not necessarily entail a search for conformity.

The Multicultural Nationalism perspective becomes easier to understand when we put the fact that Americanization Day happened as World War I raged. One NAC article explained that while European nations were locked in deadly combat, in America, "the sons of these same nations in America through common interests and loyalties could live in peaceful neighborliness."[478] In this way embracing diversity helped prepare us for the looming war. Embracing our diversity, and making it about unity, also reduced the feelings of alienation and resentment that could lead to dissent.

In Boston's Americanization Day celebration, a Reverend urged people to "lay aside race prejudice and be American citizens . . . [and declared that]"[479] "all nationalities should clasp hands and say, 'Although our brothers across the water are fighting one another, we in this country are brethren under one flag.'"[480] In Jackson, Michigan, a merchant dressed as Uncle Sam rode in the Mayor's car while the band played a medley march, including the national hymns of twelve of the foreign nations; twenty-four boys about ten years old carried the flags of those nations to Uncle Sam's car where they were received by him and taken into the machine with him.[481] The War effort required that we minimize divisions within our nation.

Defending Americanization Day

Despite the emphasis on diversity, scholars have still complained that the Americanization Day events sought conformity. One opined that to the extent that the events did not promote "boundaries fostering exclusivity, nationality and religion," all of the Americanization activities sought to meld peoples.[482] In other words, putting these folks together in an American context, despite the veneer of diversity, blurred distinctions and thus actually undermined diversity. Taken to its logical conclusion, this hard multicultural position would not allow any parades in which different groups marched together. In fact, it would require the audience always be the same ethnic group as the parade participants. Denouncing all but the most stringent separatism as intolerant efforts to create conformity sets the bar at an unreasonable level. The Americanization Day events showed an incredible appreciation for ethnic diversity.

Ultimately, participation can serve as a measure of the coercion involved in such events. It is true that social pressure to can account for some public demonstrations of immigrant fealty to the nation. But the large overflow and vibrancy of the participation speaks of more than begrudging participation. Because of space constraints, in the July 4th, 1918 New York City Americanization Day parade, whereas 35,000 Italians wanted to participate, the number had to be lowered to 10,000. Jews had to come down to the same number from 50,000![483]

And the lessons were not only nationalistic. In addition to trying to foster connections between immigrants and long-term Americans, the celebrations aimed at unity between different ethnic groups. People were nervous that the first Americanization Day parades might break down into ethnic violence. And many participants in the Americanization Day events had known strife in their nations of origin. Lillian Wald, a child of immigrants and Kellor's long time ally in fighting for immigrant rights, said in her Americanization Day speech, immigrants were particularly obligated to celebrate the day, as "there are so many among us who have known persecution."[484]

Kellor's *Immigrants in America Review*

Simultaneous with her Americanization Day efforts, under the auspices of the CIA, Kellor took her Coldwater, Michigan, trade of writing and publishing articles to a new level. Her CIA started publishing the quarterly journal, *Immigrants in America Review*, which ran from March 1915 until July 1916. Kellor served as the editor. Again, Herbert Croly, one of the *New Republic* intellectuals, was one of the CIA directors.[485] He and another major *New Republic* intellectual, Walter Lippmann, sat on the *Immigrants in America Review* advisory editorial board.

Many leaders in the field of immigration wrote for or were interviewed for that journal. The list included Peter Roberts, the head of the YMCA, Frederic Howe, the Commissioner of

Chapter Eight

Immigration at Ellis Island, and the Federal Commissioner of Education, P. P. Claxton, who wrote about how to get immigrant children into the schools. In addition, Sarah Moore, who worked for the Society of Italian Immigrants, and had her industrial worksite education facilities funded by Kellor's NACL in the early years of her Americanization work, was featured.

The *Immigrants in America Review* offered helpful information to all those working with immigrant populations. Several articles covered conferences on educating immigrant women in California. Another article profiled the night schools of Minnesota's iron range. Some focused on particular groups, such as the Levantine Jews, Italians, and Poles. Sympathetic articles discussed what the city owed the immigrant. One article included suggestions for humanizing immigrant education. Providing inspiration, a recurring article, the *Record of Progress* detailed programs that helped immigrants across the nation. Another reoccurring column, *Notes on Laws and Decisions*, covered legal decisions pertaining to immigrants. The journal facilitated national communication on immigrant issues.

A specific article worth profiling takes us back to the roots of the Americanization movement. It reported on the progress of the Educational Alliance, the same New York group whose 1893 founding can be used as a starting date for Americanization. Felix Warburg sat on the Education Alliance's board of directors in 1898 and held the post of vice-chair of Kellor's CIA in 1915. The article's author, Henry Fleischman, was the current director of the Educational Alliance. Their inclusion in the *Immigrants in*

America Review indicated that Kellor appreciated this immigrant institution's contributions to Americanization.

Fleischman's article depicted Americanization as liberating. He wrote that "Residence in the Ghetto is enforced in the majority of cases. Lack of English prevents the immigrant from applying for positions outside of the Yiddish-speaking quarter."[486] The article then highlighted the downside of too rapid Americanization of the youth. This was not a new topic to Kellor. Indeed, in 1913, the NACL had warned that "the rapid Americanization of the children, and the neglect of the parents, creates a break, and often clash in the family which is disastrous, in that it frees the children from necessary parental restraint at a time when they need it most."[487] Herein Kellor published a very sensitive reading of Americanization.

The Educational Alliance also took a stand on assimilation by declaring, "A good Jew is of necessity a good American; that a good American cannot be a bad Jew nor can a bad Jew be a good American."[488] This statement supports Multicultural Nationalism. In this context, the fact that Kellor published an article by Horace Kallen in the *Immigrants in America Review* also deserves notice.

Many historians consider Kallen the first major proponent of cultural pluralism. His article, "The Meaning of Americanism," portrayed our nation as only being a political entity.[489] Our ancestry, he pointed out, cannot be chosen and it provided "things of the spirit, the character of happiness, all that

173

constitutes the goal of living."[490] Our nation, from Kallen's perspective, constituted a neutral space in which different ethnic groups co-existed with mutual respect and mutual co-operation. So we see Kellor, via Kallen, hosting advocacy of a sort of proto-multiculturalism.

Kallen denounced any citizen who "uses his citizenship to the disadvantage of his country."[491] His cultural pluralism model did not imply hostility to the United States. Furthermore, he saw American hyphens as binding; in his eyes, all humans were hyphenated, as they were "a member of a church, one of an ethnic and social group, and the citizen of a nation."[492] Democracy allowed "people of all origins and of different gifts live and labor together in amity and co-operation in the building of a great free commonwealth."[493] Evidence suggests that Kellor had sympathy with this view that argued appreciating plurality should serve as the basis of national support. The apparent oxymoron "Multicultural Nationalism" did not seem incongruous to political scientists of the progressive era.

– CHAPTER NINE –

LIVING IN A MATERIAL WORLD

In December of 1915, Kellor's journal, the *Immigrants in America Review* (IAR) awarded its prize for an art contest under the theme, "The Immigrant in America." Gertrude Vanderbilt Whitney, later the founder of the Whitney Museum of Modern Art, and Kellor held the competition at Whitney's studio and offered $1,100 in prizes. The organizers hoped it would "awaken artistic America to its opportunity to portray the immigrant in American life." Kellor and Mrs. Whitney, as the judges, wished to see "the meaning of America to the immigrant and of the immigrant to America."[494]

Whitney and Kellor chose a fifteen-year-old Italian boy by the name of Beniamino "Benny" Bufano as the winner. In creating his art, Bufano said, he "did not try to please America, but to tell the truth." By way of clarification he continued, "the intention of this government may have been good, but time has revealed her destination, a corrupt one. It is for us to place her [America] where all her people shall have the right to enjoy her luxuries."[495] Theodore Roosevelt came to the exhibit, denounced cubism, and praised Bufano's work.[496]

A reporter noted that the fifteen-year old artist had "made of his work an indictment of those who despise the alien and exploit him." In Bufano's collection were thirty figures of "oppressed peoples who seek the Promised Land, and, finding it, find oppression there." To the reporter the collection seemed a challenge to prejudice that calls all aliens, "Dagoes," "Chinks," "Niggers," or "those ignorant foreigners."[497] Through Kellor and Whitney, the meaning of America to the immigrant had been voiced. Bufano went on to fame for chopping off a finger and sending it to President Woodrow Wilson in protest of our entry into World War I as well as creating the public statue of Sun Yat-Sen that still sits in San Francisco's Chinatown.

Historians have gotten Kellor and much of the Americanization movement wrong. Robert Carlson, for example, claimed that Kellor stood for the "imperious demand for conformity of the outsider to national norms" and that "Through her entire career, she viewed outward expressions of nonconformity by the immigrants as symptomatic of their failure to adhere to the American civic religion."[498] Herein we see her, in the heyday of Americanization, choosing a winner who denounced prejudice and exploitation. Such condemnatory quips fail to appreciate the comprehensive nature of Kellor's vision.

Out of Work's National Vision

In 1915, Kellor released a revision of her 1904 book, *Out of Work*. But, as *The New Republic* review noted, it was an "ample revision."[499] The book had nearly twice the number of pages, and its subtitle had changed dramatically. The full title of the 1904 work read *Out of Work: A Study of Employment Agencies: Their Treatment of the Unemployed, and Their Influence Upon Homes and Business.* Losing its specificity, the complete title of the 1915 book was shortened to *Out of Work: A Study of Unemployment.*

Whereas the first *Out of Work* dealt with employment agencies and largely concerned domestic employment, the newer book considered the subject of employment broadly. Chapter titles now included "Children and the Labor Market," "How America Markets its Labor," "The Marketing of Skilled Labor," and "How America Relieves Unemployment." Rather than just immigrants or women, this book addressed national topics. Nearly doubling the page count, the newness of the text, and the new development of a national perspective merited a totally new title. But Kellor's retaining the title *Out of Work* paid homage to her continuing focus on workers as workers.

Overall, the revised *Out of Work*'s newest theme was the need for a national industrial policy. It opened with a statistical lambasting of those who asserted that anyone who wanted to could find work in America and rebuked the contention that those in bread lines were "deficient" or "shirkers." It then moved on to explain that unemployment is an "*industrial* evil." [Italics in original] Kellor emphatically declared that we needed a "*national industrial policy.*"[500] [Italics in original] As such, she argued for, among other programs, a national system of unemployment offices, national unemployment statistics, and a national worker distribution system.

Characteristically, as this national economic vantage point needed to be supplemented by constant agitation, our agitating protagonist explained that "public spirited American citizens who have labored hard to secure the passage of good laws have a way of 'going to sleep' when the laws are safe on the statute books."[501] In an effort to "shorten the distance from theory to practice," the appendix of the book contained six state employment bills, a summary of Cleveland's relief measures, as well as a list of actions churches could undertake and a list of relief measures instituted by citizens.[502] As in her other work, Kellor sought to close the gap between the local and the national via activism.

Out of Work and Women

Whereas the 1904 *Out of Work* relegated men to a single chapter, this new edition relegated women to a single chapter. Outside of that chapter, Kellor generically referred to *workmen*. She argued that women needed special attention when studying unemployment: "A description of the social effects of unemployment among women would include all the aspects that have been noted for men." But she informed us that "women are at all times handicapped by not being able to take advantage of even the few resources provided for unemployed men."[503] Within the context of her times, including attention to women itself made a statement.

Showing a concern with normative morality she had not displayed in a long time, Kellor made the connection between economy and vice. She wrote, "It is impossible to evade the conclusion that increase in prostitution goes hand in hand with increases in unemployment." Though unemployment affected fewer women, she admitted, it "is more serious, and its increase carries with it social and economic dangers, not only to industry, but to the home and the community."[504] While this book has noted her continually decreasing emphasis on morality, here we see evidence to the contrary. But, whereas the topic consumed a chapter in her earlier work, here we only get a few sentences.

Kellor portrayed women as central to the moral order but simultaneously denied women belonged in the home. "The popular theory that housework is a solution of all unemployment among women is no longer tenable and does not lift the burden from the conscience of society."[505] Kellor accepted that housework existed, but this did not mean women would not work. Women would work, could be out of work, and thus merited consideration and a chapter unto themselves.

Chapter Nine

Out of Work and immigration

Immigrants also garnered a chapter in this revision. In the first edition of *Out of Work* Kellor discussed domestic work for immigrant, African - American, and long - term American women without distinction. Kellor now felt she had to address immigrants as a distinct population. As such, her chapter on immigrants included a long, direct, in-depth direct rebuttal to a leading sociologist who argued for reducing immigration, E. A. Ross.

While admitting some job displacement, Kellor attempted to prove that "the data does not show that these same displaced Americans are unemployed or employed at a lower wage-rate." She conceded that "immigrants are used both to prevent and to break strikes. But she added, "So are Americans with much greater opportunity to know the issues concerned." She also proudly noted that "[immigrants have] organized their own protests against conditions."[506] Overall, she argued that, rather than displacing American workers, immigrants helped long-term Americans move into different fields.

In terms of loyalty, Kellor wrote that immigrants' lack of attachment to America was to be expected when they were "crowded into the barest shanties, hovels or barns, with no sanitary provisions."[507] She believed that this exploitation reflected discrimination: "These conditions do not prevail for Americans. The contractor usually puts up their houses for them and often has them taken care of."[508] She blamed America for the faults of immigrants and passionately asserted that blaming the immigrants "is an easy way to explain overcrowding of cities, wretched housing conditions, increase in crime and in the number of 'public charges,' and political and social discontent."[509] Kellor routinely turned all accusations against immigrants into accusations against long-term Americans and their institutions.

As the rhetoric around immigrants was ratcheted up, in the very last page of the chapter on immigration, Kellor actually considered the idea that restricting immigration might be justified at some point. Yet her immediate caveat to whether or not it might be justified stated, "In the absence of any policy or machinery for the distribution and assimilation of the adult immigrant and of any attempt to direct immigrants into industry . . . we do not know."[510] Thus we could see this as a stalling tactic embedded in an affectation of openness.

But then she made an unprecedented statement, "*The United States should therefore take steps to determine which races are not only assimilable* (sic)*, but desire assimilation and which are not. We have already determined that certain races are not and doubtless others should be added, but this is not primarily a question of unemployment.*"[511] [Italics in original] Since this is not a question of unemployment, one might then assume that this is a question of culture. The use of the word "assimilation" is not specified. Thus, this could be read as a call for cultural homogeneity, the likes of which never again appears in her work.

Chapter Nine

The sentence that follows the previous reads, "*We need to determine what is this country's need of immigrant labor, and to insist upon a living wage.*" [Italics in original] After this, she added, "*We need to know whether we wish continually to have in this country a large number of resident aliens contributing to American industry but entirely shut off from American society and American ideals, and unable therefore to comply with American standards.*"[512] [Italics in original] For Kellor, again, American standards normally referred to clean water and decent housing. Here she leans towards this with the idea of a living wage, but then mentions ideals.

Outside of this mixed last page, *Out of Work* largely defended immigrants and asked for modes of government support for them. When off this topic, the chapter defends the immigrants from charge after charge. The days where Kellor could only discuss improving immigrants' working conditions were gone. The page is mixed and vague, but definitely hints at a desire for immigrants to assimilate and considers immigration restrictions. But the call for restriction says we will not know if it makes sense until we undertake further study and reform. Within the context of her twenty-year career, this one page seems like an attempt to enter relevant arguments with some credibility. With one exception, she never comes this close to considering the merits of immigration restriction again.

Out of Work Reviewed

Rather than put a review of the new version of *Out of Work* in its usual book review section, *The New Republic* dedicated an entire article to its release. The reviewer explained and beamed, "If we cannot know the extent of unemployment even in normal times, it behooves us none the less to try to gain an insight into its causes and significance, and into the means at hand to abate the evil. For this purpose there is no better book available than Miss Frances Kellor's Out of Work." Raving, the *New Republic* author continued, "There are few who would not agree that Miss Kellor's proposals are sound, and, if realized in permanent institutions, would go far towards coping with the evils of unemployment." [513]

Commenting on its detailed and national attention to unemployment, the *Journal of Sociology* hailed *Out of Work* as "the first important study of the kind published in this country."[514] Kellor broke new intellectual ground that moved our nation towards seeing unemployment from a national perspective. We may not have adopted her call for a national distribution program, but during the New Deal we adopted her program of "providing unemployed men with public work that is not artificial."[515] As such, overall, *Out of Work* moved us closer to a place wherein the Federal government takes responsibility for creating jobs.

Despite its Federal aggrandizement, *Out of Work* retains the fundamental Kellor attribute of trying to meld the local and the national. Substantiating the claim that Kellor sought to coordinate all sectors in collective work, the *New Republic* reviewer noted that the "plans are national in scope, but call also for cooperation of the local governments and private bodies."[516] This tension of the local versus the national appears in the juxtaposition of Kellor's grandiose unemployment scheme and her simultaneous hosting of the art competition that could have been held in her hometown of Coldwater, Michigan.

Kellor's CIA curriculum

In 1916, Kellor's Committee for Immigrants in America (CIA) organization and the New York State Department of Education published a curriculum for use with immigrants. Likely reflecting an awareness of her audience, whereas *Out of Work* largely focused on the national perspective, her immigration curriculum emphasized the local perspective. The curriculum promoted the collective activist sensibility Kellor propounded in her other work. And her private organization, the CIA, and the State working together to create it embodied the cooperative private and public model of Americanization she sought.

A mild form of fear also appears in this work. Immigrants needed to become citizens because, "Whenever there is in a democracy a large male population of voting age who have not a voice in the government, there is not pure democracy but often fertile soil for the seeds of anarchy and violent socialism."[517] On the one hand, this statement labeled immigrant populations as potential problems. On the other hand, the curriculum announced political participation as the cure. Furthermore, the fault for the danger lay not with the immigrants, but with the State that had not made an effort to integrate the immigrants into the system. And no call for restriction is even hinted at here or will be, with one exception, again in her career.

From hereon Kellor's curriculum goes back to praising immigrants. Her well-rounded view of immigrants, developed while she lived among them, shone through as she asked the teacher to remember, "They are workmen and engaged in increasing the wealth of the community. Emphasize their social membership, and what they are doing and can do for their community."[518] Rather than just workmen, and thus a boon to the nation, she acknowledges their humanity as social beings.

And Kellor's typical emphasis on activism appears herein. Her syllabi introduction declares, "Good citizenship depends not so much upon a knowledge of governmental forms as upon an ability to adjust oneself to his community so that he becomes an active force for its improvement and realizes the significance of community life." The description of one who realizes the significance of community life follows, "This means that he will take an active part in good politics, that he will vote intelligently and for the welfare of the people . . . he will not only obey the laws but be deeply concerned in the enforcement and enactment of good legislation.[519] Community adjustment meant political participation.

Chapter Nine

The CIA advocated a hands-on approach to learning. Equating curricular goals with action more than information, the curriculum prods, "*Do not only talk* about community life but get your students to think along lines of civic betterment. Suggest to them that they report unsanitary conditions to the health department." [Italics added] The syllabus asks the teacher to "tell your students of the various forms of welfare work in which they can take an active part. Have them observe their community life, analyze it, and cooperate for its improvement." The curriculum directed the teacher to "develop a community point of view with a community spirit. This will mean self-respect and development of character."[520] Spiritually, Kellor considered working on the community a road to personal improvement.

Kellor called the organization she ran for the Progressive Party "the Service." At that time she called it "an unparalleled training school in political action."[521] Tellingly, the CIA curriculum used the name of her progressive organization when it argued that "a mutual understanding with an aroused interest for community life will bring definite action for the 'New Citizenship,' the citizenship of service."[522] If we notice the continuity in which Kellor keeps using the word "service" we can understand that this "New Citizenship" ideal did not only apply to immigrants. All people in America are to be united and reborn via service.

The curriculum reminds us of her past and today's social studies curriculum. Echoes of Kellor's words resonate in the name of today's *community service* requirements for high school graduation. For the specific contents of lessons, the CIA suggested "copies of legislative bills, pictures, samples of ballot and charts" and opening up every lesson with "a discussion of current events."[523] Sample bills pervade Kellor's work and current events are a staple of social studies classes today. Her curriculum calling for the use of the stereopticon takes us back to the Education Branch of the Service and presages current classes' use of visual aids.

The Ideas Behind Americanization Curriculum

The CIA curricular guide contained a bibliography in order to foster a "deeper study of civic training."[524] Among the nine recommended books was *Moral Principles in Education* by Kellor's collaborator in the educational branch of the Service, and *New Republic* intellectual, John Dewey. By recommending his book, Kellor made it known that his goals mirrored hers. Kellor was well aware of the intellectual trends of her day.

As in Dewey's other works, *Moral Principles* distinguished between "teaching about morality" and "moral teaching." Whereas teaching about morality involved verbal formulas, moral teaching involved taking action in real social situations. Dewey's formula reminds us of the contention in *Athletic Games in the Education of Women* wherein sports would transform women's attitudes. And this recommendation to study Dewey should increase our awareness that Kellor's emphasis on action came from a theoretical perspective.

Moral teaching, for Dewey, was developed through being "a member of some particular neighborhood and community."[525]

Chapter Nine

Using the name of Kellor's progressive organization, he sought to "shift the centre of ethical gravity from an absorption which is selfish to a *service* which is social." [Italics added] In his summary, Dewey announced, "We need to translate the moral into the conditions and forces of our community life." As if providing justifications for Kellor's curriculum, he argued that moral teaching, in fact, did not matter unless the student had "the power to stand up and count for something in the actual conflicts of life."[526] Kellor's work implements this activist ideal that Dewey and the other *New Republic* intellectuals, ironically, mostly just wrote about.

Noting Kellor's connection to Dewey helps us understand Americanization. We may be tempted to search for the dogma of Americanization, but Dewey famously and repeatedly descried the "divorce between learning and doing."[527] If we look for a list of precepts with which a person must agree with in order to attain Americanization in Kellor's curriculum, we miss the point. Lived experience provided the connection between social justice work, the community, and the nation. Kellor's curriculum had no history or slogans to memorize. Action, rather than words, made Americanized the immigrant.

In the CIA curriculum, an "American Club" allowed, "coming citizens . . . to express their interest and energy for good citizenship in their community." Immigrants in the American Club would engage in such actions as, "Abating nuisances, and reporting law violations."[528] This literally was the Americanization curriculum that Kellor and the State of New York promoted. On the surface, here and in her newer version of *Out of Work*, we see Kellor's work aiming at the material conditions facing immigrants. Paralleling Dewey's concern with the division between thought and action, Kellor presented a connection between the spiritual and material.

Kellor and the state of New York's Americanization curriculum did have a cultural agenda. Again, as we discussed in Kellor's *Athletic Games,* asking women to leave their traditional domestic space, one could see it as hostile to traditional cultures. But the ideal citizen would not be passive. Kellor fought for a progressive culture with a vibrant democratic base. Again her brand of Local Nationalism required activism. Beyond being pressured to become local activists, no overt cultural content to which the immigrant might be expected to conform appeared in the curriculum.

In the long run, Kellor's impact may, in fact, run counter to the narrative established by historians of Americanization. During this time period, universities became secular. The shared religious cultural glue of these institutions dissolved as they moved towards research and vocational training. The public schools' transition from teaching pure history to including social studies, that is, the transition from teaching cultural content to sociological criticism, also began during this period. Kellor's message to immigrants presented a vision of America based more in rights and prosperity than a connection to our traditions, history or culture.

– CHAPTER TEN –

FORCED ACTIVISM

Of War and Women

Kellor entered her World War I work as a woman. On November 15th, 1915 she spoke at the Women's Conference on National Defense. At this rally, women called upon President Wilson to prepare the Navy and Army for war. Furthermore, the conference advocated a position summed up in its slogan, "America First." This was meant to summon foreign-born citizens to "pay all honor and reverence to the American flag and to do all in their power to prevent its desecration and abuse."[529]

Interestingly, the conference leaders decided not to adopt a recommendation that only English be used in schools. Loyalty, not conformity, lay at the heart of the preparedness mission of the Women's Conference. The rhetoric at this rally seems to have resonated with Kellor at this time as her organization, the National Americanization Committee (NAC), changed its slogan from "One Nations, Many Peoples" to "America First." Kellor's rhetoric moved with the times.

Perhaps significantly, there was a skirmish at the event that took place when Navy personnel mistakenly contributed money to an attending suffrage organization "for which they had no sympathy."[530] The men thought they were supporting women supporting the War. Interestingly, the newspaper's coverage inadvertently lets us know that the Women's Conference on National Defense allowed a table on suffrage to set up. This vignette showed potential tension between women's issues and the war effort.

During World War I, Jane Addams, the very famous social worker who worked for Kellor in the Service, led the crusade for pacifism. During the War, this was a very unpopular stance. It led to Addams going from being a national heroine to an outcast. Kellor worked for preparedness for war. In her day, though it would make her unpopular with social workers, it made her more mainstream. The current unpopularity of the pro-war stance in academia may, along with dislike for the Americanization project, contribute to Kellor being downplayed by historians.

Current and Historic Arguments About Progressives

The *New Republic* intellectuals were also divided over the War. The debate over support of the War between the two *New Republican* intellectuals Randolph Bourne and John Dewey has become iconic. Bourne argued that agreement with the War signified the vapidity of the *New Republic*'s philosophy, and many historians agreed. Again, the 1960s New Left historians

Chapter Ten

considered progressives to be clandestine reactionaries because their social programs served as fop to calm workers and forestall revolution. But more than any other event, some progressives – and the *New Republic* crowd generally - backing our entry into the War has marked progressives as secret reactionaries.

In the January 1916 issue of her journal, *Immigrants in America Review,* Kellor wrote her first article dedicated to getting ready for the War, "The Immigrant and Preparedness." In the article, as in her other war work, she explained that in war, machines are not enough: "Quite as important as forts and submarines is our national attitude of mind." And, on this theme, Kellor asserted that "we have discovered" danger in "strikes and sabotage and in the manning of our industries by foreign-born workmen of doubtful loyalty to the America." World War I was raging and Kellor foresaw our being drawn into it. As such, she asked a question on the minds of many, "Has America a united nation behind her defenses in her shops, on her transportation lines and in charge of her resources?"[531] Being prepared for war meant ensuring loyalty to America.

Kellor thought social justice provided the best vaccination against Bolshevik communism. But that should not, as the 1960s New Left historians did, incline us to discount the sincerity of her reforms; they were not simply fop. She did not believe in class warfare. She embraced both capitalism and reform. She advocated what has been called the "*via media,*" the middle way between reform and conservatism.[532] As we might expect from a sociologist or a girl who intimately knew both the rich and poor residents of Coldwater, Michigan, Kellor was on "everyone's side."[533]

And Kellor, as other *New Republic* intellectuals and progressives, thought of war as a way to further social justice. They thought social justice had a friend in a strong Federal government. And the War greatly increased the reach of the Federal government. It led, for example, to the Federal income tax that enables many of our social programs today. Symbolically, at the Women's Conference on National Defense, Kellor spoke on preparedness just two speakers after the Assistant Secretary of the Navy, Franklin Delano Roosevelt.[534]

Kellor was not a radical. She dreaded socialism. Kellor once invited Theodore Roosevelt to see a play put on by the New York branch of the Women's Trade Union League (WTUL), which her partner Mary Dreier headed. Kellor wrote Roosevelt, "Miss Dreier and I would be delighted to have you."[535] By way of additional enticement she argued, "I think if they [the workers] could meet you it would go a long way toward checking their advance into socialism."[536] Sometimes Kellor's statements against communist agitators seemed to be added to create urgency for adopting social programs in the minds of her audience. But in this letter Kellor decried socialism in a private letter to a good friend.

In his debates with John Dewey, Randolph Bourne, more than any other *New Republic* intellectual, recognized the danger of the overbearing state.[537] Kellor offered popular participation as

Chapter Ten

the antidote to potential abuses of the powerful state that the progressives wanted. But her democratic participants themselves had the potential to become overbearing. A lot of the popular civic participation during the War manifested in citizens spying on each other in order to stamp out dissent.[538] Popular activism and harassment were not mutually exclusive. Kellor's increased diatribes against intolerance during the War indicated that she was very quite aware of the potential for intolerance in the progressive democracy model.

Straight America Brought On

Historians agree that the Americanization movement became more hostile to immigrants with the onset of World War I. John Higham wrote that, "Nothing better illustrated the drift of wartime Americanization than the views of Frances Kellor."[539] Specifically, he claimed that a drift towards harshness in regard to immigrants manifested in Kellor's 1916 book, *Straight America: A Call to National Service*.[540] This book cemented her reputation as a militant reactionary and a nut because it recommended that civilians get sent to training camps to get ready for the War. But if we take Kellor's work and mind seriously, we see it as an extension of her basic goal of uniting the nation and furthering social justice via popular participation in progressive democracy.

The book title *Straight America* reflected the level of unity Kellor desired. Had the word *America* ended with the letter 'n' (had the title been *Straight American*), the word would have been an adjective and could have described uniform characteristics of American individuals. As it was, the first half of the title referred to America's unity as a nation. The subtitle, *A Call to National Service*, should remind us of the Progressive Service. Indeed, the main new idea Kellor introduced in *Straight America* – civilian training camps – sought to foster the same vigorous popular civic participation that the Service had.

Straight America opens with an analysis of America in the terms used by the *New Republic* intellectual, Kellor's partner in the Service and board member of her journal, Herbert Croly. His books depicted an ongoing battle between the Jeffersonian democratic vision of small farmers and the Hamiltonian vision of a strong national government. Croly sought to bend his readers towards the Hamiltonian perspective. This theory undergirded his concept of New Nationalism.

Kellor also sought the Hamiltonian national focus. But whereas Croly, in *The Promise of American Life,* sought national unity through a strong leader along the lines of Theodore Roosevelt, Kellor pursued national unity via the Jeffersonian means of a politically engaged populace demanding reform. She wanted Americans to come together via taking an interest in their fellow residents in America. Again, unity via participation constituted the backbone of Kellor's definition of Americanization. That is why *Straight America* is the ultimate Americanization tract.

Chapter Ten

In the article "The Immigrant and Preparedness" Kellor used the Declaration of Independence to condemn America for not protecting life, liberty, or the pursuit of happiness. In *Straight America,* she pointed to the passage wherein the Founders "mutually pledge to each other our lives, our fortunes, and our sacred honor."[541] She used this passage to show the "foundation stones of Americanism are exactly what they were 140 years ago – liberty, opportunity, and obligation."[542] She contended that we have nearly forgotten about the third of these attributes, "The great majority of private citizens in America recognize no compelling obligation to place themselves, their time, or their resources at the disposal of the nation."[543] "Obligation" undergirded her version of New Nationalism.

Straight Immigrant Americanization

In *Straight America,* Kellor declared that "The real matter with America is that as a nation it has not achieved within itself a permanent national consciousness." While national consciousness can sound harsh in the wake of fascism, she wrote that fealty to the ideals of the Declaration of Independence and the Constitution were "best measured by the way we have come to regard and to treat the most helpless and trusting of our people – the immigrant."[544] Kellor's brand of nationalism would take care of the vulnerable.

The War increased intolerance towards immigrants, and in *Straight America*, Kellor fought back. Seeming to agree with restrictionist logic, she accepted a social theorist's claim that "a

Russian Jew cannot in 5 years or in 25 years become English." But she then bent the agreed-upon premise in a new direction: "True, but what is an American? Is he an Anglo-Saxon racial type, and if so, by what law?" After lambasting immigration restrictionists, she unfavorably compared them to immigrants when she wrote, "Meanwhile I see all around me valiant Americans, Southern European by birth and tradition, Americans now in spirit loyalty and *tendency*."[545] [Italics in original] Make no mistake, Kellor sought to protect immigrants against attack.

Kellor's readers may have been shocked to learn that the nativism of long-term Americans and their institutions, not the attitude of immigrants, was the real threat to America's preparedness. She provided a tally, noting that "Of the many hundreds of immigrant communities which I have studied, I recall none in which American ideals were being aggressively menaced by immigrants who were determined to have none of them. Isolation, betrayal of our own minimum social and civic standards, these I have seen over and over."[546] American neglect was the greatest source of anti-Americanism.

Reflecting her castigation of the Dillingham Commission for not providing a positive domestic policy, she wrote, "There has never been a constructive effort to make the machinery of law adaptable to the immigrant."[547] In our nativism we failed to concern ourselves with immigrants' needs. "In answer to request for interpreters, for the distribution of information concerning laws, for modifications of judgments where ignorance was the

Chapter Ten

cause of the violation, we are constantly met with the unsympathetic statement that if the system is good enough for Americans and for America . . ."[548] We needed to make our legal system user-friendly for immigrants.

But all of our institutions reflected a nativist attitude that separated immigrants from our nation. This could be seen in the fact that, despite requiring English to naturalize as a citizen, we provided no English language courses. We also had no foreign language books in libraries. Sardonically, Kellor supposed that this policy is based "on the theory that although he [the American] does nothing to furnish facilities for learning English, it is better that the immigrant should read nothing while he waits."[549] Kellor also saw nativism in our banks. We worry, she wrote, "that he does not spend or invest his money here." But "the ordinary bank is not adapted to the immigrant. He is intimidated by it and is not always welcome."[550]

This defender of immigrants distilled her argument by claiming that "Americanism faces the future and is courageous. Nativism faces the past and is apprehensive."[551] In *Straight America*, Kellor often repeated that nativism led to not meeting the civic and cultural needs of immigrants. Nativism meant excluding immigrants. It led to disunity. Americanism, properly understood, consisted of meeting the civic and cultural needs of immigrants. True Americanization happened when we included immigrants in America.

Straight Nationalism

Like other progressives, Kellor saw the War as an opportunity to remake industrial relations. Dewey was glad that the War "brought into existence agencies for executing the supremacy of the public and social interest over the private and possessive interest."[552] Kellor proposed economic coordination, celebrated the new public spirit brought on by the War, and wanted all sectors of American society to think about the good of the nation. Per usual, Kellor claimed that exploitative industrial bosses were a "strong anti-American influence."[553] She wanted industrialists to cooperate and coordinate rather than compete.

Industrial cooperation would not simply result from laws. Industrial cooperation required a nationalist philosophy. She wrote that, "The nationalization of business is not a matter of legislation, or of regulation, or of coercion. It is the duty and obligation of each responsible person in industry – all working together on a national cooperative basis instead of on a local, sectional, competitive basis. It means a new spirit abroad in business – patriotic Nationalism."[554] Again, the highest vision of Americanization would be achieved when all sectors worked for the benefit of all Americans. But this required the proliferation of a shared New Nationalist sort of sentiment.

This national philosophy would also require that our laws take a national perspective. Kellor descried our having as many naturalization standards as we have states. Having to stay in one state for a year to engage in the naturalization process "creates almost insuperable difficulties for migratory laborers."[555] She also, per usual, descried state laws that discriminated against immigrants and cited laws under which aliens could not work, get relief, or own a dog. Kellor ranted, "One cannot read the hundreds of discriminating laws without a sense of the utter prostitution of American citizenship to prejudice, race hatred, greed, cupidity, and to the selfishness of groups and individuals."[556] Like industry, government itself needed to adopt a national perspective to help immigrants.

Activist Nationalism

But above all, Kellor's brand of Americanization required public service. In *Straight America,* she told the story of a town of 26,000 residents with 10,000 immigrants. The long-term Americans complained of "vice, intemperance, bad housing, and wretched standards of living resulting" from the immigrant population.[557] But as Kellor pointed out, "We in America believe in majority rule. There was a safe margin of 6,000 Americans in that town, free to establish and insist upon any standard they chose. Why were the Americans beaten in the struggle?"[558] If this statement hinted at disapproval of immigrant ways, it laid the blame for these behaviors firmly at the feet of long-term Americans' lack of civic engagement.

In high flying rhetoric, she found it both unfortunate and dangerous that "we see nothing dramatic, we see no challenge, in the fight to raise the standards of our less fortunate neighborhoods. We cannot find any inspiration in that ideal of justice which insists on law enforcement equally among all residents of a neighborhood."[559] Questioning our Americanism, she noted, "Old Philadelphians that would never have run from an Indian, that would have conquered the forests and spanned the rivers, run from the Italian and Pole. Alas!"[560] Rather than accuse immigrants of being bad Americans, Kellor's Americanization rhetoric argued that long-term Americans were poor Americans.

In *Straight America*, Kellor wanted a curriculum paralleling that advocated by Dewey. She praised the new methodology of teaching civics wherein "They have put aside the paraphrases of the Constitution . . . and they have evolved a system of "community civics" designed to teach the alien his privileges and responsibilities in their simplest form, with direct reference to his everyday life and his own immediate points of contact with the laws of public health, of property, of parents' obligations, etc."[561]

And Kellor wanted forums wherein long-term Americans and immigrants would both learn. Kellor declared, "*I should like to see the political forum in its best form, become a recognized part of American life. It is needed for the native-born. It is practically indispensable for the foreign-born.*"[562] [Italics in original] This would put the immigrant "in touch with the political issues of the day in their large national bearings."[563] This Americanizer did not want passive immigrants. She sought to bind all parties via an activist stance towards national issues. We might call this "Activist Nationalism."

In addition to civics courses and town hall type meetings, Kellor hoped we would see a rebirth of the system "tried by the Progressive Party through its Progressive Service." She hopefully prophesized, "In the interests of Americanism, I believe the political parties of this country will be forced . . . to create systems of party education." She stated that a party might stand firm for "social and industrial justice."[564] But people "who do *not* attend conventions, who are sorely in need of social and industrial justice or who would like to help in securing it for others, never learn what its concrete definition is, or how to secure it through the vote."[565] [Italic in original] Activist Nationalism required information.

Again, in this theorist's vision, political parties and people would remake each other until we had a progressive democracy. To foster a political citizenry, she recommended that "party laboratories, publicists not advertisers, a thoroughgoing machinery for getting studies and facts and opinions to people in a form in which they can weigh and use them."[566] The political party "that did its educational work best, and placed its ideas and objects most frankly in the light, would in the long run get the votes."[567] Her hopes for the Progressive Service had not died.

But the failure of the Service taught Kellor the hard lesson that its structure had not created an activist nation. With the War coming, Kellor no longer found iterations of the Service, town meetings or normal educational facilities sufficient enough to stir up the needed participation in the body politic that would unite America. Immediately after advocating the above iteration of the Service, Kellor introduced her hated idea of citizens' training camps. But people who do not understand Kellor's entire corpus of work misread the civilian training camp idea. Rather than passivity, mandatory civilian service and training were to create dynamic, active civic participants.

Connecting activism and civilian training, *Straight America* argued, "We have come to regard universal service, with a period of compulsory training in a military camp, as a measure of military defense only. We seem to think it means only learning how to shoot and acquiring a thirst for blood. I believe it has a great civic value hitherto disregarded."[568] Rather than a source of militancy, she hoped civilian training would be, "the best school of practical civics there is – a place where all Americans can meet together for the common good of America."[569] When in full swing, she hoped civilian training would "become the dynamo for national progress in America."[570] These camps were to ignite civic participation.

The *New Republic* and Military Activism

At the time of Kellor's advocacy, "universal military service was a much discussed issue."[571] In his 1906 essay "The Moral Equivalent of War," William James (whose work is closely associated with Dewey's) advocated "conscription of the whole youthful population." He claimed, "The martial type of character

203

Chapter Ten

can be bred without war," and he wanted the enlistees to work on civic improvement projects framed as a battle "against Nature."[572] James passed the idea of universal service on to the *New Republic* crowd.

Dewey's *New Republic* article "Universal Service as Education," paralleled Kellor's suggestions in advocating immigrants' "distribution" and guarding against their "industrial exploitation." Dewey also mirrored Kellor's assessment of our national consciousness. He complained that "we are overstimulated in matters of personal success and enjoyment; we have little that teaches subordination to the public good or secures effective capacity to work cooperatively in its behalf." He conceded that "we need a social ideal which is truly national; one which will unify our thoughts and focus our emotions."[573] As Kellor and James, Dewey liked the idea of universal service for education.

Although Dewey empathized with the idea of universal service, he supported eliminating the "borrowed military aspects."[574] To make the distinction between the civilian and military emphases clear, he suggested nationalizing the public schools rather than launch an institution associated with the military. Though they might have disagreed on details, Kellor's proposals were within the parameters that the *New Republic* intellectuals thought reasonable.

Randolph Bourne, who had disagreed with the *New Republic* crowd supporting the War, wrote an article entitled, "A

Moral Equivalent for Universal Military Service." He advocated national service education (as opposed to military preparedness). Like Dewey, he thought the national government should administer a program of service education via the public schools. He wanted youth between the ages of sixteen and twenty-one to "spend two years in national service." He wanted the involved youth to engage in such things as "food inspection, factory inspection, organized relief, the care of dependents, playground service, [and] nursing in hospitals." In the country, they would engage in "tree-planting, the care and repair of roads, work on conservation projects."[575] Thus Bourne too endorsed the compulsory service ideal.

But while gushing over the potential of the "army of youth" working on social projects, he claimed military models would create "uniform, obeying units." His model of civilian training would foment "stimulation, not obedience." Bourne concluded that the "advocates of 'preparedness'" are willing to spend billions on a universal military service which is neither universal nor educational nor productive." Continuing, he asked, "Can we not begin to organize a true national service which will let all serve creatively towards the toning up of American life?"[576] His main qualifier to Kellor was that he, like Dewey, sought to limit the military tint of the programs.

Bourne unfavorably reviewed Kellor's *Straight America* for *The New Republic*. Referring to *her* civilian training program, he wrote, "Miss Kellor makes a noble and eloquent plea for an

Americanism which is much broader than the 'nativism' of the Anglo-Saxon, but she yokes it to a program which is almost necessarily nativistic in its implications." Employing a bit of guilt by association, and ignoring large swaths of her short book, he claimed that Kellor's preparedness "is one held largely by the staunchly nativistic element."[577] Bourne, again, famously hated progressives who backed the War. Perhaps his slandering her as nativist reflected a dislike for her support of the War.

Positively, Bourne appreciated Kellor's point that "it is the native American who finally controls . . . the immigrant's obtaining his economic opportunity and working out an American standard of living." While apparently conveying his own opinion, he actually reiterated Kellor's point that "the community that neglects its immigrants or the corporation that leaves its workmen to take care of themselves cannot blame the alien colony for remaining a sodden and disruptive force."[578] Bourne's condemnation of Kellor had more than a hint of agreement.

Interestingly, Bourne ultimately criticized Kellor because her sense of nationalism overrode her sense of localism. He said, "Loyalty should have a foundation of locally intelligent participation in the communal enterprises that dictate the fortune of the immigrants' common life." Immigrants first require, Bourne wrote, "a sense of the functioning community and only secondly a nebulous patriotism."[579] The place of local democratic participation in a modern industrial state has been called the main focus of progressive intellectuals. With this in mind, we have framed this exact crux as source of frustration to Kellor; we have noted the tension in the term Local Nationalism. As such Bourne's focusing on the tension between the local versus the national is significant.

National Service and Americanization

In discussing civilian training in *Straight America*, Kellor wrote, "The day's drill, the camp drudgery, washing the dust off alongside a stream, the dog tent, with their magnificent opportunity for formal teamwork and informal fellowship may supply the melting pot we have missed."[580] When we hear melting pot today, we do assume the model calls for cultural conformity. And even today, as the military melds recruits, it causes some cultural blending. But, as with Multicultural Nationalism, we have to remember not to read our ideas back into history. Though it required teamwork, the goal of citizens working together for social justice did not simply imply the Anglo-conformity model historians have imagined. Kellor's only overt cultural demand was that immigrants exchange apathy for the active pursuit of improved material conditions.

Furthermore, we must always remember that Americanization did not solely or even mostly aim at changing immigrants. In *Straight America*, Kellor wrote, "When we think of a united America, our minds naturally turn to Americanizing the immigrant. Big as that task is, I do not believe that our greatest difficulty lies with him. Rather I fear that we shall have to Americanize our native Americans first. We have, I think, to return to the civilian training camp and universal service as a

Chapter Ten

melting pot for natives before we can make America a successful melting pot for aliens."[581] To the extent that Kellor had cultural intolerance, it largely aimed at long-term Americans. Nearly all of the complaints in *Straight America* aim at them, not the immigrants.

Macho Americanization

Kellor's vision of citizenship was vigorously active. In explaining America's need for cultural change, she declared that the "average boy is prompt with excuses and self-justification under discipline – and this has been seen most conspicuously in our nation's attitude in the present war." Expanding upon her denunciation of the young male, she wrote that his attitude led to "slovenly work; to indifferent citizenship."[582] In this context, she denounced individualism because it led to "play in which entertainment, not participation, is the rule; and to shifting responsibility in all walks of life."[583] Not enamored of the frivolous, consumer society, Kellor challenged the masculinity of America's young male population.

Significantly, Kellor's description of a masculine active public was gender neutral. In describing the need for civilian training, Kellor exclaimed, "We have throughout the country today a splendid expression of the desire to serve. I believe that every citizen of this republic, male or female, and of any age after childhood, should have a regular scheme of duties, a regular enlistment for service of a definite nature suited to his or her status of capacity, which must be prepared to render on demand. *And which he or she must keep in training to deliver.*"⁶⁸⁴ [Italics in original] What Theodore Roosevelt called "vigor" would come from every individual in Kellor's ideal engaged citizenry.

The New York Times called Kellor's *Straight America*, "a frank and vigorous little volume . . . [That] ought to be read from every pulpit in the country and studied by every woman's club and public forum."⁵⁸⁵ The reviewer's use of the word "vigorous" was appropriate. Kellor's frustration with her fellow citizen's complacency suffuses this work. And though the compulsory service idea might seem strange to us, it suffused the progressive discourse. Kellor's call for stridency was personal. We will see this most conspicuously in her next activist adventure.

– CHAPTER ELEVEN –

TAKING IT TO THE STREETS

Kellor's Macho Progressivism

Kellor headed the *Women's Committee of the National Hughes Alliance* in support of Charles Evans Hughes' 1916 candidacy for President of the United States.[586] In this capacity, she created "The first transcontinental campaign train, directed solely by women, in the history of American politics."[587] The train was a "31-day $40,000 transcontinental trip, during which they crossed 28 States, held 195 meetings, and addressed about 500,000 persons."[588] The *New-York Tribune* reporter that followed the train claimed they made "1840 speeches . . . indoors and out, in circus tents, movie palaces and street corners."[589] Kellor coordinated "financing and equipping the train and for organizing both the speakers that go with the train and the State and local committees that received it."[590]

The coverage of Kellor's involvement provides an intimate portrait of her personal and policy ideals. Her attitude towards gender and macho personality were on display in spades in this effort. Her public bravado, again, reminds one of the combative muscle of Theodore Roosevelt. In trying to get local populations to consider national politics, she embodied what was earlier termed "Local Nationalism." Ultimately, this nationalist's disrespect for the local and the nebulousness of her national vision derailed this effort. But Kellor's participation in this strenuous campaign modeled her ideal of a strident progressive citizen activist.

The Hughes Train publically bent gender ideals. A *New York Times* article described militaristic daily staff meetings in which "each business-like woman whose name stands for leadership throughout America is there to answer 'present' and receive orders." A writer beamed, "No military staff on the eve of battle ever suffered so amiably the ready criticism of co-workers . . . With Frances Kellor presiding the meeting was opened with historical discussion of men's campaign trains and the masculine way of working."[591]

During the campaign meeting, Kellor explained, "The men get up and say whatever they have in their heads." While the men are allowed to rant, women needed to be more efficient: "Each one must choose a line and stick to it." Kellor told one participant, "You are too long." And the reporter then reassured the reader, "The women campaigners take self-criticism like good sports – like men."[592] This snapshot confirms that Kellor's attention to gender was thought out and overt.

Class and Gender Divide

Despite Kellor's attempts to portray herself as a serious masculine campaigner, the press skewered the women with gender stereotypes. The Democrats repeatedly derided the train as "full of fuss, feathers, and femininity." Another attack announced, "Wall Street is too busy garnering money under the Democratic Administration to make the trip itself, so it is sending the women folk." Officially called the Women's Campaign Train for Hughes, the Democrat's most effective attack was to add class to gender by renaming it the Million Dollar Special, the Butterfly Special, the Billionaires' Train, and – most frequently the Golden Special.[593]

Newspapers' reports pointed to the passengers' attempts to "hide their furs and jewels from the accusing gaze of the factory girls." Mocking the participants, they wrote, "The Ladies on the train had imagined that the humble working girls in the factory towns would be much interested and impressed when given an opportunity to listen to the words of advice from ladies of wealth and position. To their astonishment, the women speakers on the train were often sneered at by the working girls, who pointed to their furs and rings with derision."[594] The press accounts were anything but kind.

Stressing the importance of local participation, Kellor tried to finance the venture through thousands of single-dollar subscriptions. She appealed to average contributors by writing, "We are especially proud that women are financing it and directing it."[595] But, in reality, the Republican Party paid for the train. As with the Service, Kellor's plan of popular financial support for national activism fell short.

Despite their not funding it, some justification for calling the train "the Billionaires' Train" existed. The extremely wealthy Mrs. Daniel Guggenheim did ride on the train (though only from New York City to Albany), and Mrs. Whitman, the wife of New York's Governor was on the train.[596] Again, Kellor's sociological perspective tried to take in the needs of all sectors of society; she eschewed class warfare. But these extremely wealthy women's presence strained attempts to create solidarity with female factory workers.

But many of the women, such as Kellor, had come from less privileged origins. Mary Antin, who urged immigrants to embrace America, had grown up as a typical impoverished immigrant. Elizabeth Freeman, who headed the National Association for the Improvement of the Colored Race (NAICR), had immigrated to America as a small child with her single-parent mother.

Since the super rich and those of humble origin and means worked together on the train, in this small instance Kellor did bridge the class divide. Creating a special level of intimacy, Kellor's partner's sister, Margaret Dreier Robins, rode on the train. As per the ideal, the participants' class-based gap was negated via activism. And while these female activists worked for the benefit of the poor, none of these women would ever again work in a factory. Kellor's band of activists were not average workingwomen.

The Wide and Shallow Platform

The name "the Hughes Alliance" was a reference to his Republican Party being a conglomeration of the old Progressive party and the Republicans. Hughes sought to "unite the Progressive and Republican parties."[597] But, actually, Roosevelt had hoped to be the Republican nominee. The New York City Women's Committee of the Hughes Alliance was originally the "Women's Roosevelt League." When the name changed, "There was much opposition by some of the women, and a majority refused flatly to let the league lose its identity."[598] Typically, Kellor called for unity transcending petty differences. But many did not see the differences as petty.

Roosevelt relented and rallied for Hughes and supported Kellor's activities throughout the campaign. But Hughes' moderation never inspired wholehearted efforts by the more progressive community. A woman who had been on the train in California said that everywhere they went, people asked why Hughes had snubbed California's Progressive Governor.[599] Political divisions likely cost the Republicans the election. Hughes' need to have the word "Alliance" in his campaign literature pointed to the division that his being the Progressive and Republican candidate sought to bridge. As always, Kellor sought to bridge gaps, to unite populations. But in this, Kellor failed repeatedly.

As with all political platforms that try to appeal to a divided base, the Republican platform was vague. One participant claimed she had "joined the alliance because it was a movement in which women could work without committing themselves to the rest of the Republican platform."[600] Hughes himself laid "particular stress on Americanism, American rights, the tariff, 'war prosperity,' the Adamson law (concerning the eight-hour work day) and the administration's attitude toward business."[601] Kellor often used Wilson's rushing our troops to the border of Mexico and leaving the families unsupported as evidence of his not understanding war preparedness. Everything under the sun, and nothing in particular, constituted the Hughes platform.

As usual, Kellor's goals were huge. She said Hughes' "election would substitute a large constructive policy applied to the issues of preparedness, nationalism and Americanism, in place of hastily conceived measures dealing with great subjects piecemeal and haphazard way."[602] One article suggested Hughes' election would afford Kellor an opportunity to revive the Progressive Service.[603] During the campaign, Kellor launched the periodical called the *Hughes Campaign Service*. It was called "The Service" for short."[604] But it did not last long.

All were for preparedness and against Wilson's "He kept us out of war" slogan. But the *New Republic* said that when

Chapter Eleven

Hughes spoke about national and international issues, he was "so vague, so commonplace and so timid that his friends were at a loss to account for him."[605] The attempted union under the Republican banner diluted, rather than strengthened, the poor campaigners' message.

Nationalism Versus Suffrage

Suffrage also divided the campaign. Hughes came out for a national suffrage amendment during the campaign,[606] but he only really supported suffrage because postponing the passage would radicalize women.[607] His lukewarm advocacy won him few female zealots.

At the first major organizing meeting, the campaign decided that the Hughes train would focus on women in states that already had suffrage.[608] They hoped with this strategy women could garner women's votes without raising the ire of anti-suffragists in states where only men could vote. As result of this set-up, men felt free to dominate the campaign in states where women could not vote and the train would not ride.

Officially, "the rule of the train" was that discussing "suffrage was strictly taboo." Still, on one stop, a speaker finished by saying, "Now that I have told you about Mr. Hughes, I wish to add personally, as it were, that I am for suffrage from first to last."[609] The crowd cheered. When logistics took them to states without suffrage, like in "strongly anti-suffrage" Trenton, New Jersey,[610] friendly suffrage workers greeted them.[611]

But some women in suffrage states were not impressed. Referring to New York's non-suffrage status, one banner used against them was, "Why do you come to teach us how to vote? Go back and get your own votes."[612] Despite their attempts to downplay the issue, the train campaign was seen as pro-suffrage.

Kellor's willingness to downplay suffrage reflected her belief that women needed to show they could stand for issues other than women's issues. She attributed the decision to limit the women to suffrage states to "the inability of the Republican leaders to grasp the idea that women can do campaign work without arguing for suffrage." Kellor denied that women "have inalienable tendencies like prohibition and suffrage which they cannot keep out of politics, an error which the train refuted."[613]

Kellor thought it disempowering that women were relegated to the "sex cloisters" of traditional women's issues.[614] Instead of suffrage, our campaigner would have women work on traditionally male topics such as war, immigration, and unemployment policy. She would have been proud of a reporter's assessment that through the train, "two and a quarter million of women who are registered to vote . . . heard a definite call to arms, not in the terms of local domestic housekeeping policies, but in behalf of great national issues."[615]

Those who might be unforgiving of Kellor's willingness to downplay the suffrage issue should recall that she did not put much stock in voting. Kellor did not like political parties in that

Chapter Eleven

they largely functioned as vote-getting mechanisms. Kellor was disappointed that "many thousands of women are of little service now because they do regard getting or opposing suffrage as the chief end of existence and have no other entry into political activity."[616] While she was on an election campaign, ultimately she thought elections could not substitute for constant political involvement. Therefore, she thought the constant focus by women on the vote aimed at a pyrrhic victory.

Our campaign coordinator particularly thought women should enter the political power arena. In jumping aboard the Hughes campaign, Kellor announced, "The bars are down to women in the national Republican Party for the first time in a national election." She thought it inefficient that "women's thought, their time, energy, and money is largely given to miscellaneous welfare and civic movements outside political lines."[617] And, in fact, Kellor's nearly unprecedented leadership in this national political campaign itself weakened barriers that had traditionally limited women.

Strangely, Kellor's argument for suffrage mirrored her argument for national Americanization. In her words, she favored suffrage because, "So long as women vote in one part of the country and not in another there will be restlessness, friction, waste, and enormous loss in the political and social life of America."[618] In a sense, Kellor did not seem to care if women did or did not have suffrage, as long as the entire nation had one position. Tellingly, upon Hughes' declaration for women's suffrage, Kellor wrote, "Mr. Hughes' indorsement [sic] of the

Federal suffrage amendment is the first important declaration of nationalism in this campaign."[619]

Kellor was much more of a nationalist and an activist than a suffragette. Still, Theodore Roosevelt personally credited Kellor with getting suffrage on the Progressive Party's 1912 platform. That was the first time that a national party made suffrage part of its platform. As the head of the *Women's Committee of the National Hughes Alliance*, Kellor had great influence on getting suffrage on the Republican Party platform of 1916. Thus, the first and second time a major national political party put suffrage on their platform, it was under Kellor's influence. This, in turn, forced the Democrats to address the issue in 1916; they supported state-by-state suffrage. By the 1920 election suffrage was won. Kellor did not obsess over suffrage; still, her contribution to in making it a national political issue, indeed enfranchising women, was significant.

The Women's Train and African-Americans

Kellor's continuing commitment to women was not the only manifestation of her constancy; the campaign included significant attention to African-American rights. Throughout the campaign, Elizabeth Freeman, the head of the National Association for the Improvement of the Colored Race, spoke to African-American organizations. In an amazing appeal to both women's rights and African-American's rights, Freeman "enlisted the aid of negro women to enfranchise the white women of the

East."[620] Again, when assessing Kellor's attitude towards minorities, one should remember that she was one.

Freeman pulled no punches. She claimed Wilson was part of a "secret Democratic organization called the Democratic Fair Play Association whose object it is to take all negroes out of Federal jobs and put 'deserving Democrats' in their places." In fact, after his election, Wilson did just this. Sensationally, Freeman said, "Even while the Fifth cavalry negro troops were fighting in Mexico a half-witted negro boy was dragged from the jail in Waco, Texas, and roasted over a fire."[621] The train's rhetoric was not moderate.

Following one of Freeman's speeches, "The singing parade of 5,000 negroes in the evening at Indianapolis marching and dancing with tom-toms and bands, put a new touch into the history of the women's campaign train."[622] The progressives' fealty to African-American liberation was not always consistent. Famously, African-American representatives from the South were excluded from the 1912 Progressive Party nominating convention. And Kellor's attempts to get W.E.B. Du Bois' plank protecting African-Americans in the 1912 Progressive Party platform were defeated.[623] In this context, this march of African-Americans that the women's train inspired burns brightly in the history of the Progressive Movement.

Kellor did not simply delegate this theme. On days with no scheduled meetings she would speak at African-American churches. A newspaper reported that in her stump speech, she,

"Opposed the whole Democratic attitude in Washington, which . . . has not only refused to dictate Federal investigation of the amazing lynching record of the South this year, but has undermined relations with Nicaragua, Hayti and Santo Domingo by substituting white Southern Democrats, with their exploitation point of view toward the colored race, for the competent, tried negro diplomats of former administrations."[624] Kellor strayed far from issues women were typically expected to address.

The Train and Immigrants

Interestingly, the Hughes' women banned "the hyphen" from their organization. The executive committee decreed that, "no local branch or auxiliary . . . shall be known or designated as representing citizens of any particular foreign extraction."[625] Kellor hoped the campaign would "build its future so wide and its foundation so sure that never again shall we be confronted with questions of hyphenism, of sectionalism or upreparedness."[626] This declaration could be taken as proof of her advocating Anglo-conformity. Yet, again, projecting our definitions back in time is dangerous.

Recall that it was Governor Hughes who first gave Kellor a government position pertaining to immigrants. Thus, relying on her own record, Kellor reminded voters of "Hughes' record as Governor in meeting, so many years before it was the fashion to discourse of hyphenates, the acuter problems of the Americanization through education and square labor deals for the vast foreign-born third of our population."[627] Hughes had, with

Kellor's help, been working to end the exploitation of immigrants for some time.

On the tour, Mary Antin spoke as an immigrant to factory workers in Yiddish.[628] Further confounding our understanding of the ban of the hypen is the fact that groups such as the Polish Women's Alliance arose and were recognized by the Hughes Committee.[629] Part of Kellor's stump speech was a denunciation of the Arizona anti-alien measure and of Wilson for signing it. We should, again, not confuse our understanding of hyphens with those of the activists of the time.

The hyphen's disappearance, in Kellor's use, meant the eradication of prejudices that justified exploitation of immigrants. She aimed the vast majority of her cultural ammunition at this very target. When residents across all of America had decent working conditions, we would have become Americanized. Only then would no hyphens would remain.

Kellor Takes it to the Streets

The divide that most immediately concerned the campaigners was that between them and their audiences. Rather than the choreographed campaigns of today, these women confronted publics in all their diversity.

Some confrontations with the public were funnier than others. In Grant's Pass and Medford, Oregon, Republican women arrived with their babies in their arms to counter the rumored plan by Democrats to bring cats in response to the "poodle dogs" on the train."[630] In many towns, the train was met with ugly banners; in one, its reception included threats with red paint and barbed wire.[631] Once, the Hughes' women were pelted with eggs as they transitioned from one theater to their cars. The crowd imitated the sound of the cries of the frightened speakers, "The women, pale, angry, trembling, clutched their hats. At this evidence mingled vanity and timidity, the chorus of jeers rose. The fusillade of eggs pursued the automobiles until extra speed put the travelers beyond their reach."[632]

When off the train, the speakers traveled in cars. And in Kansas City, mobs made the Hughes' cars bid a retreat. At one hill, cars sporting Democratic banners confronted them. When a friend of the Hughes' campaign tried to protect them, a revolver was drawn, and, in the ensuing fight, the Hughes' friend knocked down the armed confronter. With the help of the police, the sides backed down and the Hughes' cars were allowed to proceed. This was rough stuff. The delicate femininity of the campaigners, while frequently mocked, was not always respected.

Progressive intellectuals discussed the fundamental tension that existed between the idea of a democracy and the use of expert sociological managers that large government programs require. The women's train ran into this tension personally. At one stop factory workers heckled Mrs. Nelson O'Shaughnessy, who had written about her experiences as the wife of the charge d'affaires of Mexico. One laborer asked, "What do you think we want to go blowing into Mexico for – to help all sorts of rich guys?" She lost her temper and, waving her flag

Chapter Eleven

violently, told him he was ignorant and, for exclamation, added, "You're all ignorant!" Kellor tugged on O'Shauhnessy's skirt and "rose to cover the political faux pas by reviewing the Hughes' record on the eight-hour day and workmen's compensation."[633] The speech carried on to its conclusion, but after this confrontation Mrs. O'Shauhnessy quit the train.

Intellectuals rarely promulgate their ideas to the public in such intimate and vulnerable settings. Mary Dreier, who did not go on the adventure, received a letter that said in Portland, Oregon, "Our speakers held a street meeting of 5,000 for several hours. Continuously heckled by good natured crowds."[634] Kellor did not handpick her audiences. In every city, she and her associates spoke in factories or, if it was closing time, outside of factories. This campaign constituted another of Kellor's aggressive attempts to bridge the gap between political leadership and the masses via communication of ideas.

In the midst of these conflicts, Kellor proved her faith in open communication. On the morning of a scheduled appearance in a Toledo factory, an article in the most widely read labor paper in Northern, Ohio, listed the wealth of everyone on the train.[635] The workers heckled Kellor, saying, "You work for Wall Street" and, "The Republicans never did anything for labor."[636] Holding the paper, Kellor read as she was "jeered through two columns," denouncing the falsehoods.[637] With unintentional humor she stated, "Not one of the women traveling in the Hughes Special had 'more than $50,000 in her own name.'"[638]

Taking it to the Streets

According to one report, "The black-shirted oil-begrimed workers apparently thought that a modest enough sum and permitted Miss Kellor to start her speech."[639] Another exclaimed, "$50,000 smelled like plutocracy to the overalled machinists who heckled constantly."[640] Rather than quit the speech, Kellor went on to detail Hughes' "passage of the first workman's compensation act and his decisions on the right to damages of an injured workman . . . [and] his broad vision in meeting nine years ago the maladjustments of immigrants to citizenship."[641]

The heckling reignited during the same speech when Kellor denounced Samuel Gompers for endorsing Wilson. She said, "Mr. Gompers did not tell the whole truth about Mr. Hughes." When a heckler asked if she were calling Gompers a liar, she replied, "No, he is not that: he simply tells half truths. You know the difference between a liar and one who misrepresents, don't you?" Many workers turned away saying, "Mr. Gompers ain't no liar, he's our International President."[642] Some workers then asked the police to silence the crowd so Kellor could be heard. Tellingly, she responded, "Police – what nonsense! The men will listen. They believe in fair play in this campaign." In response, they shouted, "We do!" At that, she obtained some support and requests for Hughes' literature.[643] Kellor believed in open political dialogue and practiced it.

Victories for Democratic Participation

Predictably for Kellor, she supplemented her national organization with local branches of the *Women's Committee of*

Chapter Eleven

the National Hughes Alliance. Through her decentralized plan, any women anywhere in the US could affiliate directly with the Hughes organization. Any twenty-five women in the community could organize into a local branch, and obtain a charter.[644] She hoped for 100,000 members. Each of the 100,000 was "asked to do some specific task in this campaign as soon as she enrolls."[645] And, from this large group a special committee of 1,000 was to be created.[646] Donations from such women were supposed to finance the campaign.[647] While the number of people participating disappointed, Kellor again sought to recognize, organize, utilize, and, inspire grassroots participation.

Towards this end, the train had some successes. In St. Paul, Minnesota, a meeting at "the Metropolitan Theater, the largest west of the Mississippi, brought out 2,000 women who pledged to help in a campaign to get out the Republican husbands and brothers on Election Day."[648] In Spokane, Washington, it was reported that the campaigners "Packed the auditorium to its capacity to-night, and presented issues of the campaign so concisely and convincingly that Washington will be found in the Hughes column, if proper support is given these women."[649] In the small Illinois towns of "Aurora, Plainfield, Napierville, Lockport and Manhattan . . . approximately 3,000 workers heard the speakers – and didn't heckle."[650] In most cities, the crowds greeting them made a public political spectacle. In Springfield, Illinois, they were greeted "with a parade of 100 automobiles, with torches and a band."[651]

There were gender victories as well. Undoubtedly incorrect, a *New York Tribune* reporter said the train riders held "the first political meeting ever conducted by women in Trenton [New Jersey]."[652] In another inaccurate report we learn that on the first day of rest, a train speaker snuck out and spoke at a Methodist church, "where she made one of the first political speeches which have been made by a woman in the house of God."[653] This tour helped normalize the idea of women speaking about politics in public forums.

The format of the stops also reflected a strong spirit of participatory democracy. The itinerary in Chicago was typical, sending "eight different groups of women in automobiles to different parts of the city, where speeches will be made standing on the seats of cars, on street corners and in front of large industrial plants at closing time."[654] In Cedar Rapids, Iowa, two speakers in each car went "out to the eleven schools where more than 3,000 voters of tomorrow cheered with all of their little might."[655] Upon their return to New York, the train was greeted by Roosevelt, Mr. and Mrs. Hughes, and 12,000 well-wishers. Characteristically, Kellor and the speakers addressed the crowd in the streets before entering the packed auditorium.[656] Kellor's troupe showed themselves apostles for democratic participation.

Kellor Fails Again

Kellor failed to achieve her coveted goal of national alliance. She urged voters to take a national perspective, "The one big question before America today is nationalism – a united nation in which there shall be no class, sectional, racial or provincial lines."[657] Kellor complained "that the high price of wheat being an issue led to Kansas voting for Wilson." This contributed to making the "Western women's vote a *provincial vote,* as opposed to a national vote." [Italics in original] Kellor wrote, "We need, I think, to get rid of the idea that there is a New York point of view, or, indeed, a California point of view. In all parts of the country we are too far from the sense of nationalism which this country politically and economically needs most, and we do not want to increase the difficulties by any artificial cleavages."[658] Just as she put the needs of the nation above women's votes, she hoped others would consider their enlightened national self-interest.

One California woman to whom she preached nationalism replied, "We Western people may be provincial in our political expression, but we cannot help but feel that New York has arrogated to itself long enough the political destiny of this country, and if there is one thing this election shows more than another, it is the repudiation of the New York point of view in politics as in any way of expressing Americanism of the American ideal, or aspiration."[659] Thus, the correspondent fundamentally disagreed with Kellor's own provincialism. Significantly, in response to these denunciations, Kellor urged her correspondent to publish her thoughts, "for our great present need is a free expression of political thinking along national lines."[660] Again, open dialogue and democracy were bedrock values for Kellor.

Though not in the way she had hoped, Kellor's campaign may have actually had a huge national impact. An article in *The New York Times* relayed, "It is believed by many that it [Kellor's campaign train] actually was the final straw which turned the balance and defeated Mr. Hughes." The article calculated, "If 1,887 Wilson voters had voted for Mr. Hughes, Mr. Wilson would have lost California, and Mr. Hughes would have been our next President."[661] That would have only required 30 voters to have been turned off of at each of the 63 meetings that Kellor hosted in California. Kellor's divisive and controversial train campaign may have changed American history!

We might also, for the sake of fun, consider another counterfactual. If Hughes had won the 1916 election, we might have entered World War I faster. An early end to the War might have caused Germany to lose sooner. As a result, they might not have emerged from the War so bitter. Furthermore, partially to spite Wilson, Republicans refused to enter the League of Nations. With Roosevelt and the Republicans behind him, Hughes might have entered into the League of Nations and provided it with some military backing. With Germany being less bitter and a strong League of Nations, World War II might never have come to pass.

Division plagued the Hughes' Alliance. Hughes' trying to unite Republicans and Progressives weakened the message. Rhetoric about class divisions led to chronic heckling and mocking. Kellor also claimed that the train was not supported

Chapter Eleven

because women manned it. The suffrage issue limited the women. Regional division and resentments fomented hostility and division within her party. In some way, this campaign represented the most thorough repudiation of Kellor's dream of a unified nation, her New Nationalism and, therefore, her Americanization platform.

Despite the loss, in this effort Kellor and her group of women activists, at very least, successfully modeled her ideal of the aggressive progressive activists citizen. However contradictory, she modeled her ideal of local activism for national agendas, or what we have called Local Nationalism. She also challenged some of society's concepts that limited women. And, she helped keep suffrage a national issue. Kellor lost two elections, her Service program and idea of civilian training camps died, and her ideas concerning immigrants were not winning the day. Regardless, Kellor continued championing ideas. And, following this qualified Hughes debacle, this street fighter rose to Federal power.

– CHAPTER TWELVE –

WARTIME AMERICANIZATION

Kellor Goes to War

Just ten days after America entered World War I, Kellor was named the head of the Division of Aliens in the Resource Mobilization Bureau of the Adjutant General's office (DARMB).[662] Her actions in this position demonstrated the limits of her rhetoric, plans, and values. She advocated that a Federal Bureau of Immigrants (FBI) be created that would have designated "a correspondent on aliens in every industry"[663] who would investigate "destructive activities of aliens, such as spies, plots, violations of laws, censorship and the carrying out of official orders."[664] These findings would then be forwarded to the FBI so that they might formulate an appropriate course of action. In Kellor's rhetoric, she agreed that there was a real danger of alien sabotage, and to meet this possibility, she suggested transferring enemy aliens from very sensitive to less sensitive parts of the same munitions factory.

Chapter Twelve

To evaluate our suspicious leader's plan of having a correspondent in every industry, all the alternatives that had also been under consideration need to be reviewed. One proposed plan called for the wholesale dismissal of all aliens working in the manufacture of munitions and other war-related products; another proposed relocating enemy aliens from coastal areas. Kellor's plan had no employment termination component and limited workplace transfers to less sensitive areas within the same plant.

Through the recommended correspondents who would forward information concerning suspicious immigrants, Kellor argued that the individual alien could be considered, "not according to his geographical location, but according to his record and upon the merits of each particular case."[665] This intimate correspondent idea was proffered in contrast to broad decrees against aliens. These correspondents were also to provide immigrants with authoritative information about the massive amount of legislation that affected them. Thus these correspondents could support immigrants as well as inform on them.

When the plans in which enemy aliens would be fired from their sensitive jobs and restricted from parts of the East Coast were actually enacted, Kellor asked in despair, "Was any system devised for transferring or exchanging these men?"[666] She continued arguing that exploitation and neglect led to disruption. After two months on the job, with her plans still not implemented, she resigned from the Adjutant General's office.

One historian claimed that her leaving was "in protest over the handling of foreigners."[667] She tried to moderate the wholesale stereotyping of immigrant workers. When she could not, she would not take part.

While still in her DARMB position, Kellor actually became involved in labor disputes. While she admitted that the German government and German immigrants might influence enemy aliens, she reminded her readers that long-term Americans also had influence. To avoid further riots and strikes, we had to "bring the friendly aliens into closer touch with America's standard of living." No agitator, she said, "can bring about strikes and riots among workmen who . . . have fair working conditions, reasonable wages and hours and decent houses to live in." Showing leadership by example, Kellor told of a city where cessation of work was threatened by the activities of the radical socialist union, the IWW. In response, "Radical changes were recommended to the employers, who adopted them in full." As a result, the IWW representatives left town. Kellor crowed, "Their basis of their agitation had been removed and they knew it."[668]

In another case, a strike occurred because a holiday had been taken away due to increased government war work. The employees did not trust the company's motive for taking away their holiday. Kellor dispatched a member of her staff to obtain verification of the government contracts. Once the workers saw that the need that justified canceling the holiday was real, they were "willing, anxious to do their part to help the government,"

Chapter Twelve

and a strike was averted.[669] In her sole military-related post, Kellor provided evidence for her belief that disloyalty resulted from exploitation, distrust, and poor communication.

Kellor's Wartime Plan

During the War, Kellor created a multi-faceted approach to Americanization. Specifically, she created four types of Americanization: Educational, Neighborhood, Industrial, and Political.[670] Educational Americanization expressed America's point of view to immigrant communities. Neighborhood Americanization occurred in the homes of immigrants. Industrial Americanization dealt with the workplace. Finally, political Americanization simply attempted to continue Federal support of Americanization efforts.

Educational Americanization

Kellor's largest wartime Educational Americanization endeavor came through her leadership in the Federal government's wartime Americanization program. Our nationalist subject had finally achieved a Federal position. In 1913, Kellor's National Americanization Committee (NAC) began working with the Division of Immigrant Education (DIE) in the Federal Bureau of Education (FBE) under the Department of the Interior (DOI). By the next year, the DIE was fully dependent on the NAC. And Kellor was the NAC liaison to the DIE.

Kellor's official position within the FBE in the DIE was Special Advisor on War Work among Immigrants.[671] But she had power because her NAC funded the DIE, FBE, and DOI. That

Kellor considered the NAC funds to be hers, was reflected in a letter to the FBE Commissioner of Education, P. P. Claxton, on NAC stationery, "I am willing to undertake its [DIE] financing until such time as the government funds can be secured for this work."[672] In one letter, she asked the Commissioner to provide itemized records of expenditures.[673] In a rather pathetic letter, the Commissioner of Education asked Kellor for "two new typewriters" to replace their rentals.[674] NAC funding "furnishing a staff of 36 headquarters' workers in Washington and New York City, including field officers, translators, writers, speakers and especially workers among the races."

Sitting atop of so much bureaucracy, pinpointing Kellor's personal voice at this time sometimes proves difficult. But one set of documents detailed Kellor's specific ideas for the movement during wartime. Sounding more worried than at other times, she said teaching English and civics and reducing illiteracy was good, but "we cannot wait for them with the active anti-American influences at work."[675] Kellor worried that there were, "Thousands of foreign-language organizations in the US . . . [who] fought among themselves for independent and united native countries or to preserve their racial solidarity [but] few such organizations whose first interest is Americanization or to help America win the war."[676] Rather than oppress the immigrants, to confront the situation, Kellor engaged them in a battle of ideas.

Chapter Twelve

Kellor laid out five educative strategies to communicate to immigrants. First was "the organization of the foreign-language groups among themselves and by themselves into loyalty bodies for America." Second, she wished to find leaders in the racial groups who would "suggest, advise and assist in securing the co-operation of each racial group and to get right material to them in a form they will use."[677] The third prong requested "the selection of Americanization correspondents in schools, industrial plants and existing racial and native-born organizations" to give information to said groups. Fourth, she called for "an official bulletin on this work and a press service to foreign-language newspapers."[678] Lastly, Kellor hoped to have industrial and labor organizations to lobby for a Federal immigrant communication bureau. Hers was a thorough communication strategy.

Though what we have seen so far only advocated information from the government to immigrants, Kellor also continued to push for immigrants' civic participation. The Americanization Division of the FBE published the monthly *Americanization Bulletin*. One issue announced the results of a NAC-sponsored conference on the training of teachers, in which the main theme was that schools should "prepare citizens for democracy." Another bulletin article conveyed that preparing citizens for democracy "should be the preeminent, not the secondary or incidental, purpose of all public teaching."[679] Kellor did not put ideas of participatory democracy to the side for the War.

As ever, Kellor's Educational Americanization pushed the progressive education method of activity rather than reading or listening to lectures. The *Americanization Bulletin* explained, "Social activity must develop within the neighborhood itself" and "serve the real needs of the group"[680] The National Committee of One Hundred, to which Kellor belonged, published a curriculum with the FBE that stressed democratic participation. Students used foods to show the interconnectivity of the world and then were to "demand clean food from the milk dealer . . .[and] report careless handling of food or the selling of spoiled food . . . to the health department." Another lesson advocated inspection of clothing factories to ensure sanitary work conditions.[681] Rather than a passive audience, Kellor sought active learners.

Kellor's typical decentralized organizing strategy attempted to reach people individually. The FBE's coordination with the Council of National Defense (CND) resulted in "Americanization work in 32 states and hundreds of local Councils of Defense,"[682] which, in turn, created War Information Offices that were instructed to "handle the request of each immigrant as an individual personal matter as sympathetically as possible."[683] The FBE also spent four months surveying 50,000 local Americanization agencies, and Kellor's organization, at the very least, communicated with the 15,000 respondents. In 1918, Kellor compiled a list that included the names and addresses of over 140,000 groups involved in Americanization.[684] Kellor struggled mightily to bridge the gap between the local and the national.

Chapter Twelve

During this time of War, Kellor's Federal efforts included a wide spectrum of immigrant voices. One of her field agents, Frances Rumsey, tried to recruit racial advisors to the DIE. However, dissention and division within the Greek community made finding a Greek racial advisor difficult. One BOE report noted that the Greek factions were so antagonistic to each other that Rumsey and Kellor were unable to see "how they can be induced to work together or how any good result could be achieved."[685]

The Greek Constantinist group was well organized, pro-German, and neither "representative nor democratic." It would neither work with the Panhellenic group nor the Greek-American National Union. Kellor recommended a committee of seven with two Constantinists, two from the Panhellenic Union, and three neutrals.[686] The remarkable feature of this arrangement was that Kellor's team sought to include the pro-German Greeks in the discussion. Interestingly, when Rumsey worked in a group that included a "Zionist socialist," she reported that "the meeting was full of constructive interest and possibilities. The elements included were many of them essentially antagonistic. Yet we have the promise of good cooperation."[687] Remarkably, rather than restrictive coercion for conformity during wartime, Kellor's encouragement of civic participation even extended to pro-Germans immigrants and socialists.

Neighborhood Americanization

Kellor's Neighborhood Americanization program conveyed a faith in participatory democracy. Appropriately, rather than only promulgate it in publications or policy, she personally gave several speeches on the topic in 1918. Whereas her other efforts emphasized ideas and reform in male-dominated spaces, Neighborhood Americanization specifically sought to reach women. And, although Kellor's Industrial, Political and Industrial Americanization were humanistic, they also relied upon systematic implementation. Neighborhood Americanization, by way of contrast, advocated unorganized intimate contacts between long-term American and immigrant individuals.

Before getting to the meat of Neighborhood Americanization, a quote must be mentioned. At the beginning of one speech on the topic, Kellor uttered her harshest words ever. For the few disloyal immigrants, she rang, "there must be – Internment and Imprisonment. Expulsion from the country. A restriction on such immigration in the future. There is no use temporizing."[688] She may have made this unprecedented, unrepeated statement to prepare her listeners to take her seriously, as she then launched into a twenty-seven page speech filled with farfetched idealism. Ending her mention of expulsion and restriction, she announced, these topics were "not my field today" and turned to her topic, Neighborhood Americanization.[689]

Chapter Twelve

Neighborhood Americanization simply required that long-term Americans visit the homes of immigrants and, in turn, invite immigrants into their homes. Kellor urged her female audiences to "adopt an immigrant family. Some of you can adopt a whole neighborhood. Then do everything for and with that family."[690] She included a long list of services that the Neighborhood Americanizers could provide the family, with friendship being the most important component.

The close friend of Kellor's and wealthy socialite, Ms. Astor, participated in neighborhood Americanization by opening her home to seventy-six tenement residents and social workers. Echoing Kellor, Astor announced that it was necessary to "bring Fifth Avenue and First Avenue together, which will make acquainted as neighbors and friends, not as charity workers."[691] Here again the Americanization dream of bringing all sectors, long-term American and immigrant, as well as rich and poor, in friendship manifest itself.

Rather than instruction, Kellor claimed, "What the immigrant wants is simplicity and friendliness and new contacts."[692] To this end, she advocated "inviting her to your home and going to hers, not with the idea of uplift, but of getting acquainted for mutual benefit."[693] To highlight the importance of simple contact, Kellor reminded her listeners of the happy immigrants who, during Americanization Day, had stated that "it was the first time they had shaken hands with an American!"[694] This literally homey wartime program cannot but help remind one of the social events this Federal leader covered as a young gossip columnist in Coldwater, Michigan.

The sensitivity to snobbery in Neighborhood Americanization could also have stemmed from her history as one of the poorest children, the daughter of a domestic servant, in the small town of Coldwater. She denounced the "snob – whether it is the patriotic snob, who can't find good in other peoples and organizations; the social snob who lets class lines stand in the way; the intellectual snob who is so busy criticizing with his superior mind that he never does anything himself; or the moral snob who is intolerant of the man or woman who is climbing the heights more slowly."[695]

One wonders how Kellor being lifted from poverty by the Eddy sisters in Coldwater played into her explanation of how Neighborhood Americanization differed from settlement house work. She wrote that unlike settlement work, these visits to immigrants were not to come "From the top down . . . . The settlement worker wants to do something for her, to improve her. The church wants to make her better. The club wants her to come to meetings; the suffragists want her to vote . . . [This] is all manipulation . . . [and so the immigrant woman] becomes suspicious and resentful and sullen and that unforgivable thing you call unappreciative."[696] Rather than coercion, here we see a call for pure connection for connection's sake.

Kellor cautioned that those involved had to carefully scrutinize their attitudes for lingering racism. Success particularly

Chapter Twelve

required the "disappearance of racial prejudice and of Anglo-Saxon superiority and condescension."[697] Kellor warned that if the potential participant were to "have "racial prejudice and inhospitality in your heart and a sense of Anglo-Saxon superiority in your mind and go with your hands bearing gifts, you will ultimately set America back rather than forward."[698] The proper attitude also required the *"conveyance to her of the belief that we understand her traditions, culture and background and that we want to make it a part of America and to use and not destroy it."*[699] [Italics in original] Here again, we see Americanization and cultural acceptance going hand-in-hand.

Still, subtle ironic manipulation could be said to underlay this program's determination not to manipulate. Kellor wanted immigrant women to *"feel at home in America and that she is our guest and entitled to real courtesy and hospitality and consideration until she joins America."*[700] [Italics in original] Kellor hoped immigrant women would wish to learn English so that conversations could be had across linguistic divides. And throughout, there was a goal of wanting the women to become citizens. Neighborhood Americanization had a goal.

Ultimately, Kellor asked the women to distance themselves from manipulation by honestly offering choices. Rather than give pat correct civic answers to immigrant women, she sought to *"give her* [the immigrant woman] *the information necessary for her to make her own choice* . . . The great element in individual and social progress is to give men and women the chance to choose – whether it is a job, a home . . . their officials or laws."⁷⁰¹ [Italics in original] Kellor again showed faith in persuasion rather than coercion when she declared, "If they [immigrants] have a range of choices we more often get a right decision that endures more than where it is imposed from the outside."⁷⁰² Ultimately choice, rather than conviction, showed the greatest potential for bonding people.

Finally, Kellor sought political participation. She told the women in her audience, "Whatever you undertake, do it yourself. Do not delegate it someone else . . . When the government calls you for service it does not want your maid or your secretary or your stenographer or even your pet charity. It wants you . . . Don't rush off and join an organization to do this work. Be a neighbor by way of yourself and not by way of a headquarters. So many of us get stuck at headquarters and never get into the field.⁷⁰³ She noted that 300 organizations, not including churches and schools, were conducting Americanization work in New York City, and then challenged, "How many of you have ever met immigrants at the meetings where we discussed their Americanization?"⁷⁰⁴

Seemingly incongruously for someone concurrently leading several government agencies, she asked, "Have we gotten into the habit of asking too much of our government – thinking of it as something impersonal – unfailing, like air and sunshine? The governments cannot impersonally Americanize the home. The government cannot impersonally get women to take men's places in factories. The government cannot

Chapter Twelve

manufacture loyalty and devotion from Washington."[705] The irony of a government worker asking for local help illustrates Kellor's relentless aim at Local Nationalism.

Social circumstances, culture and gender necessitated Americanization specifically targeted at women. Men became Americanized at their jobs and now had the added benefit of being Americanized in military training and combat. Children became Americanized at school. However, Old World customs kept women isolated. This hurt women, as "the child comes home from school in her American clothes; the husband and brother come home in American uniforms or store clothes, but the mother still wears her shawl on her head . . . and as picturesque though she is, pretty soon the daughter and husband go without her. She loses her hold and the family morale is gone."[706] As we discussed when looking at Kellor's programs for female empowerment via athletics, we can see this attitude as disrespectful of cultural diversity.

Yet Neighborhood Americanization sought female empowerment. Kellor also decried "old world ideas on a woman's education" and the social isolation that lacking English enforced.[707] But this lack of access applied to all women. In discussing Neighborhood Americanization, Kellor asked her audience, "Do you know that with two possible exceptions there isn't a woman today heading a national movement of *ideas or politics* – that isn't strictly a woman's concern or division?"[708] [Italics in original] Rather than ineptitude, Kellor left home visits to women because only they could gain entry. Thus, beyond having a hidden agenda for immigrants and Americanizers, Neighborhood Americanization's plan for fostering unity held a hidden agenda for all women.

Educational - Industrial Americanization

During the War, Kellor declared, "Industrial justice is the essence of Americanization." And she elaborated on this vision: "Not less important is equality before the law. All men and women must be given an opportunity to be heard and to receive fair treatment or Americanization will fail because it can find no response from the hearts of the men and women in whom an injustice reigns." [709] Kellor's Industrial Americanization effort gave a great boost to the adoption of welfare capitalism wherein industries provide workers benefits to retain them as loyal employees.

In 1915, a combination of Kellor's Committee for Immigrants in America (CIA) and her NAC carried out an ambitious plan to "Americanize a city" in Detroit. To this end, night school appropriations were doubled. The CIA and NAC printed 150,000 "America First" posters in seven languages touting "the advantages of attending night school and learning the English language"[710] and showing Uncle Sam "welcoming the immigrant and directing him to the public school."[711] Industrial Americanization began by bringing Educational Americanization to the factory.

Public libraries displayed these posters and also placed advertisements for the English courses inside children's books to

Chapter Twelve

surreptitiously target parents. Pastors from all foreign churches publicized the schools. The Ford Motor Company produced a film promoting education that was shown in theaters. Foreign language newspaper editors met with members of the Chamber of Commerce, and, subsequently, local Italian and Polish papers used their columns to campaign for the night schools.[712] Social agencies, visiting nurses, courts, YMCAs, small stores, and employment agencies, among others, were enrolled in the publicity campaign. Five hundred billboards were donated to the cause. Kellor's journal reported that the educational endeavor was "absolutely dependent upon a *systemized co-operation between the educational authorities, industries and various social agencies.*"[713] [Italics in original] As in Kellor's other endeavors, Americanizing Detroit welded the city together via collective participation on a civic goal.

Industries' responses to these efforts varied. Nearly all put a safety officer in charge of publicizing the program within each factory. Some businesses, when told that workers were too tired to go to a public school after work, set up schools on their factory grounds. Some publicity reminded potential students that non-English-speaking workers were the ones fired first when industry slowed. Other industries made promotion contingent upon one's trying to learn English. Thus Kellor's group fostered many worker-friendly education efforts.

Punitively, some companies announced that they would fire workers who did not attend any English classes. An NAC pamphlet admitted that "these are drastic measures,"[714] while adding that "certain employers" thought this a necessary step towards teaching English to the city. Kellor's journal explained, "They regard the paternalism involved in making night school attendance mandatory as a temporary exigency."[715] Most employers took a more positive approach. One gave those who learned a raise of two cents an hour.[716] Henry Ford famously not only set up English courses, but created Americanization plays. Variety bloomed as a result of Kellor's usual decentralized organizational structure.

Immigrant participation was the ultimate measure of success for Kellor. One historian of the Americanization movement described the results as "phenomenal" because attendance at classes rose "153%."[717] Still, only a small fraction of the immigrant population attended the courses. But these Industrial – Educational Americanization efforts in Detroit lasted until at least 1931.[718] Beyond the immediate goal of Americanizing Detroit, this Industrial Educational Americanization effort greatly aided in the spread of adult education throughout America.[719] Undoubtedly, they did some good.

Full Industrial Americanization

The Educational - Industrial Americanization courses mentioned industrial democracy. And the unions used Kellor's standard language of the "American standard of living" to argue for reform.[720] Interestingly, the historian James Barrett singled out the organization that Kellor's life partner Mary Dreier and her

Chapter Twelve

sister Margaret Dreier Robins ran, the Women's Trade Union League, for creating English language primers designed to lure immigrant women into unions.[721] It could be inferred that Kellor approved of her partner's use of her techniques for collective bargaining. Clearly, coercion was not the only potential result of Kellor's Educational - Industrial Americanization efforts.

Kellor undertook other Industrial Americanization efforts apart from the NAC's Detroit effort. She spoke to the leaders of the Chamber of Commerce as early as 1913.[722] In 1915, she helped create the Immigration Committee of the National Chamber.[723] In 1916 she became the Assistant to the Chairman of the Immigration Committee of the national Chamber of Commerce.[724] And by 1918, her NAC funded the Immigration Committee of the National Chamber. And the Immigration Committee, in turn, paid for Americanization Committees in 150 cities.[725] Despite the NAC's publicity efforts in Detroit, Kellor spoke of similar efforts in such cities as Syracuse, Youngstown, Dayton, and Utica. Bringing attention to her networking style of organizing, she called the Chamber "the best clearing house for all other agencies and departments, public and private."[726]

In her profile of the Chamber's efforts in Detroit, Kellor praised features that the official NAC reports had overlooked. The NAC saw to it that passing classes in industrial settings automatically qualified one for citizenship. They then held receptions for newly naturalized citizens. Reflecting her more traditional concerns, the Chamber, Kellor relayed, also opened emergency employment bureaus as a part of the Detroit effort.

They had "canvassed employers in an effort to maintain a certain level of employment, avoid too rapid variations, have good workmen carried over the slack period at part pay and part time."[727] To the extent that Kellor agitated for English courses, they took place within a web of social justice initiatives.

Engineering Industrial Americanization

As was her wont, Kellor created a comprehensive theoretical reform ideal surrounding wartime Industrial Americanization. In her capacity as a leader of the Chamber of Commerce, she wrote the article "Engineers and the New Nationalism." In it she argued that engineers are the new heroes of industrial Americanization. Pointing to a wartime effort she wrote, "In the selection of 30,000 engineers to take an inventory of industries, to serve as the basis for mobilization, the Naval Consulting Board is revealing the engineer as the future big civic factor in . . . the nationalization of business." Herein the War revised her hope that we would create a national system to inventory employment and distribute workers. She hoped that providing a glimpse of national needs would "give the engineer training and a vision of industrial organization and responsibility which he has but dimly realized."[728] She created the vision of industrial engineer as a New Nationalist leader.

One problem the engineer could address were those Kellor termed "birds of passage." In Kellor's parlance, these were workers who moved from plant to plant or nation to nation. This created a lack of attachment to any particular place. As she said, they had "no job stakes or home stakes."[729] As a result, American wages were spent in other nations, and industries were forced to hire 300 workers in order to keep 100. Widespread exploitation fueled this wandering. Engineers were expected to solve this problem through the "regularizing of industry and employment of men."[730]

Engineers were also expected to fix living conditions outside of the factory gate. Factories owners often owned the land surrounding their facility. In addition, the owner was "probably the determining factor in transit facilities, water power, etc."[731] He alone had power over the industrial and civic future of a town. Whether or not he wanted the role, the factory owner was the town planner. As such, he needed the help of the engineer.

On the heels of the Detroit English teaching campaign, Kellor ran a contest for architects. The winner would be one who could design an inexpensive structure that could "take the place of the derailed freight car as the home for the railroad construction gangs."[732] Cash prizes were offered to those who could provide plans for four types of dwellings that met American standards, as defined by sanitation, lighting, ventilation, comfort, privacy, and aesthetic values. The designs needed to have economy of construction and maintenance.

By focusing on infrastructure, professionals like architects and the factory engineers could "translate the industrial – welfare movement into a sound industrial and community movement."[733]

Even the educational aspects of Americanization, Kellor noted, were "largely determined *by the actual physical provision* in the way of schoolhouses."[734] [Italics in original] In this brand of Industrial Americanization, infrastructure trumped ideology and Americanization depended on material conditions.

Kellor laid responsibility for the sorts of problems she uncovered in her early tours of labor camps with Lillian Wald at the feet of engineers, noting, "When we see day after day splendid buildings put up to house machines and store materials . . . with little or no thought for the necessities, comforts and conveniences for workmen, then we know the engineer is neglecting the human phases of his work."[735] She told readers that the worker who "cannot get a drink of water on a hot day, who must go home sweat-smeared in his dirty clothes, who must eat his lunch alongside his machine, or must take his turn in a three-shift bed" feels injustice.[736] Previously, she had laid such problems at the feet of the legislator. Now engineers joined legislators in culpability.

Ultimately, however, Kellor sought to inspire potential engineers with possibilities, declaring, "We have a whole, relatively speaking, unexplored field before us in the way of insurance, pensions, profit sharing and cooperative management, worthy of the best intelligence in the country."[737] She suggested keeping records on employees, accidents, labor turnover, and incentives, such as providing shorter hours and high wages for efficient employees. There were psychological components. Housing, education, aid in naturalization, social and recreational work were tools the engineer would use to create contented employees. Racial prejudice also needed to be actively stopped, as "a few hours spent in almost any plant will uncover most astonishing and often quite unconscious discriminations, based largely upon racial prejudice."[738] Kellor hoped to entice the engineer to embrace New Nationalism by displaying all of the areas they could control.

Democratic Industrial Nationalism

By 1918, Kellor had come up with a totalizing variation of Industrial Americanization that she entitled "War Americanization."[739] In this formulation, she advocated a variation of the British War system, explaining that the British controlled all aspects of the national economy by designating everything used in the War, including the housing of workmen and munitions, as war work. The government took excess profits from munitions industries, and the wages of those who switched industries were protected. Arbitration replaced the right to strike in Britain. Kellor embraced this nationalization of the economy.

By contrast, Kellor descried our system as disorganized. Evidence for her charge included thousands of strikes and alien enemies excluded from coastal zones without any attempt to find them other work. This national industrial organization was to be coordinated from the top, yet take care of those on the bottom. She wanted employers and labor to get together and "stabilize the situation and help win this war."[740]

Kellor sometimes framed her policies as being aimed at combating Bolsheviks. Yet, interestingly, in one lengthy article she compared her plan to Lenin's, and the depiction of him was not entirely unfavorable. She announced that "American business men will do well to set their denunciatory powers aside and to develop their analytical and critical faculties" by studying Lenin's policies.[741] In the article, she presented national industrial management as a science that had not yet discovered its basic principles. And she assured the reader that the rules for this industrial science would emerge. This anti-Bolshevik applauded Lenin's national economic coordination.

Still, Kellor had a fundamental argument with Lenin's approach to national economic management. Lenin hoped "to discover these secrets by the use of force through communistic organization," whereas America would find them "by the use of science through a democracy in which all men . . . will be the master of production."[742] Lenin's defect was authoritarianism. Our nationalism had to be based on a blend of science and democracy. Kellor did not dislike the Bolshevik's dream of a nationally coordinated society (that was her goal); she only denounced their authoritarian means.

The Human in the Machine

Kellor's Industrial Americanization took on board a broader movement, called scientific management. There were varieties of scientific management. The movement's founder, Frederick Taylor, thought it axiomatic that workers did not work as hard as they should.⁷⁴³ Thus, he focused on increasing their output. His ideological message "required the suppression of all evidence of workers' dissent, of coercion, of any human motives or aspirations other than those his vision of progress could encompass."⁷⁴⁴ At heart, his vision separated thought from manual labor. The scientific managers would do the thinking, and the workers would only perform movements.

Kellor supported worker participation in management. Therefore, she did not fall into Taylor's camp of scientific managers. In Samuel Haber's classic analysis of scientific management, *Uplift and Efficiency*, the biggest categories of scientific managers were "systemizers" and proponents of "Industrial betterment." Those in the former camp worried about increasing industry's profit and would have been the persons behind Taylor's unpopular "regime of the stop watch" and the techniques that undercut the importance of craftwork and "hinted at standardization."⁷⁴⁵ Those in the latter camp, who embraced industrial betterment, thought, "human happiness was a business asset."⁷⁴⁶ Kellor clearly fell into this second category.

As mentioned, human happiness required good facilities. Kellor said these made life pleasant and fostered "a quickened sense of *industrial justice.*"⁷⁴⁷ [Italics in original] Subtly, however, material improvements could not suffice without a sense of communality, which needed to come from a shared interest among members of the industrial community. Kellor denounced mere *ad hoc* features as paternalism, believing that a community created by shared understanding of industrial justice would knit management and workers together.[748]

To this end, our scientific managment proponent lauded a program in which, during their training, engineers spent six years as factory workers. This was an intensive form of experience-based learning. This work requirement "equipped the men to *interpret one group to another* – which is the very secret of national industrial organization."[749] [Italics in original] We see the hoped for community and intimacy she reported on in Coldwater, Michigan following her into the factory.

Though Kellor, in her scientific management phase, used the popular language of efficiency, her content reflected humanistic values. She warned that we should not conceive of efficiency as a "cold mechanical thing." Rather, it needed to touch "the spiritual or social springs of action in men."[750] Instead of a mechanical top-down solution, she held that we "must find a way to satisfy the creative instinct in men; we must find a way to give them a share in management; we must establish a personal relationship based upon understanding and community of interest, with co-operation as its keynote."[751] Having all classes engaging in progressive industrial democracy together would create a meaningful unity.

Kellor sought to coordinate the national economy much like fascists and communists did. This bold fact should give us pause to recognize how much of her Americanization efforts concerned labor. Again, living up to American standards, in her

255

world, had much more to do with economic conditions than cultural conditions; the fact that so much of this chapter on wartime Americanization focused on Industrial Americanization is not an accident. But, though this economic centralization led to great abuses in the twentieth century, her basic premise, her insistence on worker input, her making participation the crux of feeling connected with the factory, economy, and nation, aimed at putting the brakes on the abuses of centralization.

Political Americanization

The NAC funded the Federal Bureau of Education's Bureau of Immigrant Education for nearly five years.[752] Effective July 1, 1919, a law prohibited Federal bureaus from taking private funds.[753] Because the FBE's BIE had no independent funding, it largely died on that date. Kellor had long been calling for a "National Board of Aliens."[754] Now she worked to have the Federal funding of such a bureau make up for the loss of philanthropic support, and bills were introduced in Washington to obtain such funding.

Her groups backed the Smith-Bankhead Americanization bill, which "provided sufficient funds for administration and for state aid for the reduction if illiteracy and the teaching of English."[755] Samuel Gompers, speaking for the American Federation of Labor, with some reservations, said he was "heartily in accord with the purposes and principles of the bill."[756] Wilson endorsed the bill, but it did not pass. The Kenyon Americanization Bill in January of 1920 sought to "combat the menace of Bolshevism in this country by educational means instead of through repressive measures."[757] This bill also failed. Kellor's Political Americanization program largely consisted in efforts to get Federal funding for Americanization efforts. After July of 1919, the American government would not support national Americanization.

Before it died, Kellor's FBE education bureaucracy fought a turf war with the Department of the Labor's (DOL) Bureau of Naturalization (BON) for Americanization monies and responsibilities. The BON's Americanization program largely consisted of straightforward preparation for naturalization. To this end, they distributed over 100,000 textbooks and kept meticulous records, with each teacher continually recording such details as the number of students per teacher, students' nationalities, weeks in the program, etc.

In addition, the BON coordinated the Flag Day event, which mirrored Americanization Day, but seems to have mostly transpired in the confines of factories. While very impressive, BON's Americanization efforts were dwarfed by Kellor's FBE efforts under the DOI. Yet the BON was no more coercive or intolerant than Kellor's FBE. President Wilson backed efforts to harass immigrants and their communities. But the Americanization efforts of both of the Federal government's official wartime Educational Americanization bureaus were persuasive, not coercive.

Chapter Twelve

Throughout her Americanization work, Kellor used a variety of means to change public opinion. Haranguing against prejudice in print was her most common means. But she also taught via action in her athletic work, street battles, Service program, civilian training concept, curriculum, and Americanization Day efforts. Her networking organizational structure taught teamwork and fostered buy-in. Laws protecting immigrants demonstrated care and thus won immigrant hearts. In this chapter we saw approaches ranging from Neighborhood Americanization's attempt to foster direct intimacy to calls for engineers to manage the economy. The work she now moved towards showcased a whole new strategy – Media Americanization.

– CHAPTER THIRTEEN –

MEDIA AMERICANIZATION

Permanent Disunity

On July 1, 1919, when a law made it illegal for Federal bureaus to take money from private institutions, Kellor could no longer unite all the disparate Americanization efforts across the nation. As such, she retreated to working with a private organization, the Inter-Racial Council (IRC). In a very real sense, this law killed her vision of Americanization. If private and governmental agencies were no longer allowed to overtly support each other, the all-encompassing, nation-wide integration of our governance, industry, and population that she had called Americanization could not happen. America would forevermore be made of separate sectors.

The IRC was Kellor's last organized Americanization effort. In 1919, the National Americanization Committee (NAC)

Chapter Thirteen

voted that the IRC would take over all of the work previously performed by the NAC and the Committee for Immigrants in America.[758] As the name might indicate, the IRC's official mission was to "create a better understanding and a better feeling among the races in America."[759] So once again we see another iteration of Kellor's desire to bridge divisions.

Kellor's methodology of coordinating pre-existing organizations appeared in the announcement that the IRC would supplement and reinforce other Americanization efforts. The organization pledged to work "from the ground up, rather than from the top down."[760] The IRC had thirty racial conference boards consisting of various racial leaders well known in the business, educational, professional, and journalistic affairs of their respective racial groups.[761] Immigrants were involved. But with the IRC rank and file immigrants were involved less directly than in previous efforts.

The heads of two small unions participated in the creation of the IRC. But we must note that industrial giants paid for and formed the vast majority of the permanent membership of this organization, which included hundreds of the largest corporations in the U.S.[762] As she had in her other endeavors, in creating the IRC, Kellor ran her organization with the help of businessmen. In fact they often were the official leaders of organizations Kellor ran. Coleman DuPont was the titular chairperson of the IRC; Kellor headed the group under the title of Secretary of the Executive Committee.[763]

We might pause here to pose tantalizing personal questions. In the years leading up to 1919, newspapers' social columns frequently listed Kellor as attending and speaking at charities hosted by Mrs. Vanderbilt and Mrs. Astor.[764] In terms of class, one wonders if Kellor reflected on having gone from cleaning richer people's homes to help support herself and her single mother, to being a guest of honor in them. Kellor might have suspected that the rich saw her as a poster child of what a determined person could do in America. Her Horatio Alger type story might have served to relieve their guilty feelings concerning exploitation.

A gendered consideration also comes to mind. These charity dinner parties often supported good causes such as recognizing artists, funding stone removal in parks, and helping war widows. But all the causes had a dilettante tone to them. Again, Kellor got Mrs. Astor to open her home to the poor for Neighborhood Americanization. But these ad hoc charities did not seek to systematically address the mechanisms of national power as her work with industry and politics did. Kellor disliked the corralling of women into small feminine charitable areas of concern. Might she have done these events to maintain leadership among women? Was this a way to make men feel she did not mean to challenge women's domestic roles?

The newspaper announcements often noted that she came to these social events in the company of her girlfriend, Mary Dreier. Kellor's mercurial style allowed her to penetrate the world of the rich. In doing so, she both navigated the world of the charitable wealthy women and the policy boards of their powerful rich husbands. Her roots in Social Gospel with its disdain for class antagonisms, likely guided her apparent lack of resentment towards the world's wealthiest people. But one has to wonder if this once impoverished daughter of a single working mother found a mixture of elation and dislocation as she entered these feminine elegant events hosted in the homes of the world's wealthiest women.

The Battle for Free Speech

The IRC's most noteworthy adventure was its effort to foster Americanization through the American Association of Foreign Language Newspapers (AAFLN). This organization supplied 50% to 60% of the advertising in U.S. foreign-language newspapers.[765] That is, the AAFLN placed ads for American producers of American products who wished to advertise in America's foreign-language newspapers. And, again, as a result of Kellor's networking organizational style, the distinction between her organizations was not always clear. As such, we will often toggle back and forth between attributing actions to the AAFLN and the IRC.

The IRC bought the AAFLN in early 1919 and installed Kellor as its president. Kellor had written for her hometown newspaper, *The Coldwater Republican* as a teen. During this time she attended meetings of the Woman's Press Association.[766] She also served as the chief editor of her journal,

The Immigrants in America Review. When she became the President of the AAFLN, it earned half a million dollars annually. Kellor's insights as a theorist of media deserve respect.

The AAFLN fell into controversy when its founder and owner, Louis Hammerling, was indicted for violating the Espionage Act.[767] He published an advertisement in some 800 newspapers, signed by publishers of several hundred foreign papers, calling on foreign workmen to cease generating munitions.[768] Worse for Hammerling, the advertisement was funded by a financial attaché of the German Embassy.[769] Moreover, German companies paid for pro-German articles distributed in the AAFLN's industry publication. Worse yet, prior to running the advertisement, Hammerling sent men to gather information about the number and type of immigrants in munitions plants. Hammerling burned all of his records prior to the Senate investigation of the AAFLN. Seventy-five percent of the editors whose names appeared in the advertisement calling for the disruption of munitions production, claimed they had not given permission for the use of their names.[770] The Senate investigation of the AAFLN heavily sullied the reputation of the foreign press in America.

At this dark point, the IRC bought the AAFLN from Hammerling and gave Kellor control. Under her, the organization successfully worked to protect the immigrant press from attacks. She immediately called a conference of 500 foreign press editors. The attending editors issued a joint statement expressing their intention to uphold American institutions and ideals against "the menace of bolshevism."[771] The AAFLN then publicized statistical analyses showing that the foreign press "is loyal" and "for Americanization" and "for American Citizenship."[772] In advertisements, the AAFLN touted the foreign press' role in aiding our war efforts. While this smacked of forced jingoism, Kellor was trying to save the foreign language press in America.

The conference of foreign-language editors denounced a pending New York legislature bill that would discriminate against foreign papers in city and state advertising.[773] One speaker warned of a "deliberate and decided movement to eliminate foreign language newspapers."[774] A Congressman told the assembled editors that suppressing the foreign-language press would be a "great mistake."[775] And Kellor warned those assembled that "to take away the means of communicating with the intelligence of millions of people is to lay the foundation for Bolshevism in America."[776] Beyond jingoism and fighting Bolshevism, Kellor wished to save free speech.

During the War, Kellor publically mocked Wilson's suppression of dissent as an "obey the law and keep your mouth shut" policy.[777] With the AAFLN she continued to fight what she deemed the "suppress everything" crowd.[778] When the Senate moved to bar foreign-language papers from second-class mailing privileges, the IRC and the AAFLN sent her long-time Americanization partner, Louis Marshall, and others to argue the bill was unconstitutional. He told the Senate that "probably not more than 1 percent" of foreign papers were "Communistic or I.W.W."[779] This law would have harmed or destroyed "approximately 1,500 newspapers and magazines . . . with a circulation aggregating 8,000,000."[780] One historian surmised that the IRC "was unquestionably influential in preventing the passage of the bill."[781]

The Battle Against Authoritarianism

The AAFLN's disparagement of Bolshevism was not purely strategic. As seen in a previous chapter, Kellor did not despise Lenin's aim of national economic coordination. In fact, she thought that it represented the way of the future. Kellor simply disliked the authoritarianism of Lenin's plan for coordinating all aspects of society. Kellor battled this authoritarianism with information. Authoritarianism was anathema to one who spent so much of their career trying to get citizens involved in public life. And, appropriately, she fought this perceived threat to freedom with contributions to the marketplace of ideas.

Sharing information was a basic goal of what Kellor called her "clearinghouse" organizational model. It was the official justification for her journal, the *Immigrants In America Review*. In her Neighborhood Americanization advocacy, Kellor spoke openly about her faith that with information and freedom people would make positive choices. The educational branch of her National Progressive Service organization worked hard to distribute information about political events. And Kellor saw both

Chapter Thirteen

of the presidential campaigns she embarked on as methods by which to educate the public. With the AAFLN, Kellor did not try to control the editorial content of the foreign papers. Suppression of dissent would have violated her ethics. Instead, she provided content for the papers.

An IRC survey of the foreign press in Chicago seemed to confirm Kellor's assumption that authoritarianism constituted part of the Bolshevik agenda. The survey found that "of the fourteen Russian publications four are dailies, three of which are I.W.W. and Bolshevist." The same report concluded, "The eight Bolshevist publications have three-quarters of the circulation, reaching over 100,000 people."[782]

In response, the IRC supported the only anti-Bolshevik Russian publication in Chicago, the *Russkoye Slovo*. According to the IRC investigation, Russian organizations threatened the livelihoods and lives of the shops and individuals who distributed the paper. The IRC asked industries to subscribe to the *Russkoye Slovo* and provide issues for their workmen. Rather than shutting down the many Bolshevik papers, the IRC fought to keep the dissenting paper in business.

The AAFLN contributed to American dialogue via paid editorials. Often their paid editorials reached 6,000,000 readers.[783] These editorial pieces were placed in between 230 and 313 newspapers in some 25 to 30 languages. The AAFLN paid regular advertising rates for these messages. Some few newspapers refused to run them. There were no reprisals.

Editors of foreign papers did not have to publish the copy. The IRC and AAFLN used open dialogue, not compulsion, to spread their messages.

Some of the advertisements explained the problems with Bolshevism. One article, "When America Practiced What Lenin Preaches," told of the experience of Captain John Smith. The settler community Smith led, according to Kellor's editorial, originally believed in "the ideal of common ownership." But because of the free-rider problem, starvation ensued. That only ended with "the introduction of individual ownership." Succinctly, their advertisement announced the commonplace that, "The reason for the failures of communism is human nature."[784]

Another paid AAFLN editorial argued that the same failure to take human nature into account appeared in the Soviet's expectation that men would work their hardest on different jobs for the same wage. To compel this unnatural behavior they had to "give the bosses what they never had before – absolute power over the workers." The IRC advertisement pointed out that Soviet workers "can not strike. They can not even complain."[785] It added, "Some people say we ought to have bolshevism in America; but we ought to first learn how it is working out in Russia."[786]

It is interesting that the AAFLN editorial, financially supported by these wealthy businessmen, celebrated the right to strike. These editorials also confirmed that Kellor disliked Bolshevism due to its propensity for authoritarianism. The placement of these editorials, apart from their content, also demonstrated Kellor's faith in the power of rational arguments and, therefore, the goodness of people.

The IRC and Immigrants

Apart from media work, the IRC focused most of its efforts on keeping America's borders open. Louis Marshall told an IRC conference that he "deemed the present law well framed in excluding the mentally, morally and physically unfit." But, he "denounced as absurd" the Dillingham policy of selecting immigrants on the basis of nationality. In front of Congress, speaking for the IRC, Marshall argued, "The literacy test should be repealed at the earliest possible moment."[787] At one IRC conference, the keynote speaker told the audience, "Americans would starve and freeze to death if immigration were eliminated from our national life."[788] Throughout her career, Kellor's Americanization efforts encouraged immigration.

In her fight for open borders, Kellor cannot be said to have been anti-immigrant. But the charge of her rich friends undermining the rights of workers has more justification. A 1919 report the IRC produced warned that between low immigration during the War, poor post-war immigration, and the estimate that "1,000,000 men will return [to Europe] as soon as passport regulations are let down . . . the labor market is short 4,000,000 men and women."[789] Immigration, they argued, was needed to make up for the impending lack of laborers. In 1920 the IRC claimed, "Labor unions are disturbing themselves needlessly if they fear ruinous competition from newcomers." Somewhat antagonistically, the IRC surmised, "The need of production was never greater than now. Yet labor is apparently bent on restricting its outcome."[790] Another IRC member called the literacy test "the unions pet-child."[791] She took immigrants' rights over workers' rights.

Kellor not only fought against legal restrictions on immigration, she tried to convince immigrants not to leave America. In 1920, the IRC ran the following advertisement entitled "America Wants You to Remain Here":

> America has room for your ideals and welcomes your ideas; and your race has a future in the building of America. Enterprises, hopes, and rewards, are in the New World.
> Do you remember the long days and nights of doubt and fear on the deck of the steamer? How painfully you were longing for the home you left behind?
> The beautiful day when your ship arrived - and the first thing which greeted you was the statue which stands on watch at the entrance to the New World - the Statue of Liberty . . . .
> You landed. You got a job.
> Soon you became happy and contented. You saw that "Liberty" lived up to its promise . . . .
> Then war came! . . . .
> You were a man through and through. And you answered like a man.
> You helped to build ships.
> You made ammunitions of war.

Chapter Thirteen

> You bought Liberty Bonds. . . .
>
> And now your new land wants you for an American, in every sense of the word – she wants to share with you the victory she has won. . . .
>
> The employers everywhere recognize that the working man has come to his consciousness – recognizing the rights and honor of labor.
>
> This means better working conditions, better living conditions, and better wages.
>
> It took "pluck," as it is called by Americans – for you to leave your home and to begin to live in a new country. Now that you are already here and that you have begun – begun successfully – why not remain?[792]

In 1920, on behalf of the IRC, Louis Marshall testified to Congress against the raids of immigrant organizations aimed at deporting Communists. In an earlier 1920 report, the IRC had said raids were "interpreted by many as a campaign of repression against the foreign – born element in general." Making an interesting argument, they said, "The person of foreign birth participating in activities aimed at destruction of the government by force, is arrested and held for deportation, whereas an American [doing the same] . . . is not molested."[793] This inconsistency convinced the alien that there was "one kind of justice for them and another kind for the native residents."[794] Again, the IRC took a strong pro-immigrant position.

Educating long-term Americans, the IRC told the public that, "80% [of the foreign press] are as conservative as the great majority of American publications." They denounced the "grotesquely exaggerated statements about these publications."[795] and stated, "Some regard for the sensibilities of the foreign-born should be shown in the present crusade against destructive radicalism."[796] In this time of upset, they tried to remind America "that the great majority of them are loyal and are doing everything they can to understand America and aid in promoting its welfare."[797] In addition to protecting immigrants, Kellor's Americanization efforts always assumed that total unity would require acceptance of immigrants by long-term Americans.

Kellor's Media Theory

Since she began working with immigrants, Kellor showed sensitivity to the immigrants' point of view. She now showed understanding of their media needs. Defensively, she prefaced one article with a disclaimer, "So that there be no misunderstanding or cries of treason. I take it we all agree . . . English is recognized as the current language of the country."[798] She then explained the importance of the foreign press as an institution, in that it "Helped the immigrant find out what was happening to his family on the other side in the war . . . . It carried the specific news about his own province, lost in the generalities of the English-language paper. It helped him write letters home, and to get a job and to send money to his family."[799] Kellor protected foreign-language newspapers because they provided vital services to immigrant communities.

271

Kellor's praise of the foreign press implied the failure of the American press in that "it was his friend and his guide and a lot of things that an American newspaper is far too busy and impersonal to be."[800] She argued that foreign-language press advertisements in America failed because "the usual method is to take the English text of an advertisement and translate it literally without any regards to the psychology, habits, traits, culture or any other force in the particular group's life." American papers needed to understand the immigrants' political situation. She told advertisers, "The Jewish salesman will be about as popular in a Polish district as he would be abroad, and vice versa." This cultural analysis came on top of her usual refrain that "The American-born salesman full of race superiority and prejudice" would likely fail.[801] Americanization via media, Media Americanization, required deep appreciation and understanding of immigrants' point of view.

But while reaching immigrants required understanding them, Media Americanization also aimed to amalgamate immigrant identity. In a public advertisement, the AAFLN claimed, "National Advertising is the Great Americanizer."[802] The IRC found that approximately 70% of advertisements in the foreign-language press maintained connections, attention, and investments with the Old World.[803] They advertised "products made abroad, or specially prepared by racial people for distribution among their own people."[804] Foreign products created foreign attachments. In declaring that, "Americanization is an Invention," the IRC argued that we should put "the products of America in the homes of all who have not yet learned our language."[805] Kellor used the equation between product consumption and identity to convince businesses that it was their duty to buy AAFLN advertising.

Presenting a product-centered definition of American identity, the AAFLN claimed that "the American Standard of Living is developed through the use of American products, such as Tooth-brushes, Graphophones, Soaps, Tools, Sewing Machines . . . Toilet Articles and Tobacco."[806] But this was not only a matter of consumption; the same forward-looking progressive approach to the world activism fostered could be learned through our products.

For the magazine *Advertising and Selling*, Kellor wrote, "The history of America is the history of American pluck, invention and achievement." Consumer products conveyed this American story. And, "The immigrant is ready to read about it whenever the American is ready to tell it to him. There is romance in a harvester or an automobile if properly told; there is good will and good friendship in the story of the successful industries which the immigrant would like to hear from American business men themselves . . . Advertising can be made to tell the great adventure of America both here and abroad."[807] Products conveyed secret lessons.

Financial interest also built loyalty. The IRC thought that the "income generated by American advertising dollars would cause foreign editors to slowly become increasingly interested in

Chapter Thirteen

American affairs."[808] Kellor argued that, "One million dollars of American money spent in selling American goods to the foreign born in America will do more good than all the investigations and detecting ever set on foot *simply because the publishers will feel that America cares and is their friend and wants them to make good and they will return it."* [Italics in original] Repeating her long refrain about the power of material, rather than ideological persuasion, Kellor declared, "Men who have American securities, own homes in America, have accounts in American banks and have a little land stake, have the making of steady citizens."[809] Advertising would encourage all foreigners to invest financially in America. Financial investments would lead to emotional investments.

And, per usual, in her Media Americanization work, Kellor blamed American industry for the alienation of immigrants. She chided, "If any of the banks, or salesmen interested in American homes have taken the trouble to interest the immigrants, I have failed to find their appeal in the advertising columns of this American foreign language press."[810] Businesses, via advertising, had to interest immigrants in America and its products. Rather than coercion, Kellor's Media Americanization theory used the persuasion of advertising and the lure of the products themselves to cultivate immigrants' love.

Reckoning

The IRC spent over $200,000 a year on this movement. A fundraising letter claimed that, in return for contributions, the

IRC would furnish employers, "information on the immigrant labor situation, assistance in the reduction of labor turnover" and help in "stabilizing of labor conditions and other plant matters."[811] To this end, foreign-language speaking IRC employees would analyze the factory working conditions, and then explain both sources of unrest and how to ameliorate them via improving the working conditions. The IRC would then provide speakers of the majority of foreign-born employees to plants in order to explain steps being taken and placate labor discontent.[812]

The Industrial Americanization movement has been portrayed as a corporate effort to fend off radicalism and thereby create a docile workforce.[813] Knowing that contributors expected help with undercutting strikes and turnover, one could argue that the IRC's programs only seemed to be welcoming and protective towards immigrants. From this vantage point we could conclude that the IRC only sought the corporate agenda of having a compliant and steady workforce. One could argue that love of immigrants had nothing to do with Americanization.

Those who would characterize the Americanization movement as a trick by the wealthy to co-opt workers assume class antagonism and discount the possibility of mutual interest. In 1919, the IRC had Herbert Hoover speak on "how the races in America can cooperate in the relief work for children of their own race in Europe."[814] Cynically, one could argue that this effort to get money overseas only provided a reason for the immigrants to continue working in America. But helping their families

Chapter Thirteen

devastated by the War in Europe was a vital concern to immigrants. And Kellor's Social Gospel roots would argue that industrialists and immigrants, indeed all Americans and sectors in America, could have mutual interests. Indeed this was the only way our nation could be united, that we could truly be Americanized.

– CHAPTER FOURTEEN –

INTERNATIONALISM VERSUS AMERICANISM

Kellor's Final Writing on Americanization

Kellor led the Inter-Racial Council until 1921. During that time, she wrote two final books on immigration and several lengthy articles. In 1920, she published *Immigration and the Future*.[815] and in 1921, she released the shorter *The Federal Administration and the Alien: A Supplement to Immigration and the Future*.[816] The latter book was actually a compilation of articles written for the magazine *Public Ledger*. After nearly twenty years working with immigrants and Americanization, in these volumes Kellor spoke her last words on the topics.

The Chicago-based Americanizer, Edith Abbott, unfavorably reviewed both books in *The Journal of Political Economy*. Abbott wrote, "They have apparently been so carelessly or so hastily written that they contain numerous inaccuracies."[817] She disputed Kellor's historical details and found several typographical errors. On the other hand, the *New-York Tribune* wrote that the first book was "an expert, authoritative study, based upon wide experience and knowledge."[818]

The discrepant estimates likely reflected different expectations. These books were not about details; rather, they presented a total rethinking of the Americanization movement as immigrants increasingly came under attack. Kellor spent much of 1920 in Europe researching international immigration policy and developing her new outlook. These writings may not have shown much attention to detail, but they enthusiastically announced a new and, at that time, path-breaking political theory that showed Kellor transitioning from being an advocate for Americanization to an advocate of internationalism.

Kellor Denounces Americanization

In her post-War writing, Kellor distanced herself from the word *Americanization*. She noted that due to such efforts as the "noisy and generally futile hunt for spies . . . many immigrants have come out of the war with a sense of resentment and, in some instances, bitterness."[819] She explained that the word *Americanization* "antagonized the [foreign] editors. They have come to believe that this movement meant that Americans wished them to forget their language homeland and heritage."[820] The immigrant began to "Conceive a thorough dislike for the word *Americanization* and for everything connected with it. It was more than dislike; it was distrust. He saw no vital connection between Americanization and his daily life, a life usually so hard . . . he did not believe greatly in its sincerity."[821]

In arguing for cultural manipulation, Kellor wrote, "Nation building is to be in the future a deliberate formative process, not an accidental, dynastic, geographical, and economic arrangement."[822] But, "it is obvious that, with the best intentions in the world, Americanization cannot be established by propaganda."[823] She contended that as long as an America "tolerates discrimination in sanitation, housing and enforcement of municipal laws, he can serve on all the Americanization Committees that exist and still fail in his efforts."[824] The immigrants rejected Americanization and Kellor did not blame them.

In a 1919 article entitled, "What is Americanization?," Kellor definitively surmised, "The English language campaigns in America have failed because they have not secured the support of the foreign – born. Men must have reasons for learning new languages, and American never presented the case conclusively."[825] No reason to love America, no care could had been shown to counterbalance the general squalor. Worse yet, during the War, the U.S. trammeled on the very items that made us worthy of adoration: "The rights of free speech, of opportunity to be heard, of representation of justice, have all been imperilled [sic] in the campaigns and action taken in the name of a one-language country."[826] America had not lived up to its own ideals.

Chapter Fourteen

True Americanization

True unity, true Americanization, Kellor contended, would require acceptance of diversity. She wrote that, if we want the immigrant to stay, our law must "permit him to use his own language and go to his own meetings and realize his dreams in freedom in America."[827] To have true unity, we had to realize that America had no true cultural traditional core. She claimed that in America, "There is not a common interest in language, science, art or literature. There is not a common possession of moral, intellectual, artistic or political gifts, nor is there common sense sympathy in the use of them."[828] Here again, Kellor promoted an early version of what became multiculturalism to a generation. Our unity would not come from conformity to a cultural ideal we did not actually share.

Still, Kellor hoped for unity. Provocatively, she asked, "What is it that will hold together members of all races, and native American, in an identity of interest which embraces the spiritual as well as the material needs of men?" She answered, "opportunities to better conditions, to be equal to other men, to have the right to be heard, freedom of thought, worship and speech, and to enjoy life, liberty and the pursuit of happiness." She explained that "the failure of Americanization in the past years is identical with the failure of these guarantees."[829] Freedom and opportunity could unite America.

Commonality in America could come from participation in industrial governance. In the 1920 she announced, "The great fusing power of a nation is community of interest. The common interests in America are work and wages."[830] But she continued by saying of the common interest that "it is a share in the management of business." It resulted from giving immigrants a "voice in determining their own working conditions."[831] She stated clearly, "If a way could be found to include racial leaders of the foreign born workmen in industrial deliberations . . . much would be prevented which now leads to unrest."[832] Industrial democracy could help to fuse us.

Our common interest also required participation outside of the factory. We needed Neighborhood Americanization. As before, Neighborhood Americanization involved immigrants and long-term Americans inviting each other into their homes. But after the War, it also involved "mutual co-operation in neighborhood affairs."[833] It needed to incorporate activism. With this premise, Kellor theorized that "From participation in neighborhood activities and in governing their own communities, the immigrant will grow into the larger responsibilities of the State and nation."[834] The local and national poles in the phrase "Neighborhood Americanization" would be bridged via activism.

The chapter in *Immigration and the Future* entitled "Principles of Assimilation" listed them as recognition, reciprocity, and participation. For reciprocity, we needed to "bring together native and foreign born bankers; racial and American trade and merchants' associations; English and foreign language newspaper editors; and native and foreign born workmen in plants."[835] Recognition fed participation in that it meant "the elimination of discriminations, of a sense of race superiority, of impositions without consultation, and of many similar attitudes of mind which now limit the immigrants' participation in American affairs."[836] Though other Americanizers used coercion and hoped for conformity, Kellor pioneered a different vision.

Kellor's vision of Americanization required intimacy. She wrote, "If assimilation, then, is identity of interests, its principles are recognition by both the immigrant and the American of the capacities, qualities, and potentialities of each other; the exchange of ideas, opinions, and goods; and the participation of each in the life of each other.[837] As she experienced in Coldwater, Michigan, this intimacy required contact. She sadly acknowledged that advocates of immigration restriction "have no thought of coming into contact with the immigrant or contributing to his advancement."[838] These restrictionists wished to "retire into lofty seclusion to observe the struggle going on below."[839] Distance and abstraction doomed the potential for intimacy that Americanization required.

Introduction of International Perspective

In her final two books on immigration, Kellor developed an international perspective that reflected what she had found during the six months she spent in Europe surveying the immigration policies of various countries. This international sojourn not only mirrored her transition from a strictly national perspective to an international point of view about immigrants, it foreshadowed the internationalism of her post-immigration career, wherein she helped launch the field of international arbitration.

While the permanence of her switch to the international perspective provides evidence for Kellor's finding the point of view intrinsically valuable, she also began to use internationalism to help frame her arguments against immigration restriction. At the time she was writing her final two books on Americanization, Congress was enacting increasingly strict and permanent immigration restrictions. Kellor herself spoke to the Senate Immigration Committee denouncing the proposed restrictions.

This head of the Americanization movement told the Senators that labor flow was becoming increasingly international.[840] She used this framing to show that restrictive legislation ran contrary to world trends. The title of her book, *Immigration and the Future,* referred to the increasing internationalism of labor. While she continued asserting that immigrant restriction would prove financially ruinous and insulting to immigrants, Kellor now also argued that America needed laws that facilitated, rather than impeded, the increasing trend of international business travel to be out in front of world trends.

In an argument that did not likely impress anyone committed to restricting immigration, Kellor explained why America would soon suffer from a shortage of immigrants. Lowered immigration levels would stem from nations needing their laborers. Before the War, "European countries were flush with population. They seemed fairly secure in their power. They

283

had men to spare, and when their subjects did not like conditions in their own countries their emigration was encouraged."[841] Post-War situations were, according to Kellor, "making European Governments exceedingly reluctant to contribute gratuitously an adult population to build up a greater America."[842]

And future emigration would not inevitably come to America; for example, Kellor tried to convince the Senate that German immigrants were heading to Russia and South America rather than the U.S.[843] We needed to understand, as other nations did, that immigrants were assets that needed to be pursued aggressively. Immigration arrangements were being increasingly achieved through cooperative international agreements. The U.S. would soon have to become involved in international conferences with European countries so as not to be a casualty of those extremely "intelligent plans."[844]

The unfolding world order, in Kellor's explanation, looked a lot like her domestic distribution plans writ large. The object of such treaties was to "locate the surplus populations of one country in a country that needs labor, under conditions that will not prove burdensome to either."[845] One such agreement provided that "immigrant workmen, for equal labor, shall receive the same rate of pay as nationals in the same category, and that they will enjoy the same protection to native workmen." Furthermore, it provided for "payment of pensions, indemnities and compensation for injuries."[846] If America wished to be a part of the new international coordination of labor flow, it would have to guarantee labor rights and bid competitively for immigrants.

International Americanization

Internationalism increased the need for Americanization. Fearing a return to war, our exiting spokesperson claimed that every country believed it now had to keep track of its racial members and sustain feelings of loyalty.[847] To this end, the governments were going to increase their efforts to protect their emigrants, engage in cultural outreach, and even facilitate the sojourning members' voting in the home nation's elections.[848] Kellor feared that when unassimilated immigrant voters did vote, their vote would depend upon what their European kinfolk thought about the President, rather than the interests of America. Kellor's alarmist conclusion read, "A situation of this kind cannot continue with safety to the nation."[849]

When the Dillingham Commission fomented cultural concern over immigrants, Kellor used the fears they stoked to argue for social justice. When Bolshevism and War sabotage became hot topics, Kellor used fears of them to push social justice measures too. Kellor now used Internationalism to argue for such measures. Discussing international aggression after the War she told us, "America unconsciously permits exploitation which necessitates that foreign governments shall protect their own people here."[850] Kellor argued that this new aggressiveness on the part of immigrants' home countries made it more imperative than ever that America help immigrants "participate more fully in our national life."[851]

Chapter Fourteen

Since the War ended, Kellor could no longer argue for aiding immigrants in the name of being prepared for war. In this context, Kellor now argued that internationalism justified our continuing the same sort of personal outreach her Federal bureaus had cultivated during the War. Kellor thought it unfortunate that "when the war machine was dismantled, these relationships seemed to have no value in peace time and they were consequently rather ruthlessly abandoned."[852] She recommended renewing and fortifying these relationships because, "The more foreign born leaders are brought into contact with leading Americans, the more their leadership becomes identified with the American government and American interests."[853] Either Kellor's programs solved all perils America faced or she simply used different threats to justify her programs.

Kellor also used the international perspective to augment her previous arguments concerning consumption. Previously, she had argued that product usage helped immigrants identify with America, but now she stressed that when an immigrant returned to his home country he would become a great ambassador for our products. Since the returning immigrant would have some status "in the councils of his nation, where future contracts are to be arranged, and where the terms of commercial treaties are to be negotiated, his may well be the deciding voice for or against American products."[854] Immigrants having fond feelings for America and its products would help our international balance of trade.

Characteristically, rather than just dealing in theory, Kellor had an active plan to facilitate her vision. The very immigrant factory workers we derided as slow often spoke several languages and could be recruited to sell our goods abroad. She suggested our nation "create a training school in America for American salesmen to be sent abroad; to take the cream of the foreign born leadership for American business enterprises; to make sure that returning immigrants are salesman for American products abroad . . . and to participate in the direction of the affairs of foreign chambers of commerce."[855]

As for the average worker, our American salesperson asked, "Cannot the immigrant, while in America, be taught the use of American-made goods, so that his choice will be for American–made goods even when he is back in his homeland?"[856] Remorseful over America's loss, she lamented that "every immigrant who goes back could have been made a missionary of the American spirit, an advocate of American business, a salesman of American goods, as well as a champion of democracy."[857] Here products and democracy became linked through an international purpose.

The End of Sovereignty

Whereas Kellor had earlier hoped Federal law would overrule discriminatory State laws, she now called on international law to do the same to our Federal laws. Kellor's Inter-Racial Council denounced raids and deportation for despoiling immigrants' feeling about America. Now she added that since deportation only happened to immigrants, the raids gave the false impression that immigrants were more likely to be radical than long-term Americans. But she also added an international legal perspective, arguing that increased deportations lacked strict legal sanction and in that they "tend, therefore, to break down the safeguards of law" and undermined our "good faith in keeping our international agreements."[858] Our law had to recognize international law.

Treaties frequently specified that there should be no discrimination against foreign – born citizens or subjects. Seeking fidelity, Kellor reminded her readers that Serbia's treaty with America required that their foreign nationals "shall not be subjected to taxes or conditions of any kind that are more onerous than those imposed upon natives."[859] She recommended that America "improve assimilation" by "studying the laws of the various states and municipalities and pointing out to the states wherein these laws conflict with treaty rights."[860] Kellor's internationalism had totally superseded her concern for America's national sovereignty.

Our New Nationalist had become a total internationalist. She claimed that "we face a period in the world's history when the immigration of people will be the phenomenon of the world. The United States itself is fast becoming an emigration as well as an immigration country. It is a time when the lure of foreign markets and ease of transportation will lead Americans to go to all parts of the world. It is for us to plan – for as we treat aliens here so will the American be treated abroad."⁸⁶¹ We were rapidly entering a world in which borders would not have much meaning.

Amazingly, this ex-Americanizer now also thought naturalization an unreasonable demand. She noted that "Sweden, for instance, is not concerned whether or not the foreign born living in Sweden declare their allegiance to the Kingdom. Italy disavows any interest as to whether the Basques or the Greeks living in Rome enroll themselves as subjects of Italy."⁸⁶² In South America, she informed her readers, the subject of citizenship was not raised, unless by the immigrant himself. America's concern with citizenship made it abnormal.

Pressing a new philosophical point, Kellor noted, "Nearly every other country makes a distinction between the political and the economic aspects of immigration. They regard those who intend to remain as distinct from immigrants who intend to depart." Arguing that we distinguish between the two types of immigration, Kellor pointed out, "If we are to consider immigration as economic rather than as political, then we must bear in mind that economic influences are flexible whereas the political remain fixed."⁸⁶³ During economic downturns, did we really want international workers permanently bound to America? With hope, Kellor related that "American thought is beginning to correct the misshapen idea that every alien is a potential citizen and that economic opportunity and political opportunity are identical."⁸⁶⁴ Immigrants who did not wish to stay in America permanently, should not be pressed into citizenship.

Chapter Fourteen

Globalism had arrived. In the 1919 article "Immigration in Reconstruction," she noted that currently "no international discussion more than suggests the world-wide migration of people which will soon begin from every quarter of the earth and which will cross and recross each other's lines for many years to come."[865] She then radically asked if our harsh naturalization laws could be "amended to give international citizenship which shall be good the world over and having but one meaning and standard at home?"[866] And the very last sentence of her last book on immigration asked America to formulate a plan for "international human beings."[867] While the nation geared up for immigration restriction, Kellor championed the end of borders.

Kellor's Americanization programs entailed a profound disregard for culture. It originally solely focused on material betterment. This tactic discounted the role of ideology. The Multicultural Nationalism she promoted with the Americanization Day events assumed no fundamental cultural antagonisms existed. Now from her international perspective, she saw peoples as interchangeable international workers. In her early writing Kellor utilized moral arguments. She denounced African-American morals and prostitution. But even then, social structures and economics, rather than poor morals or cultural proclivities, motivated such depravity. Traditional cultural tendencies did not worry Kellor.

Rather than fret over culture, Kellor largely focused on economics. Apart from economics, she mostly decried passivity. And all cultures, in her assessment, were equally inclined to activism. As such, over her Americanization career, Kellor easily transitioned from a perspective that included a bit of Protestant morality to one wherein culture proclivities held no importance. The name "the Americanization movement" implies a distinct national group. Yet Kellor's easy switch to promoting "the International Human Being" indicated how little import she had given to the distinctive nature of different cultures all along.

Kellor Leaves Americanization

In 1925, Kellor released her analysis of the early years of the League of Nations entitled *Security Against War*. In researching the book, she "went to the scene of each of the League's activities, resided there and researched all available records. In all she visited 21 countries."[868] The book was released in two volumes that collectively had over 800 pages. The book profiled the disastrous results of bypassing the World Court in the settlement of international controversies.[869] Kellor contended that not utilizing the Court made finding conflict resolutions, "political questions not constitutional questions."[870] Political partisanship in the League of Nation's system would, Kellor argued, preclude security against war.

Kellor's long-time friend, Florence Allen, the first woman to sit on a State Supreme Court bench, claimed that the U.N. charter has the form it has because the "great nations of the world later agreed with Miss Kellor's conclusion as to why the League of Nations failed." This influence could be seen, Allen claimed, in the fact that the U.N. charter said the Security

Chapter Fourteen

Council should take it as a "general rule" that conflicts primarily be referred to the International Court of Justice.[871] Thus Kellor even had a hand in shaping the modern global order.

Kellor also blamed some of the failure of the League of Nations on America's failure to include immigrants in the negotiations, saying, "It was a subject of comment at the Peace Conference that our representatives had so little racial understanding." This ignorance reflected the "fact that English – speaking Americans seldom get close to foreign – speaking Americans."[872] Despite this reference to immigrants, after 1921, the all-consuming focus of Kellor's life would be the arbitration of domestic and international conflict.

Personal Motives

Kellor's private letters were about private matters. Her public life did not speak to her personal motives. As such, we can only guess the why she left Americanization. When the 1921 Emergency Quota Act passed, which limited the annual number of immigrants who cold be admitted from any country to 3% of the number of persons from that country living in the U.S. in 1910, Kellor was 42 years old and had been working for immigrants for nearly 20 years. The law passed the Senate 78 to1. And in 1922, 1923, and 1924, as the law was toughened and extended, Kellor kept largely silent on the issue. A cynic would argue that Kellor simply gave up.

As a sort of Americanization encore, in 1923 the retired Americanizer wrote the article "Humanizing the Immigration

292

Law." Bitterly, Kellor asserted that our immigration laws could not be humanized as they "disregarded natural law, and outraged the canons of civilized society."[873] The article categorized the many horrors befalling immigrants who had bought tickets and did not know if they were going to come within the quota limits. But the article held no real hope for stopping restriction legislation. It only hoped that, via efficient administration, the potential immigrants' "hardships may be minimized."[874] Kellor had clearly lost any hope that the America would accept her point of view concerning International Human Beings.

Yet, over her career, when Kellor faced her numerous defeats, she did not give up. After her defeat regarding Roosevelt's Presidential campaign, she immediately formed the National Progressive Service. After that failed, she launched her journal, the *Immigrant in American Review*. She put up a major battle for Hughes, but lost. Simultaneous to this endeavor, she published *Straight America*. Her idea of civilian training camps failed to garner public or political support. After these failures, during the War, Kellor became powerful in the Federal government. And when she failed to obtain support for a permanent Federal Americanization Bureau, she created the IRC. This incomplete list highlighting Kellor's resiliency undercuts the argument that Kellor quit Americanization because of failure.

Manically active, Kellor did not seem to linger long enough to feel the sting of defeat. But this list of failed initiatives also showed that Kellor was frequently out of step with the

Chapter Fourteen

public. This must have been more painfully obvious than ever as she developed her international perspective while America enacted extremely restrictive immigration legislation. During her transition out of Americanization work, Kellor wrote, "A leadership not constantly in jeopardy loses its edge; and if not held on merit loses its power."[875] Now with her exhaustive League of Nations study completed, our sociological warrior moved on to a career that was on the cutting edge of international arbitration.

– CHAPTER FIFTEEN –

KELLOR TAKES OFF

Sex Cloisters

It is not hyperbole to say that Frances Kellor was politically and theoretically in advance of her time. She fought for and theorized about women's basketball before men played it much. She became the first of many women to run a State agency. She normalized women taking part in national politics. She was instrumental in getting women's suffrage put on a major political party's national platform, twice. And after Kellor's Americanization work she launched the now thriving field of international arbitration. This chapter will look at Kellor's visions for the future.

Respectively, Kellor's first three books concerned incarcerated, domestic, and athletic women. In 1917 Kellor wrote an analysis of women in the Presidential Hughes campaign. In the early 1920s, Kellor wrote her last extended piece on women and politics. The title was "Cloisters in American Politics." This new twelve-page article was never published. Perhaps she did not publish the article because it presented such a negative view of women's political achievements after gaining suffrage. Regardless, in the article, this gendered warrior provides us with provocative final thoughts concerning women and activism.

Near the article's beginning, Kellor lamented, "Neither friends nor foes of enfranchisement foresaw the rapid decline of the ascendency women had gained over the American mind during suffrage activities." No one thought women would so quickly "slip down from that brilliant arena and disappear into the nothingness of political thought."[876] As the roaring 1920s brought the flapper, Kellor lamented the disappearance of the serious female activist.

In the article, she argued that, "political thought is rather well cloistered within sex lines."[877] The title, "Cloisters in American Politics," referred to women's segregation. Women were only allowed policy input concerning areas traditionally relegated their gender. To stop women, men employed gender stereotypes. Controversially - since so many women then and now have taken pride in it - Kellor's portrayed the creation of the female-headed Federal Women's Welfare Department as a conscious ploy designed to limit women's influence.[878] Letting women run that traditionally feminine area of control kept them away from areas of real power such as war, immigration policy, and industrial relations.

Kellor ventured that men limited women's access due to a fear of "subordination." But, Kellor mostly laid blame at the feet of women. Paralleling arguments she made during the Hughes campaign, Kellor blamed women's weakness on suffrage leaders' single-minded focus. Ever cynical about electoral politics, Kellor argued that these battles led women to think that winning the vote was enough. And, preening gendered sophistication, she wrote, "This judgment showed little real understanding of that highly sensitized masculine organization called the political machine."[879] Suffrage battles had habituated women to militant action. As such, American women were prone to "exaggerate the evil and to work indefatigably for sweeping reform."[880] As a result of this militancy, women "came to the electorate in possession of neither the theory nor practice of political science."[881] Breaking the cloister walls required understanding the subtlety of politics and the use of the political machine.

To end sex cloisters, women "must have a philosophy of life which political thought occupies a larger place in their scheme of existence."[882] Women would not, however, learn the essentials from the political arena because, "As an intellectual center, its activity is chiefly noticeable in those periods of irrational thought called campaigns." Rather, "If women are to have truly educated minds and independent thought, it would seem that their experience should be in the broader fields of art, science, philosophy, economics and business administration." It was in these broad fields that "problems are studied, policies formulated, and important candidates nominated."[883] Intellectuals such as herself, and others with experience, devised policies; politicians merely implemented them. Integration in society at large would facilitate women's political power.

While arguing for equal access to influence over political issues, Kellor claimed that women had "a deeper moral impulse," than men and "keener spiritual insight stirring beneath our sluggish political thought," as well as an appreciation of "the need for more fundamental action," and "warmer sympathy in dealing with the facts of life."[884] Women's particular sensibilities were being excluded from politics. Once sex cloisters were demolished, politics would "be defined in nobler terms and follow finer lines than now prevail."[885] Women needed access to men's traditional areas of purview because they were different.

Controversially, in response to women's and men's attempts to cloister women, Kellor asked if it might not be time for the "elimination" of the "network of women's organizations." She hoped "the increase in contacts between men's and women's minds in dealing with practical impersonal affairs might well take the place of some of these women's activities."[886] She argued that if women continued only interacting with their own gender, it would "*kill independent thought* among women."[887] [Italics in original] Gender integration, so to speak, might lead to a "community of thought between men and women."[888] It is interesting to note that in 1916, Kellor told a confidant that she had never led a women's movement.[889] As with immigrants, women would help themselves and America most by making their experience a part of the general fabric of society.

In regards to the future impact of women's striving, Kellor conceded, "it may be that generations must pass before its effects are visible."[890] Reflecting a belief in difference, and echoing the centrality of aesthetics in athletic work, she claimed that when granted access, "women's political influence will be traced in terms of fine feeling, spheres of thought and in accents of beauty, for such is our judgment of values and aspirations toward perfection." The closing of her farsighted feminist tract ended: "The contributions made by women to political thought during the next centuries, in this great democratic experiment, are likely to be an index to its civilization."[891] Incredibly, this masculine woman looked forward to the development of more feminine politics.

Kellor Launches International Arbitration

Kellor held the post of Vice-President of the American Arbitration Association (AAA) from its inception in 1926 until her death on January 4th, 1952. Arbitration, Kellor explained, differed from litigation and mediation. In litigation, two lawyers fought until one side emerged victorious and the other defeated. This technique cost too much, could take years to reach a conclusion, and fostered acrimonious relationships. Under mediation, the two sides bargained in the presence of a person who facilitated the conversation. Thus, mediation mirrored her Americanization hope of unity via engagement.

Chapter Fifteen

However, just like Kellor's sectors failed to unite under the banner of Americanization, an agreement would not necessarily be reached under the mediation model. In such cases, a neutral arbiter would be called in to make a decision. A contract signed by the disputants upon entering into the arbitration process made the arbiter's decision binding. And, hopefully, the fairness of the process and decision would entice the involved parties to accept the arbiter's decision with equanimity. Kellor's new organization hoped for mediation, but specialized in arbitration.

In some respects, the AAA just seemed to be an extension of principles found in small towns applied to larger arenas. In discussing the attitudinal outcomes of arbitration, Kellor made a statement that could have been uttered in her hometown of Coldwater, Michigan. She hoped she would hear a businessman say, "Well, if Harry Smith our busiest banker, will take his time to straighten out our troubles for nothing, it's up to me to straighten them out without bothering him."[892] Even her international work harkened back to the small town of her youth.

But simply casting Kellor as a nostalgic fails to recognize her achievements. The AAA was maintained via membership fees paid by participating businesses as well as very low fees per arbitration. Not reliant on government taxes, the AAA worked outside of and parallel to the legal system. Thus, as with the National Progressive Service, Kellor's quasi-governmental organization circumvented an entire entrenched bureaucracy. With the AAA she created yet another alternative governmental system. And this time the form of government she envisioned has lasted for nearly one hundred years and become international.

The results of Kellor's meticulous analysis of the League of Nations found that international "controversies were settled by political machinery because no settled rules of law existed to meet the claims."[893] As such, she was not only noting and filling a small vacuum in existing governance. In the year before Kellor's death, eleven governments recognized the arbitration guidelines she helped craft. That same year her organization helped arbitrate conflicts between forty-seven countries including six major European countries, six Middle Eastern ones, Japan, and "several colonial possessions."[894] The AAA currently has thirty-four offices and negotiates over 200,000 disputes a year.[895] And, again, the legal analysis she undertook to lay the foundations for the AAA likely influenced the prominence of the World Court in the United Nations.[896] Her political inventions were not just the reactions of a hayseed to the loss of small town life. Kellor, as a lawyer, sociologist, and intellectual, designed and implemented a very successful international extra-governmental system.

Arbitration and Culture

As with all of Kellor's work, arbitration sought to bring out the best in people. To get people to agree to their decisions, it was vital that arbiters had absolutely "no interest whatever in the outcome of the controversy." With delight, Kellor told us that the

Chapter Fifteen

arbiters, who were some of the busiest Americans, pledged to make themselves available "with no compensation other than the privilege of being of service to their fellow businessmen and for the honor of being selected." Proud of the altruism her organization had inspired, Kellor beamed, "Lawyers and accountants and bankers, who are supposed to do nothing but chase the American dollar, make up a considerable part of this body of men intent upon maintaining commercial peace." By 1930 the AAA had enlisted over 7,000 men as volunteer arbiters.[897] Kellor appealed to the powerful as people. She believed in the humanity of all.

As with Americanization, arbitration's implied ethic would rework society. Giving businessmen credit for the AAA's creation in spiritual terms, Kellor chimed, "The business man has gone on constructing his edifice of peace and working out his own salvation through the self-regulation of industry."[898] Kellor considered arbitration "the one proceeding adapted to an industrial society which wishes to govern itself wisely and justly and to render what is the just due of all its members."[899] She saw arbitration as attempting to "drive disputes out of American industries in a manner befitting the democracies in which we live." As Kellor said, "Arbitration is a civilian self-regulative procedure."[900] With good will and a social outlook, division and hostility could give way to social cooperation.

Whereas Kellor failed to bring social unity to America through Americanization, arbitration showed promise of uniting the world. As a member of the executive board of the Pan

American Union, Kellor "promoted arbitration and better economic relations between North and South America."[901] She developed a twelve-part vision of universal commercial arbitration which she ended by noting that disputes' "systematic settlement, through a science of arbitration designed to avoid the mounting menace of conflict, is a part of the realization of a vision of universal arbitration." Even after World War II, she hoped that arbitration would serve as a "counterbalance to the organized forces of destruction let loose through conflict and war."[902] While somewhat utopian, the AAA, again, still arbitrates hundreds of thousands of disputes a year. As with Americanization, hoping the AAA would end all divisions looked too far into the future.

Final Words

Confirmation of Kellor's ending her immigration work due to her being out of step with the public can be seen in the last three paragraphs of her final full-length book on immigration, *Immigration and the Future.* Her last thoughts on immigration focus on the disappointing current state of society at large. And they display a very far-reaching aesthetic visionary mind. The words she ended her writing on immigration with were,

> When the commercial age has exhausted the treasures to be gained by adventures into the resources of the earth, and we have found a way to assure to all men the necessities and comforts of life, then men's

Chapter Fifteen

minds may create the age of beauty in which their thoughts will turn to quality rather than toward quantity; to simplicity rather than toward ostentation; to form rather than toward bulk; to color and line rather than toward size; to continuity and precision rather than towards loose idealism. Perhaps, then, the best architects will build the shops and home of immigrants and native born alike, and the best designers will decorate them, and perfection will not be reserved for state occasions, but will find its way into the common things of life.

Then the ordinary problems of economic assimilation will no longer hold, for we shall have passed from the freedom we have gained by subduing brute force by science and skill by controlling the oppressions of men by politics and economics, to the conquest of ourselves. Thus we will be freed from petty ambitions; and peace and unity, which the end of the war has so signally failed to achieve, will become realities.

In the meantime, we must live through the practical age in which the instruments given to us for use are commercial. We are cheered within the narrow confines of the day's work by the hope that the age which succeeds this will hold the keynote of beauty instead of profits. It is possible that we hay have to wait until then for the full assimilation of the immigrant – for it may be that full identity of interest consists less in sharing what money alone will buy, than in the mutual appreciation of the spiritual qualities of men. It is the vision of this which keeps many in the economic treadmill though they know that the day of perfection is not for them to see.[903]

Kellor Creates Modern America

Kellor's last words on immigration convey her messianic visionary qualities; she looks forward to a day when economic well-being will allow aesthetics to flourish as a consideration. And she had to concede that she was looking far into the future when foreseeing women's input being totally infused into politics. Yet the American Arbitration Association demonstrated Kellor's amazing ability to implement visions via practical programs. Her visions' sensitivity to slights and reliance on personal contact, reveal a person dedicated to the humanity in all humanity. But her many successes in changing our national character and assumptions remind us of just how strategically Kellor worked to implement her humanistic ideals.

Our subject worked hard to create the expanded opportunities modern women enjoy. When women today engage in sports, they reflect an ideal of Kellor's. When women vote, they can know that Kellor first brought this idea to national political party platforms. This feminist's 1916 campaign across America for Charles Evans Hughes specifically aimed at letting females know they could publically engage in politics. In Kellor's time, women doing these activities scandalized. So Kellor overtly, directly, and constantly warred with the cultural assumption that women's temperament naturally suited them to

Chapter Fifteen

the home and only the home. To the extent that modern women take active public lives for granted, Kellor succeeded.

By replicating Cesare Lombroso's measurement of women, Kellor demolished the ascending idea that criminality reflected bad genes. And with her full analysis of the South's culture and institutions, she launched the idea that criminality comes from poor environments.[904] She emphasized the same theme when she exposed the scandal of "White Slavery;" limited economic conditions led women to their life of immorality. As a society we no longer buy into the idea that some people have innate criminal tendencies. Instead, our conversations frequently note the role of poverty in the creation of crime. Thus our modern assumptions directly echo the contributions of Kellor in her role as a leading criminal sociologist of the Progressive era.

We also see the legacy of Kellor in our education systems. Her work with female athletics foreshadowed Title IX, wherein women have equal access to sports.[905] Kellor can take some credit for the existence of female athletic departments in our nation today. More and more states are asking young people to do community service as a graduation requirement. Kellor wrote such curriculum for the State of New York in 1916 and gave it the modern title of "Service Learning." And, her organization's "Americanize a City" campaign gave significant momentum to the adult education movement in America.[906] Promoters of women's sports, Service Learning, and adult education should have a common gratitude for Kellor's penchant for creation. And, if you have ever engaged in such activities, Kellor has touched you personally.

This social pioneer significantly furthered the creation of today's system of unemployment offices and relentlessly passed worker protection laws.[907] But more fundamentally, with the second edition of her book, *Out of Work*, Kellor provided one of the first analyses of unemployment as a national problem.[908] And, in terms of labor, Kellor contributed heavily to the rise of what now gets called, "welfare capitalism," wherein employers strive to keep workers happy by providing them with services and benefits. When we work and when we do not, Kellor directly impacts our lives. Our assumptions about work life and unemployment reflect Kellor's work.

Traditionally, to be American was to be Protestant. In Kellor's time, the government used the Dillingham Commission's logic to stop immigration from Southern and Eastern Europe (Jews and Catholics). Kellor taught us that engaging in political activism aimed at improving America, and the belief in democracy, were the most important components of American identity. Thus she fulfilled the trajectory from Christian Sociology to secular sociology embodied in her Coldwater mentor, Henry Collin. To be sure, we had pride in our democratic form of government prior to Kellor. But Kellor pushed us towards a solely secular definition of what it means to be an American, one that does not discriminate on the basis of national origin, religion, race, disability, sexual orientation, gender or other characteristics.

If engagement with the political system constitutes the primary qualification for American identity, the stage has been set for multiculturalism. The Americanization Day parades Kellor championed on the Fourth of July, taught our population that America consisted of different ethnic groups living side by side. Significantly, her discussions of disloyalty always denounced industrial exploitation rather than cultural traits. This Americanizer promoted and saved the ethnic press. Kellor thought that love for America would bloom when people were treated well and felt free to celebrate express their cultural heritage as they sought fit. Kellor promoted an early formulation of America as a multicultural nation.

One might argue that Kellor sat astride rather than created the changes being discussed. These ideas concerning the transformation of prison reform, race relations, multiculturalism, the emergence of women into public life, Federal responsibility for the economy, benefits in the workplace, women's sports, and the like, were "in the air." Industrialization itself might get credited with our increasing secularization. Such arguments sadly argue against the importance of thought and individual action. But, there are other reasons to credit Kellor with being a creator of modern American identity, rather than just being someone with a knack for recognizing forward-looking trends.

A lawyer, Kellor studied under the most prominent sociologists of her time. These men wrote of creating a science of guiding society. Thus, rare among her contemporaries, Kellor had been expertly trained in the art of guiding and transforming societies. This training showed itself in her multi-faceted account of the mechanisms that perpetuated the racist Southern penal system, *Experimental Sociology*. Her sociological reform bent manifested itself in the first edition of her *Out of Work* being a how-to-manual on sociological activism. An eye towards social design also appears in her promotion of civilian training camps in *Straight America* and her use of sports to change women in *Athletic Games*. Kellor's Bundle Day, Americanization Day, Industrial Americanization, Neighborhood Americanization, Education Americanization and industrial reform, were consciously designed to impact our national identity. Unlike other social workers, Kellor long studied the science of being a Founding Mother.

Kellor's special status as a creator of national identity also stems from her penchant for implementing her sociological visions. In addition to constructing a theory of gender, Kellor spent a decade coaching actual basketball teams. Launching the National Urban League and getting women's suffrage on a national party platform, arguably did more to change our nation than many of the academic sociological tomes published in Kellor's lifetime. We cannot quantify the social impact of this very public intellectual promoting the inspection of employment

Chapter Fifteen

agencies in popular women's magazines such as *Harper's Bazaar* and *The Ladies' Home Journal*. But, Kellor, unlike her sociological mentors, she did not only craft her sociological visions for other academics. Appropriately for a Founding Mother, Kellor literally created many organizations, policies, and events in an effort to guide America.

More than One Hundred Million modern Americans have an ancestor that came through Ellis Island. During this peak period of immigration, Kellor created and ran the New York Bureau of Industry and Immigration. Having official responsibility for this population makes Kellor unique among those who would claim the status of founders of modern American identity. In her official capacities, and as the informal head of the Americanization movement from 1906 – 1921, she undoubtedly impacted the family lines of many of our current national population. The rise of the modern era coincided with the Progressive Era's peak in immigration; Kellor was in a unique position to impact this swollen generation.

Kellor's transgender lesbian status fit well with the notions of national identity she crafted. In her promotion of active public women, we see an ideal of a person with priorities other than traditional feminine roles. Her secular sociological position promoted more potential acceptance of homosexuals than traditional Christianity. She made room for her own existence in society, perhaps one day for her own gay marriage, when she set up structures designed to have people celebrate diversity.

But, in her announcement of the International Human Being concept, we see the ultimate in social and legal inclusion. Kellor's LGBT orientation meshed well with the welcoming and protective plans this Founding Mother had for strange people in a foreign land. Thus, as the global order Kellor helped create emerges, we relive her struggle to both be free and belong in this modern world.

Frances Kellor's Timeline

1873 Born in Columbus, Ohio on October 20th
1873 Moved to Coldwater, Michigan
1889 Possibly shot her own hand and moved in with the Eddy sisters
1895 Entered Cornell Law School
1897 Graduated from Cornell Law School
1898 Entered University of Chicago
1899 Journeyed south for prison research
1901 Published *Experimental Sociology*
1902 Moved to the New York College Settlement House
1903 Moved in with the Dreier sisters
1904 Published *Out of Work*
1906 Founded the National League for the Protection of Colored Women
1908 Appointed to the New York Commission on Immigration
1909 Organized a New York branch of the North American Civic League
1910 Became the head of the Bureau of Industries and Immigration and thus the first woman to run a state agency
1911 Merged her National League for the Protection of Colored Women with two other groups to form the National Urban League
1912 Left the Bureau of Industries and Immigrants to lead in Theodore Roosevelt's Presidential campaign
1912 Launched the Progressive Party's activist branch, The Service
1914 The New York Department of the Service became the Committee for Immigrants in America (CIA)
1915 Created Bundle Day
1915 Began funding the Division of Immigrant Education under the Bureau of Education
1915 Published a new version of *Out of Work*
1915 Began publishing her journal, *Immigrants In America Review*

1915 Launched Americanization Day
1916 Ran the Women's Campaign Special for Charles Hughes' Presidential bid
1916 Became the Assistant to the Chairman of the Immigration Committee of the National Chamber of Commerce
1916 Published *Straight America: A Call to National Service*
1917 Named the head of the Division of Aliens in the Resource Mobilization Bureau of the Adjutant General's Office
1917 Appointed Special Advisor on War Work among Immigrants for the Federal Government
1918 Launched the Inter-Racial Council
1918 Installed as President of the American Association of Foreign Language Newspapers
1919 Stopped subsidizing the Bureau of Education
1920 Published *Immigration and the Future*
1921 Published *The Federal Administration and the Alien*
1924 Published *Security Against War*
1926 Became Vice-President of the American Arbitration Association
1952 Died January 4th

INDEX

A

American Arbitration Association (AAA) 134, 299 - 303, 312
Abbott, Edith, 277
Activist Nationalism, 200 - 202
Addams, Jane, 42, 90, 104, 105, 144, 147, 149, 150, 155, 191
Advertising, 272 - 274
African – Americans, 50, 56 - 58, 60, 62, 64, 80, 88, 97 - 99, 102, 109, 305
American Arbitration Association, 134, 299, 312, 321
American Association of Foreign Language Newspapers (AAFLN), 21, 262 - 267, 272, 273
Americanization Day, 5, 161 - 171, 240, 257, 258, 290, 307, 311
Americanization Movement, 5, 7, 9, 30, 58, 81, 95, 143, 172, 176, 194, 247, 275, 278, 283, 291, 304, 308, 309
Americanizers, 1, 240, 245, 282
Antin, Mary, 213, 222
Art, 2, 3, 322
Astor, Mr. & Mrs. Jacob, 240, 261
Athletic Games, 39 - 42, 44 - 48, 64, 77, 88, 187, 189

B

Basketball, 31, 32, 34 - 37, 39, 40, 42, 64, 91, 295, 312
Berenson, Sarah, 31, 32, 35
Bolshevism, 192, 253, 257, 264 - 267, 285, 306
Booker T. Washington, 101
Bourne, Randolph, 191, 193, 204 - 206
Bufano, Beniamino, 175, 176
Bundle Day, 160, 161, 320

Bureau of Industries and Immigration (BII), 105 - 107, 109, 116, 121, 124, 143, 320
Bureau of Naturalization (BON), 137, 257

C

Carlson, Robert, 176
Chambers of Commerce, 163, 246, 248, 249, 287
Chautauquas, 17, 18, 153
Christianity, 14, 17 - 19, 23, 42, 43, 45, 80
Claxton, P.P., 171, 235
Coldwater, Michigan 1 - 10, 12, 14 - 16, 18, 19, 21, 23 - 25, 27, 33, 42, 49, 51, 58, 75, 137, 138, 141, 167, 171, 183, 193, 241, 255, 262, 282, 300, 305,
Coldwater Republican, 1, 21, 22, 322
Collin, Henry P., 16 - 20, 23, 42, 43, 64, 80, 83, 322
Columbia University, 74, 322
Committee for Immigrants in America (CIA), 91, 158, 159, 162 - 164, 167, 171, 172, 184 - 187, 245, 260, 320
Cornell, 23 - 27, 29, 30, 32 - 34, 39, 50 - 52, 127, 129, 154
Croly, Herbert, 140, 141, 144, 156, 162, 171, 195
Culture, 2, 8, 32, 33, 36, 37, 48, 60, 64 - 66, 77, 81, 88, 92, 95, 106, 111, 112, 173, 174, 181, 189, 198, 207, 208, 222, 242, 244, 256, 272, 279, 280, 285, 290, 301, 305, 306, 309, 311

D

Division of Aliens in the Resource Mobilization Bureau of the

Adjutant General's office (DARMB), 231, 233
Deegan, Mary Jo, 67
Department of the Interior (DOI), 234, 257
Department of the Labor (DOL), 257
Dewey, John, 46, 140, 143, 151, 157, 187, 188, 191, 193, 199, 201, 203 - 205, 306
Dillingham Commission, 136, 137, 139, 143, 197, 285
Division of Immigrant Education (DIE), 234, 238
Dreier,
  Dorothea, 89, Mary, 26, 69, 70, 72, 73, 89, 90, 103, 108, 109, 124, 128 (ill.), 131 (ill.), 193, 224, 247, 261, Margaret, (Robins) 70, 73, 90, 116, 128 (ill.), 144, 213, 248
  Theodore, 89
Dudley, Gertrude, 39, 42, 43, 45, 46, 47, 50
DuPont, Coleman, 260

E

Eddy,
  Mary, 11 - 18, 23, 25, 27, 44, 50, 72, 73, 138, 241 Frances, 11, 12, 14 - 18, 24, 25, 27, 50, 72, 73, 241
Edison, Thomas, 154
Educational Alliance, 91, 92, 94, 96, 107, 124, 172, 173
Educational Americanization, 234, 245, 247, 257
Ely, Richard T., 17 - 20, 83
Experimental Sociology, 52, 58 - 64, 66, 67, 77, 78, 81, 88, 99, 101, 306

F

Federal Bureau of Education, (FBE), 234, 236, 237, 256, 257
Federal Bureau of Immigrants, (FBI), 231

Federal government, 75, 141, 142, 160, 163, 183, 193, 234, 257, 293
Female dominion, 25, 26
Fleischman, Henry, 172, 173
Foucault, Michel, 62
Franzen, Trisha, 26
Freeman, Elizabeth, 213, 219, 220

G

Gender, 10, 12, 30, 32, 33, 35, 38, 49, 51, 67, 70, 71, 147, 208, 211, 212, 227, 244, 296
Gompers, Samuel, 225, 256

H

Haber, Samuel, 254
Hammerling, Louis, 263
Hartmann, Edward, 92
Henderson, Charles, 68
Higham, John, 194
Hill, Lucille, 28, 32, 34, 322
Hoover, Herbert, 275
Hughes, Charles Evans, 90, 105, 106, 210 - 212, 214 - 216, 218, 219, 221 - 227, 229, 230, 293, 295, 297, 321
Hyphen, 168, 221, 222

I

Immigration Commission, (IC), 105 - 109, 113, 123
Inter-Municipal Committee on Household Research, (IMCHR), 84, 85, 100
Immigrants in America Review, (IAR), 171 - 173, 175, 192, 263
Immigration and the Future, 277, 281, 303
Immigration Committee of the National Chamber, 248
Industrial Americanization, 234, 239, 245, 248, 251, 256
Intellectual history, 46, 68, 75
International Human Beings 291, 293, 311, 312

315

Internationalism, 278, 282, 283, 286, 288, 306
Inter-Racial Council (IRC), 259, 260, 262 - 264, 266, 267 - 270, 272 - 275, 277, 287, 293, 321

J

James, William, 31, 61, 203, 204, 247

K

Kallen, Horace, 173, 174
Kellar, Alice, 1, 3 - 21, 24, 33, 322
Kellar, Mary Sprau, 8, 9
Kymograph, 54, 58, 60

L

Ladies' Library, 12, 13, 15
League of Nations, 229, 291, 292, 294, 301
Legal Aid Society (LAS), 117, 119
Lenin, Vladimir, 253, 265, 267
Lesbian, 53, 69
Lippmann, Walter, 140, 143, 148, 157, 171
Local Nationalism, 153, 156, 189, 206, 211, 230, 244
Lombroso, Cesare, 53, 54, 67, 305

M

Marshall, Louis, 107, 264, 268, 270
Masculine, 11, 37, 38, 49, 71, 208, 211, 212, 297, 299
Matthews, Victoria Earle, 99 - 102
Mattson, Kevin, 75
Mead, George Herbert, 67
Media Americanization, 258, 272, 274
Melting pot, 207
Moore, Sarah, 96, 97, 171
Multicultural Nationalism, 48, 161, 167 - 169, 173, 174, 207, 290, 310

N

National Americanization Committee, (NAC), 162, 165, 168, 169, 190, 234, 236, 245, 246, 248, 256, 259
North American Civic League for Immigrants, (NACL), 106, 107, 109, 111, 114, 115, 117 - 124, 150, 162, 172, 173
National Association for the Improvement of the Colored Race, (NAICR), 213, 219
National League for the Protection of Colored Women (NLPCW) 100 - 103
Nativism, 198
Neighborhood Americanization, 234, 239, 244, 258, 281, 307
New Left Historians, 191, 192
New Nationalism, 141 - 144, 150, 151, 157, 162, 195, 196, 199, 230, 249, 252, 288
New Republic, 140 - 144, 148, 150, 153, 157, 162, 171, 176, 182, 183, 187, 188, 191, 193, 195, 203 - 205, 215
New Republic intellectuals, 141 - 143, 148, 151, 153, 157, 171, 188, 191, 193, 204
New York Summer School of Philanthropy, 74

O

Okin, Susan, 49
Out of Work, (1904), 73, 74, 77, 78, 80, 85 - 88, 99, 109, 116, 147, 176, 177 - 179, (1915), 176, 177 - 179, 182 - 184, 188

P

Park, Robert, 99
Participate, 170, 285, 287, 308, 313
Participation, 86, 90, 92, 107, 142 - 144, 147 - 149, 153, 156, 163, 165, 170, 184, 185, 193 - 195,

202, 203, 206, 208, 211, 212, 226, 227, 236 - 238, 243, 246, 247, 254, 256, 280 - 282, 307, 312
Participatory, 47, 102, 227, 236, 239
Pinochet, Gifford, 150
PNLS, 153, 155
Progressive intellectuals, 46, 76, 156, 223
Progressive National Lyceum Service, 153
Progressive Party, 73, 130, 144, 145, 146 - 149, 152, 155, 186, 191, 195, 202, 213, 214, 219, 220, 320
Progressive Service *see* The Service
Prostitution, 55, 78, 79, 80, 123, 179, 200, 290, 309
Protestant, 2, 18, 42, 75, 80, 104, 112, 291

R

Robins, Raymond, 70, 144, 156, 213, 248
Roosevelt, 38, 71, 141, 144 - 148, 152, 156, 158, 161, 163, 168, 193, 195, 209, 211, 214, 219, 227, 229, 293, 320
Rosenberg, Carol Smith, 25
Rosenwald, Julius, 163
Rumsey, Frances, 238

S

Schiff, Jacob, 91, 92, 94, 95, 107
Security Against War, 291, 321
Servant problem, 18, 82, 83
Service *see* The Service
Settlement Houses, 25, 36, 40, 47, 74, 79, 90, 104, 105, 124, 144, 241
Sexism, 26, 55, 66, 67, 99
Small, Albion, 67
Social Gospel, 17, 18, 83, 262, 276, 305
Society of Italian Immigrants (SII), 96, 97, 171

Sociology, 4, 19, 40, 52 - 54, 58, 64, 66 - 68, 71, 80, 82, 85, 87, 99, 109, 141, 143, 145, 146, 151, 154, 156, 161, 180, 189, 192, 213, 223, 294, 301, 305, 310
Soltes, Mordecai, 95, 96
Sports, 29, 31, 34, 36 - 38, 43, 44
Sports and Pastimes Association, 29, 31
Straight America, 194 - 196, 198, 200, 201, 203, 205, 207, 209, 293, 321
Suffrage 15, 147, 148, 150, 191, 216 - 219, 230, 241, 295 - 297

T

Taylor, Frederick, 253, 254
The Service, 143, 145, 146, 149 - 158, 162, 186, 187, 191, 195, 202, 213, 215, 265, 293, 300, 320

U

Unions 43, 48, 216, 233
University of Chicago, 33, 35, 36, 39, 51, 52, 58, 67, 68, 72, 320

V

Vanderbilt, Mr. & Mrs. 38, 163, 261
Veblen, Thorstein 67
Victorian, 42, 44, 49, 66, 70, 112, 310

W

Wald, Lillian, 90, 96, 104, 105, 108, 109, 123, 124, 171, 251
Warburg, Felix, 91, 107, 172
Ward, Lester Frank, 151
Women's Christian Temperance Union, (WCTU), 14, 15, 16, 18, 23
Weyl, Walter, 140, 151, 157
White slavery, 78, 79, 81
Whitney, Gertrude, 175, 176

Wilson, Woodrow, 163, 190, 215, 220, 222, 225, 228, 229, 256, 257, 264
Woman's Press Association, 21, 262
Women's Trade Union League, 73, 193, 248
Woolley, Celia Parker, 51, 52, 58, 72
World War I, 166, 167, 169, 190 - 192, 194, 229, 231
World War II, 302

ENDNOTES

----- CHAPTER ONE -----

[1] Wiebe, Robert, *The Search for Order, 1877 – 1920*, (New York: Hill and Wang, 1967), 141
[2] Collin, Henry P., *A 20th Century History and Biographical Record of Branch County, Michigan*, (New York: The Lewis Publishing Company, 1906), 93
[3] Ibid., 94
[4] Kellar, Alice, "Coldwater, Michigan," *Coldwater Republican,* Aug. 1, 1893, 3
[5] Conover, J. S., *Coldwater Illustrated,* (Coldwater: J. S. Conover, 1889), 12
[6] "Death of an Art Patron; Henry C. Lewis, of Coldwater, Mich. Expires at Clifton Springs," *New York Times,* Aug. 19, 1884, 1
[7] Kellar, Alice "Coldwater, Michigan," *Coldwater Republican,* Aug. 22, 1893, 3
[8] Putnam, Robert, *Bowling Alone: The Collapse and Revival of American Community,* (Simon and Schuster: New York, 2001), 19
[9] Kellar, Alice, Coldwater *Republican*, Feb. 23, 1894, 3
[10] Kellar, Alice, *Coldwater Republican*, Sept.15, 1893, 3
[11] Kellar, Alice, *Coldwater Republican*, Feb. 23, 1894, 3
[12] Kellar, Alice, *Coldwater Republican*, Feb. 23, 1893, 3
[13] Kellar, Alice, *Coldwater Republican*, July, 27, 1894, 3
[14] Kellar, Frances, "Industrial Americanization: A Discussion of the Conditions of the Labor Market Now and After the War," Address Delivered at a Conference of the National Association of Cotton Manufacturers in Boston, Copley-Plaza Hotel, January 18, 1918, p. 8
[15] Kellar, Alice, *Coldwater Republican*, Oct. 6, 1893, 3
[16] Kellar, Alice, *Coldwater Republican*, Sept. 15, 1893, 3
[17] Kellar, Alice, *Coldwater Republican*, July 27, 1894, 3
[18] Kellar, Alice, "Coldwater, Michigan," *Coldwater Republican,* July 14, 1893, 3
[19] *Coldwater Republican*, Aug. 4, 1893, 1
[20] Kellar, Alice, "Coldwater, Michigan," *Coldwater Republican*, Aug., 1, 1893, 3
[21] Kellar, Alice, "Coldwater, Michigan," *Coldwater Republican*, May 15, 1894, 3
[22] Kellar, Alice, "Coldwater, Michigan," *Coldwater Republican*, Aug. 11, 1893, 3
[23] Kellar, Alice "Coldwater, Michigan," Coldwater Republican, July 10, 1894, 3
[24] Kellar, Alice "Coldwater, Michigan," Coldwater Republican, Feb. 23, 1881, 3
[25] Kellar, Alice Coldwater Republican, Aug. 4, 1893, 3
[26] Kellar, Alice Coldwater Republican, Sept. 15, 1893, 3
[27] Maxwell, William J. "Frances Kellar in the Progressive Era: A Case Study in the Professionalization of Reform," (Ed.D. diss., Columbia University, 1969), 66
[28] Gordon, Linda "Social Insurance and Public Assistance: The Influence of Gender in Welfare Thought in the United States, 1890-1935," *The American Historical Review*, Vol. 97, No. 1. (Feb. 1992), 23
[29] Maxwell, William J. "Frances Kellar in the Progressive Era: A Case Study in the Professionalization of Reform," (Ed.D. diss., Columbia University, 1969), 67
[30] Faderman, Lillian *To Believe in Women: What Lesbians Have Done for America – A History,* (Boston: Houghton Mifflin, 1999), 146

[31] "Former Coldwater Girl Honored By Appointment: Frances Kellar Promoted to Head of Bureau of Immigration in New York City," *The Courier*, Oct. 4, 1911, 1
[32] Maxwell, William J. told this author that none of Kellar's childhood associates mentioned the story. Interview via phone (May 18, 2007)
[33] "Kellar, Frances," *Coldwater Daily Republican*, May 4, 1961, 1
[34] (Faderman 1999, 139)
[35] Maxwell, William J. "Frances Kellar in the Progressive Era: A Case Study in the Professionalization of Reform," (Ed.D. diss., Columbia University, 1969), 66
[36] "Former Coldwater Girl Honored By Appointment: Frances Kellar Promoted to Head of Bureau of Immigration in New York City," *The Courier*, Oct. 4, 1911, 1
[37] Fitzpatrick, Ellen, *Endless Crusade: Women Social Scientists and Progressive Reform*, (New York: Oxford University Press, 1990), 18
[38] "Coldwater, Michigan," *Coldwater Republican*, Oct. 28, 1892, 3
[39] Letter sent to H.M. Utley by Mary Eddy, July 6, 1891, in the possession of the Coldwater Public Library, Holbrook Heritage Room.
[40] Conover, J. S., *Coldwater Illustrated*, (Coldwater: J. S. Conover, 1889), 29
[41] Letter from Mary Eddy to H. M. Utley, July 6, 1891, in possession of the Coldwater Branch Library.
[42] "State Library Association – Coldwater as Ever at the Front," *The Republican*, Sept. 4, 1892, 3
[43] Kellar, Alice "Coldwater, Michigan," *Coldwater Republican*, July 27, 1894, 3
[44] Kellar, Alice "Coldwater, Michigan," *Coldwater Republican*, Aug. 1, 1893, 3
[45] Kellar, Alice "Coldwater, Michigan," *Coldwater Republican*, Feb. 23, 1894, 3
[46] Kellar, Alice "Coldwater, Michigan," *Coldwater Republican*, July 29, 1892, 3
[47] Blocker, Jr .Jack S.. "Separate Paths: Suffragists and the Women's Temperance Crusade," *Signs*, Vol. 10, No. 3 (Spring, 1985), 470
[48] Kellar, Alice "Coldwater, Michigan," *Coldwater Republican*, Sept. 1, 1893, 3
[49] Kellar, Alice "Coldwater, Michigan," *Coldwater Republican*, July 12, 1892, 2
[50] Holbrook, Phyllis, Letter to Ms. Patricia King of Schlesinger Library, Apr. 23, 1987. In the possession of Ellen Fitzpatrick.
[51] Maxwell, William J. "Frances Kellar in the Progressive Era: A Case Study in the Professionalization of Reform," (Ed.D. diss., Columbia University, 1969), 84
[52] "Coldwater, Michigan," *Coldwater Republican*, Oct. 28, 1892, 5
[53] Ely, Richard T., *Social Aspects of Christianity and Other Essays*, (New York: Thomas Y Crowell & Company, 1889), 11
[54] Ely, Richard T., *Social Aspects of Christianity and Other Essays*, (New York: Thomas Y. Crowell & Company, 1889), 92
[55] Collin, Henry, P., "Educated Men in American Life," *Coldwater Republican*, June 29, 1894, 2
[56] *Coldwater Republican*, Aug. 9, 1895, 8
[57] "Tuesday Night's Meeting at the Presbyterian Church," *Courier*, Apr. 25, 1896
[58] Collin, Henry P., "Sermon: Delivered by Rev. Collin," *Coldwater Republican*, Apr. 28, 1896, 6
[59] Maxwell, William J., "Frances Kellar in the Progressive Era: A Case Study in the Professionalization of Reform," (Ed.D. diss., Columbia University, 1969), 72
[60] Kellar, Alice "Coldwater, Michigan," *Coldwater Republican*, July 7, 1893, 3

----- CHAPTER TWO ------

61 Muncy, Robyn, *Creating a Female Dominion in American Reform, 1890 – 1935*, (New York: Oxford University Press, 1991), 4
62 Conable, Charlotte Williams, *Women at Cornell: The Myth of Equal Education*, (Ithaca: Cornell University Press, 1977), 77
63 Ibid., 108,109
64 Smith-Rosenberg, Carroll "The Female World of Love and Ritual: Relations between Women in Nineteenth-Century America," *Signs*, Vol. 1, No. 1, (Autumn, 1975), 9
65 Muncy, Robyn *Creating a Female Dominion in American Reform, 1890 – 1935*, (New York: Oxford University Press, 1991)
66 Bishop, Morris & King, Allisson, *A History of Cornell*, (Ithaca: Cornell University Press, 1962), 301
67 "The Women's Debating Club," *Cornell Daily Sun*, Volume XVI, Issue 44, 15 Nov.1895, 1
68 Franzen, Trisha, *Spinsters and Lesbians: Independent Womanhood in the United States*, (New York: New York University Press, 1996), 108
69 Gordon, Linda, "Social Insurance and Public Assistance: The Influence of Gender in Welfare Thought in the United States, 1890 – 1935," *The American Historical Review*, Vol. 97, No. 1 (Feb. 1992), 26
70 Barringer, Emily Dunning, *Bowery to Bellevue: The Story of New York's First Woman Ambulance Surgeon*, (New York: W. W. Norton & Company, Inc., 1950), 59
71 Bishop, Morris & King, Allison, *A History of Cornell*, (Ithaca: Cornell University Press, 1962), 301
72 Letter from Mary Dreier to Phyllis Holbrook, Nov. 23, 1960, 3, in possession of Ellen Fitzpatrick.
73 Fitzpatrick, Ellen, *Endless Crusade: Women Social Scientists and Progressive Reform*, (New York: Oxford University Press, 1990), 19
74 "The Woman's Crew," *Cornell Daily Sun*, Vol., 16, Issue, 81, Jan. 22, 1896, 1
75 "Athletic Council Decides Against the Women's Proposed Crew – Manager Elected for Athletic Team," *Cornell Daily Sun*, Vol., 16, Issue, 81, Jan. 23, 1896, 1
76 "From Wellesley," *Cornell Daily Sun*, Vol. 16, Issue 84, Jan. 25, 1896, 1
77 "Freshmen at Cornell: They Want Their Canes – The Question of Supremacy Not Denied," *New York Times*, Mar. 2, 1896
78 "Meeting of Sports and Pastimes Association," *Cornell Daily Sun*, Vol. 16, Issue 119, Mar. 6, 1896, 1
79 "Permanent Organization Effected," *Cornell Daily Sun*, Vol. 16, Issue 115, Mar. 2, 1896, 1
80 "The Women's Crew: History of the Sage College Boating Club," *Cornell Daily Sun*, Vol., 18, Issue 137, Apr. 23, 1898, 3
81 "Sage College: The Sports and Pastimes Association – History of the Organization," *Cornell Daily Sun*, Vol. 17, Issue 141, Apr. 30, 1897, 3
82 Ibid., 3
83 Grundy, Pamela, *Learning to Win: Sports, Education and Social Change in Twentieth – Century North Carolina*, (Chapel Hill: University of North Carolina Press, 2001), 43
84 Ibid., 13
85 "Growth of Basket Ball: Most Popular of Indoor Sports for Young Women," *Chicago Daily*, Feb. 25, 1900, 18

[86] Grundy, Pamela, *Learning to Win: Sports, Education and Social Change in Twentieth – Century North Carolina,* (Chapel Hill: University of North Carolina Press, 2001), 40, 41
[87] "Wellesley College Representative Says Physical and Moral Effects on Girls are Bad," *New York Times,* Oct. 11, 1903
[88] "Wellesley College Representative Says Physical and Moral Effects on Girls are Bad," *New York Times,* Oct. 11, 1903
[89] Faderman, Lillian, *To Believe in Women: What Lesbians have Done for America – A History,* (Boston: Houghton Mifflin Company, 1999), 140
[90] Smith, Daniel, Bar-Eli, Michael, Essential Readings in Sport and Exercise Psychology, (Champaign: Human Kinetics Publishers, 2007), ix
[91] "A Psychological Basis for Physical Culture," *Education,* Vol. 19, No. 2, (Oct. 1898), 102
[92] Ibid., 102
[93] "A Psychological Basis for Physical Culture," *Education,* Vol. 19, No. 2, (Oct. 1898), 104
[94] Ibid., 104
[95] "Growth of Basket Ball: Most Popular of Indoor Sports for Young Women," *Chicago Daily*, Feb. 25, 1900, 18
[96] Johnson, Scott, "Not Altogether Ladylike: The Premature Demise of Girl's Interscholastic Basketball in Illinois," Illinois High School Association, 1991, http://www.ihsa.org/initiatives/hstoric/basketball_girls_early.htm
[97] Ibid.
[98] Nellie Comins Whitaker, "Book Reviews," *The School Review,* Vol. 18, No. 7 (Sep. 1910), 499
[99] Verbrugge, Martha H., "Recreating the Body: Women's Physical Education and the Science of Sex Differences in America, 1900-1940," *Bulletin of the History of Medicine,* Vol. 71, No. 2, (1997), 273-304.
[100] "Ethical Value of Sports for Women," *American Physical Education Review*, Vol. 11, 1906, 164
[101] "Ethical Value of Sports for Women," *American Physical Education Review*, Vol. 11, 1906, 165
[102] Ibid., 168
[103] Ibid., 164
[104] Ibid., 168
[105] Ibid., 168
[106] Ibid., 163
[107] Leovy, Jennifer, "Chicago Pioneer Got Women onto Courts, Fields for Variety of Competitive Athletics," *The University of Chicago Chronicle,* 18, No. 4, (Nov. 12, 1998)
[108] Dudley, Gertrude, Kellor, Frances, *Athletic Games in the Education of Women,* (New York: Henry Holt and Company, 1909), 135
[109] Ibid., 4
[110] Ibid., 19
[111] Ibid., 10
[112] Ibid., 8
[113] Ibid., 15
[114] Ibid., 4
[115] Ibid., 110

[116] Ibid., 136
[117] Ibid., 14
[118] Ibid., 140
[119] Ibid., 30
[120] Ibid., 12
[121] Ibid., 154
[122] Ibid., 15
[123] "Ethical Value of Sports for Women," *American Physical Education Review*, Vol. 11, 1906, 162
[124] Dudley, Gertrude, Kellor, Frances, *Athletic Games in the Education of Women*, (New York: Henry Holt and Company, 1909), 142
[125] Deegan, Mary Jo, *Jane Addams and the Men of the Chicago School, 1892 – 1918*, (New Brunswick: Transaction Books, 1990)
[126] Ibid., 27.
[127] Dudley, Gertrude, Kellor, Frances, *Athletic Games in the Education of Women*, (New York: Henry Holt and Company, 1909), 20
[128] Ibid., 22
[129] Ibid., 60
[130] Ibid., 141
[131] Ibid., 93
[132] Ibid., 169
[133] Ibid., 166
[134] Ibid., 141
[135] Okin, Susan, "Feminism and Multiculturalism: Some Tensions*," *Ethics*, Vol. 108, No. 4, (July, 1998), 667
[136] Dudley, Gertrude, Kellor, Frances, *Athletic Games in the Education of Women*, (New York: Henry Holt and Company, 1909), 3

----- CHAPTER THREE -----

[137] Woolley, Celia Parker, *The Western Slope*, (Evanston: William S. Lord, 1903), 84
[138] Ibid., 85
[139] Moyer, Imogene, *Criminological Theories: Traditional and Nontraditional Voices and Themes*, (Thousand Oaks: Sage Publications, 2001), 30
[140] Freedman, Estelle, *Their Sisters' Keepers: Women's Prison Reform in America, 1830 – 1930*, (Ann Arbor: The University of Michigan Press, 1981), 109
[141] Lombroso, Cesare, *The Female Offender* (New York: D. Appleton and Company, 1895), 98
[142] Lombroso, Cesare and Guglielmo, Ferrero, *Criminal Women, the Prostitute, and the Normal Woman* (Durham: Duke University Press, 2004), 176
[143] Freedman, Estelle, *Their Sisters' Keepers: Women's Prison Reform in America 1830-1930* (Ann Arbor: University of Michigan Press, 2000), 113
[144] Ibid., 112
[145] "Discloses the Inner Nature of a Person – Successful Experiments," *New-York Tribune*, Oct. 7, 1900, 3
[146] Kellor, Frances. "The Criminal Negro: Physical Measurement of Females." *The Arena*, Vol. 24, No. 2, (1900), 195
[147] Kellor, Frances. "The Criminal Negro: A Sociological Study." *The Arena*, Vol. 25, No. 1, (Jan. 1901), 64

148 Kellor, Frances. "The Criminal Negro: Physical Measurement of Females." *The Arena*, Vol. 23, No. 3, (Mar.1900), 306
149 Kellor, Frances, "A Psychological Basis for Physical Culture," *Education*, Vol. 19, No. 2, (Oct. 1898), 102
150 Kellor, Frances, "Sex in Crime," *International Journal of Ethics*, Vol. 9, No. 1, (Oct. 1898), 74
151 Ibid., 78
152 Kellor, Frances, *Experimental Sociology: Descriptive and Analytic* (New York: The MacMillan Company, 1901), 29
153 Freedman, Estelle, *Their Sisters' Keepers: Women's Prison Reform in America 1830-1930* (Ann Arbor: University of Michigan Press, 2000), 144
154 Fink, Leon, *Progressive Intellectuals and the Dilemmas of Democratic Commitment*, (Cambridge: Harvard University Press, 1997), 5
155 Ibid., 9
156 Walkowitz, Daniel, *Working with Class: Social Workers and the Politics of Middle-Class Identity*, (Chapel Hill: The University of North Carolina Press, 1999), 33
157 Parker, Celia Woolley, *The Western Slope*, (Evanston: William S. Lord, 1903), 87
158 Kellor, Frances, "Social Conditions in the Southern States: Results of Investigations Made by Frances Kellor Under Direction of the Federated Women's Clubs of Chicago and Their 'Tribune,'" *The Chicago Sunday Tribune*, Oct. 14, 1900, 53
159 Kellor, Frances, *Experimental Sociology: Descriptive and Analytic* (New York: The MacMillan Company, 1901), 138
160 Kellor, Frances, *Experimental Sociology: Descriptive and Analytic* (New York: The MacMillan Company, 1901), 138
161 Ibid., 7
162 Ibid., 194
163 Ibid., 154
164 Ibid., 138
165 Ibid., 140
166 Deegan, Mary Jo, *Jane Addams and the Men of the Chicago School, 1892 – 1918*, (New Brunswick: Transaction Books, 1990)
167 Kellor, Frances, Experimental Sociology: Descriptive and Analytic (New York: The MacMillan Company, 1901), 82
168 Ibid., 91
169 Ibid., 85
170 Ibid., 99
171 Ibid., 94
172 Kellor, Frances, *Experimental Sociology: Descriptive and Analytic* (New York: The MacMillan Company, 1901), 103
173 Kellor, Frances, "Anthropology in its Relation to Criminal Jurisprudence," *The American Journal of Sociology*, Vol. 4, (Jan. 1899), 519
174 Ibid., 520
175 Ibid., 523
176 Kellor, Frances. *Experimental Sociology: Descriptive and Analytic* (New York: The MacMillan Company, 1901), 233
177 Kellor, Frances. "The Criminal Negro: A Sociological Study." *The Arena*, Vol. 25, No. 1 (Jan. 1901), 60

[178] Kellor, Frances. *Experimental Sociology: Descriptive and Analytic* (New York: The MacMillan Company, 1901), 191

[179] Kellor, Frances, "Social Conditions in the Southern States: Result of Investigation Made by Frances Kellor Under Direction of the Federated Women's Clubs of Chicago and 'The Tribune,'" *The Chicago Sunday Tribune,* Oct. 14, 1900, 53

[180] Kellor, Frances. *Experimental Sociology: Descriptive and Analytic* (New York: The MacMillan Company, 1901), 218

[181] Ibid., 211

[182] Ibid., 149

[183] Ibid., 149

[184] Pittenger, Mark, "A World of Difference: Constructing the "Underclass" in Progressive America," *American Quarterly,* Vol. 49, No. 1, (1997)

[185] University of Chicago, Office of the University Registrar, official transcript of the scholastic work of Frances Alice Kellor, number 6991

[186] Deegan, Mary Jo, *Jane Addams and the Men of the Chicago School, 1892 – 1918,* (New Brunswick: Transaction Books, 1990), 2

[187] Ibid., 74

[188] Gordon, Linda, "Social Insurance and Public Assistance: The Influence of Gender in Welfare Thought in the United States, 1890 – 1935," *The American Historical Review,* Vol. 97, No. 1 (Feb. 1992), 26

[189] Fitzpatrick, Ellen, *Endless Crusade: Women Social Scientists and Progressive Reform,* (New York: Oxford University Press, 1990), 72

----- CHAPTER FOUR -----

[190] Faderman, Lillian *To Believe in Women: What Lesbians Have Done for America – A History,* (Boston: Houghton Mifflin, 1999)

[191] Ibid., 3

[192] Miss Naumburg to Mary Dreier, Mary Elizabeth Dreier 1875 – 1963 Collection, Box 5, MC 309 folder 85, Schlesinger Library. Feb. 5, 1952

[193] Mary Dreier to Miss Curtis, Mary Elizabeth Dreier 1875 – 1963 Collection, Box 5, MC 309 folder 85, Schlesinger Library, Jan. 31, 1952

[194] Frances Kellor to Mary Dreier, Mary Elizabeth Dreier 1875 – 1963 Collection, Box 5, MC 309 folder 77, Schlesinger Library, Oct. 10 1904

[195] Frances Kellor to Mary Dreier, Mary Elizabeth Dreier 1875 – 1963 Collection, Box 5, MC 309 folder 77, Schlesinger Library, Jan. 3, 1905

[196] Faderman, Lillian, *To Believe in Women: What Lesbians Have Done for America – A History,* (Boston: Houghton Mifflin, 1999); 143

[197] Mary Dreier to Phyllis Holbrook, Mary Elizabeth Dreier 1875 – 1963 Collection, Box 5, MC 309 folder 77, Schlesinger Library, Jan. 11, 1960

[198] Mary Dreier's nephew would not let researchers read Mary Dreier's letters until 1977. He then donated them to the Schlesinger Library at the Radcliffe Institute for Advanced Study.

[199] Chauncey, George, *Gay New York: Gender, Urban culture and the Making of the Gay Male World, 1890 – 1940,* (New York: Basic Books, 1995), 116

[200] Frances Kellor to Mary Dreier, Mary Elizabeth Dreier 1875 – 1963 Collection, Box 5, MC 309 folder 77, Schlesinger Library, Oct. 30, 1906

[201] Frances Kellor to Mary Dreier, Mary Elizabeth Dreier 1875 – 1963 Collection, Box 5, MC 309 folder 77, Schlesinger Library, July 28, 1905

202 Franzen, Trisha, *Spinsters and Lesbians,* New York (New York University Press, 1996), 113

203 Frances Kellor to Lillian Wald. Lillian D. Wald Papers, 1889 – 1957 New York Public Library Humanities and Social Sciences Library, Manuscript and Archives, Reel 8, Box 10, Folder 4

204 "Woman Chief Investigator: Miss Kellor Appointed to Place in Department of Labor," *New – York Tribune,* Oct. 5, 1910, 11

205 Woolley, Celia Parker, *The Western Slope,* (Evanston: William S. Lord, 1903), 88

206 Faderman, Lillian, *To Believe in Women: What Lesbians Have Done for America – A History,* (Boston: Houghton Mifflin, 1999), 142

207 Harper, Ida, "Fight to a Finish for Woman Suffrage," *New – York Tribune,* Nov. 5, 1912, 10

208 Letter from Elizabeth Robins to Margaret Dreier Robins, (Aug. 6, 1910); Papers of the Women's Trade Union League. Microfilm Reel 21. Tamiment Library, New York University.

209 "Mary Dreier's Arrest: Utterly Shameful, and Quite Worthy of Tammany's Attitude Toward Women, *American-Journal –Examiner,* Nov. 9, 1909

210 Recchiuti, John, *Civic Engagement: Social Science and Progressive – Era Reform in New York City,* (Philadelphia: University of Pennsylvania Press, 2006), 95

211 Faderman, Lillian. *To Believe in Women: What Lesbians Have Done for America – A History.* (Boston: Houghton Mifflin Company, 1999), 141

212 Mattson, Kevin, *Creating A Democratic Public: The Struggle for Urban Participatory Democracy During the Progressive Era,* (University Park: The Pennsylvania State Press, 1998), 14

213 Kellor, Frances, *Out of Work: A Study of Employment Agencies: Their Treatment of the Unemployed, and Their Influence Upon Homes and Business* (New York: G. P. Putnam's Sons, 1904), 5

214 Katzman, David, *Seven Days a Week: Domestic Service in Industrializing America,* (Urbana: University of Illinois Press), 44

215 Feldman, Egal. "Prostitution, the Alien Woman and the Progressive Imagination, 1910 – 1915." *American Quarterly*, Vol. 19, No. 2., Part 1, (Summer, 1967), 205

216 U.S. Immigration Commission Reports. Vol 37. 61st Congress. 3rd session. Document no. 753. (Washington Printing Office, 1911). Importation and Harboring of Women for Immoral Purposes. 59-60

217 Kellor, Frances. "The Problem of the Young Negro Girl from the South: Lured Away From Her Rural Home by Unscrupulous Agents to Find Herself Here Confronted by a Choice Between Starvation and Unworthy Associations . . . Here is an Opportunity for Practical Philanthropists," *New York Times,* Mar. 1905, X8

218 Kellor, Frances, *Out of Work: A Study of Employment Agencies: Their Treatment of the Unemployed, and Their Influence Upon Homes and Business* (New York: G. P. Putnam's Sons, 1904), 7

219 Kellor, Frances, "The Servant Question Plus the Employment Bureau, *Harper's Bazaar*, Jan. 1905, Vol, 39, No. 1, 17

220 Ibid., 18

221 Kellor, Frances, "The Housewife and Her Helper," *Ladies' Home Journal,* Feb. 1905, Vol. 23, No. 1, p. 32

222 "Treatment of Domestics," *New – York Tribune,* Mar. 5, 1905, C7

[223] Kellor, Frances, "The Housewife and Her Helper," *Ladies Home Journal,* Jan. 1906, Vol. 23, No. 2, 36
[224] Kellor, Frances, "The Servant Question Plus the Employment Bureau, *Harper's Bazaar,* Jan. 1905, Vol. 39, No. 1, 18
[225] Kellor, Frances, *Out of Work: A Study of Employment Agencies: Their Treatment of the Unemployed, and Their Influence Upon Homes and Business* (New York: G. Putnam's Sons, 1904), 16
[226] Ibid., 156
[227] Ibid., 157
[228] Ibid., 166
[229] Ibid., 165
[230] Ibid., 170
[231] Ibid., 177
[232] Ibid., 178
[233] Ibid., 178
[234] Ibid., 166
[235] Ibid., 258
[236] Ibid., 282
[237] Nicholson, Jan, *Frances A. Kellor: Social Reform in the Progressive Era,* Senior Project (B.A.), Antioch College, 1974, Call No. 1974 NIC, 31
[238] "Current Events," *Friends' Intelligencer,* July 9, 1904, 440
[239] Kellor, Frances, *Out of Work: A Study of Employment Agencies: Their Treatment of the Unemployed, and Their Influence Upon Homes and Business* (New York: G. Putnam's Sons, 1904), v
[240] "Out of Work," *New York Times,* Oct. 8, 1904, BR673
[241] Kellor, Frances, "The Housewife and Her Helper," *Ladies' Home Journal,* May 1906, Vol. 23, No. 6, 30
[242] Kellor, Frances, *Out of Work: A Study of Employment Agencies: Their Treatment of the Unemployed, and Their Influence Upon Homes and Business* (New York: G. Putnam's Sons, 1904), 130

----- CHAPTER FIVE ------

[243] Dreier, Mary, *Margaret Dreier Robins: Her Life, Letters and Work,* (New York: Van Rees Press, 1950), 8
[244] "Notable American Women: The Modern Period," Edited by Barbara Sicherman and Carol Hurd Green, (Cambridge: The Belknap Press of Harvard University Press, 1980), 394
[245] O'Connell, Lucille, *Notable American Women: The Modern Period, A Biographical Dictionary,* Eds. Sicherman, Barbara, Green, Carol, (Cambridge: The Belknap Press of Harvard University Press, 1980), 394
[246] Wald, Lillian, *The House on Henry Street,* (New York: Henry Holt and Company, 1915), 292
[247] Official Souvenir Book of the Fair In Aid of the Educational Alliance and the Hebrew Technical Institute 1895, (New York, Frederick Spiegelberg, 1895), 19
[248] "The Educational Alliance," Center for Jewish History, Call N. 312, Box 2, Folder 2, (Apr. 7, 1905), 1
[249] Ibid., 4
[250] Abelson, Paul, "The Education of the Immigrant by the Education Alliance," *Journal of Social Science,* Vol. 44, (Se 1906), 167

251 Ibid., 168
252 Ibid., 16
253 Gustave, Straubenmueller, "The Work of the New York Schools for the Immigrant Class," *Journal of Social Science,* Vol. 44, (Se 1906), 177
254 Hartmann, Edward, *The Movement to Americanize the Immigrant,* (New York: Columbia University Press, 1948), 24
255 "Summary of Labor and Living Conditions in Camps and Small Communities," L. Hollingsworth Wood papers, Haverford College Special Collections, Call No. 1175, Box 66, National Civic League for Immigrants, date unknown, but based upon the 1911 Bureau of Industries and Immigration report, 12
256 Kellor, Frances, "Who is Responsible for the Immigrant?" *Outlook,* Apr. 25, 1914, 912
257 Ibid., 913
258 "Distributing the Immigrant," *The Independent,* May 18, 1914, 287
259 "League to Protect Aliens From Fraud: New Organization Plans Also to Assist Immigrants in Many Other Ways: Will Urge Distribution," *New York Times,* 10 Jan. 1910, 8
260 Topics of the Times: Important Work in Good Hands," *New York Times,* Oct. 7, 1910, 10
261 Soltes, Mordecai, *The Yiddish Press: An Americanizing Agency,* (New York: Arno Press and the New York Times, 1969), 114
262 Ibid., 176
263 Ibid., 177
264 Wald, Lillian, *The House on Henry Street,* (New York: Henry Holt and Company, 1915), 308
265 Hartmann, Edward, *The Movement to Americanize the Immigrant,* (New York, Columbia University Press, 1948), 27
266 "Camp Schools for Italian Laborers: To be Installed Among Erie Canal Workers Following Successful Test in Pittsburg," *New York Times,* Oct. 6, 1907
267 Letter from Warren C. Eberly to L. Hollingsworth Wood, L. Hollingsworth Wood papers, Haverford College Special Collections, Call No. 1175, Box 66, Correspondence 1914 – 1915, National Civic League for Immigrants, Dec. 9, 1913
268 "To Help Italian Immigrants: Society Formed to Protect New Arrivals and to Secure Them Employment," *New York Times,* May 12, 1901
269 "How Salovatore Zamanti, An Italian Immigrant, Was Swindled," *The Society for the Protection of Italian Immigrants,* New York, 1904, Harvard University Library, http://pds.lib.harvard.edu/pds/view/4902915?n=1&s=6
270 "Italian Immigrant Work: Recently Formed Society Has Nearly Broken Up Boarding-House "Runner" System," *New York Times,* Feb. 23, 1903
271 Kellor, Frances, "The Problem of the Young Negro Girl from the South," *New York Times,* Mar. 19, 1905, X8
272 "Colored Girls From South," *New – York Tribune,* Mar. 18, 1905, 7
273 Kellor, Frances, "The Problem of the Young Negro Girl from the South," *New York Times,* Mar. 19, 1905, X8
274 Kellor, Frances, "Southern Colored Girls in the North: The Problem of Their Protection," *Charities,* Mar. 18, 1905, 584
275 "What the Urban League Has Meant to the U.S.," *Afro-American,* Se 3, 1938, 12
276 "Colored Girls From South," *New – York Tribune,* Mar. 18, 1905, 7

277 Kellor, Frances, "Assisted Emigration From the South: The Women, *Charities: A Review of Local and General Philanthropy,* Vol. 15, No. 1, (Oct. 7, 1905)
278 Letter from Frances Kellor to L. Hollingsworth Wood, Haverford College Special Collections, Call No. 1175, Box 67, Apr. 7, 1911
279 "Minutes of Meeting: New York – New Jersey Committee of the North American Civic League for Immigrants," L. Hollingsworth Wood papers, Haverford College Special Collections, Call No. 1175, Box 66, National Civic League for Immigrants, Mar. 14, 1912, 5
280 Ososky, Gilbert, *Harlem: The Making of a Ghetto, Negro New York, 1890 – 1930,* (Chicago: Elephant Books, 1963), 56
281 Parris, Guichard and Brooks, Lester, *Blacks in the City: A History of the National Urban League,* (Boston: Little, Brown and Company, 1971), 7
282 Weiss, Nancy, *The National Urban League, 1910 – 1940,* (New York: Oxford University Press, 1974), 18
283 Kellor, Frances, "Associations for Protection of Colored Women," *The Colored American Magazine,* Vol. 9, No. 6, 1905, 699
284 Ososky, Gilbert, *Harlem: The Making of a Ghetto, Negro New York, 1890 – 1930,* (Chicago: Elephant Books, 1963), 58
285 Weiss, Nancy, *The National Urban League, 1910 – 1940,* (New York: Oxford University Press, 1974), 18
286 "To Shield Colored Girls: National Society for Their Protection About to be Formed," *New – York Tribune,* Aug. 11, 1905, 5
287 Weiss, Nancy, *The National Urban League, 1910 – 1940,* (New York: Oxford University Press, 1974), 40
288 "Urban League Marks Fortieth Anniversary," *Atlantic Daily World,* Mar. 29, 1951, 1
289 Parris, Guichard and Brooks, Lester, *Blacks in the City: A History of the National Urban League,* (Boston: Little, Brown and Company, 1971), 7
290 "Breeding Places of Crime," *The Southern Workman,* Vol. 33, No. 7, (Jul. 194), 373
291 Ososky, Gilbert, *Harlem: The Making of a Ghetto, Negro New York, 1890 – 1930,* (Chicago: Elephant Books, 1963), 57
292 Kellor, Frances, "Some Old Needs of the New South," *Charities,* Vol. 10, No. 18, (May 2, 1903), 439 - 440
293 Weiss, Nancy, *The National Urban League, 1910 – 1940,* (New York: Oxford University Press, 1974), 42, 43
294 Ibid., 40
295 Scheiner, Seth, *Negro Mecca: A History of the Negro in New York City, 1865 – 1920,* 153
296 "Kellor, Frances, "Associations for Protection of Colored Women," *The Colored American Magazine,* Vol. 9, No. 6, 1905, 697
297 Parris, Guichard and Brooks, Lester, *Blacks in the City: A History of the National Urban League,* (Boston: Little, Brown and Company, 1971), 8
298 "Late Literary News," *Afro-American,* Aug. 19, 1905, 4
299 National League for the Protection of Colored Women Stationary, L. Hollingsworth Wood papers, Haverford College Special Collections, Call No. 1175, Box 53, National League for the Protection of Colored Women. Also see "Kellor, Frances, "Associations for Protection of Colored Women," *The Colored American Magazine,* Vol. 9, No. 6, 1905, 699

----- CHAPTER SIX ------

[300] "'Rose Pastor' Speaks," *New – York Tribune,* Apr. 8, 1906, 7
[301] Wald, Lillian, *The House on Henry Street,* (New York: Henry Holt and Company, 1915), 293
[302] "Call for a State Industrial Bureau: The Immigration Commissioners Think Such a Department Would Protect Immigrants," *New York Times,* May 24, 1909, 6
[303] "A Good Samaritan for Hapless Alien Hosts is Miss Frances A. Kellor," *New – York Tribune,* May 12, 1912, A4
[304] "League to Protect Aliens From Fraud," *New York Times,* (Jan. 10, 1910), 8
[305] "Special Meeting: New York – New Jersey Committee North American Civic League for Immigrants," L. Hollingsworth Wood papers, Haverford College Special Collections, Call No. 1175, Box 66, National Civic League for Immigrants, Jan. 30, 2
[306] "Report of the Extension Secretary: March 1 – September 30, 1912," L. Hollingsworth Wood papers, Haverford College Special Collections, Call No. 1175, Box 66, National Civic League for Immigrants, Correspondence 1912 (September - December), Se 30, 1912, 2 (author's pagination)
[307] "Call for a State Industrial Bureau," *New York Times,* (May, 24, 1909), 6
[308] "Woman Chief Investigator: Miss Kellor Appointed to Place in Department of Labor, *New – York Tribune,* Oct. 5, 1910, 11
[309] Letter from Frank Trumbull to L. Hollingsworth Wood, L. Hollingsworth Wood papers, Haverford College Special Collections, Call No. 1175, Box 66, Correspondence 1910 - 1911, National Civic League for Immigrants, Dec. 18, 1911
[310] "Bi-Weekly Report, North American Civic League for Immigrants," L. Hollingsworth Wood papers, Haverford College Special Collections, Call No. 1175, Box 66, 1912, National Civic League for Immigrants, July 26, 1912
[311] "Minutes of the meeting of the New York – New Jersey Committee of the North American Civic League for Immigrants," L. Hollingsworth Wood papers, Haverford College Special Collections, Call No. 1175, Box 66, 1912, National Civic League for Immigrants, May 23, 1912
[312] Hartmann, Edward, *The Movement to Americanize the Immigrant,* (New York: Columbia University Press, 1948), 54
[313] Kellor, Frances, Wald, Lillian, "The Construction Camps of the People: The Findings of an Automobile Tour of Investigation of Cap Conditions Along the Line of New York State's New Barge Canal and New York City's New Aqueduct," *The Survey,* Jan. 1, 1910, Vol. 23, 433
[314] Ibid., 449
[315] Ibid.,465
[316] Ibid., 464
[317] "Summary of Labor and Living Conditions in Camps and Small Communities," L. Hollingsworth Wood papers, Haverford College Special Collections, Call No. 1175, Box 66, National Civic League for Immigrants, date unknown, but based upon the 1911 Bureau of Industries and Immigration report, 15
[318] Ibid., 5
[319] "Summary of Labor and Living Conditions in Camps and Small Communities," L. Hollingsworth Wood papers, Haverford College Special Collections, Call No. 1175, Box 66, National Civic League for Immigrants, date unknown, but based upon the 1911 Bureau of Industries and Immigration report, 2, 4
[320] Ibid., 7

[321] "Preying Upon Helpless Immigrants After They Land," *New York Times*, Apr. 14, 1912, SM10
[322] "Summary of Labor and Living Conditions in Camps and Small Communities," L. Hollingsworth Wood papers, Haverford College Special Collections, Call No. 1175, Box 66, National Civic League for Immigrants, date unknown, but based upon the 1911 Bureau of Industries and Immigration report, 13
[323] Ibid.,, 8
[324] Ibid., 14
[325] "Preying Upon Helpless Immigrants After They Land," *New York Times*, Apr. 14, 1912, SM10
[326] "Summary of Labor and Living Conditions in Camps and Small Communities," L. Hollingsworth Wood papers, Haverford College Special Collections, Call No. 1175, Box 66, National Civic League for Immigrants, date unknown, but based upon the 1911 Bureau of Industries and Immigration report, 2
[327] "Favor Sunday Selling: Proposed Amendment to Excise Law Finds Many Supporters," *New – York Tribune*, Mar. 21, 1909, 5
[328] "Evils Abound in State Canal Camps," *New York Times*, Jan. 1, 1910, 9
[329] "Summary of Labor and Living Conditions in Camps and Small Communities," L. Hollingsworth Wood papers, Haverford College Special Collections, Call No. 1175, Box 66, National Civic League for Immigrants, date unknown, but based upon the 1911 Bureau of Industries and Immigration report, 4
[330] "League to Protect Aliens from Fraud: New Organization Plans Also to Assist in Many Other Ways: Will Urge Distribution," *New York Times*, Jan. 10, 1910, 8
[331] "To End Fleecing of Immigrants: Bill in Legislature Aimed at Fake Bankers and Steamship Agents. Hundreds Are Victimized," *New York Times*, 12 May 1907, 7
[332] "League to Protect Aliens from Fraud: New Organization Plans Also to Assist in Many Other Ways: Will Urge Distribution," *New York Times*, 10 January 1910, 8
[333] "Protection for Aliens: Report to Governor," *New – York Tribune*, Apr. 6, 1909, 7
[334] "Annual Report of the New Jersey Committee of the North American Civic League for Immigrants," L. Hollingsworth Wood papers, Haverford College Special Collections, Call No. 1175, Box 66, National Civic League for Immigrants, Correspondence 1912, Oct. 1, 1912, (September - December), 2
[335] "Protect the Immigrants: Miss Morgan, F. A. Vanderlip, and Felix Warburg in New Society," *New York Times*, Apr. 2, 1910, 2
[336] Maxwell, William J. "Frances Kellor in the Progressive Era: A Case Study in the Professionalization of Reform," (Ed.D. diss., Columbia University, 1969), 181
[337] "League to Protect Aliens From Fraud," *New York Times*, (Jan. 10, 1910), 8
[338] Higham, John, *Strangers in the Land, Patterns of American Nativism, 1860 – 1925*, (New Brunswick, Rutgers University Press, 1955) 249
[339] "Annual Report, 1911 – 1912," L. Hollingsworth Wood papers, Haverford College Special Collections, Call No. 1175, Box 66, National Civic League for Immigrants, Correspondence 1912 (September - December), 1
[340] Kellor, Frances, "Assisted Emigration From the South: The Women, *Charities: A Review of Local and General Philanthropy*, Vol. 15, No. 1, (Oct. 7, 1905), 16
[341] "Frances A. Kellor Sponsored New State Policy Toward Immigrant," *Industrial Bulletin*, (Mar. 1952), 16
[342] Maxwell, William J., "Frances Kellor in the Progressive Era: A Case Study in the Professionalization of Reform," (Ed.D. diss., Columbia University, 1969), 194
[343] "Frances A. Kellor Sponsored New State Policy Toward Immigrant," *Industrial Bulletin*, (Mar. 1952), 16

344 Bennett, Helen Christine, *American Women in Civic Work*, (New York: Dodd, Mead and Company, 1915), 172
345 "Current Events," *Friends' Intelligencer,* Vol. 61, No. 28, July 9, 1904, 440
346 "Agent Law Amendments: Miss Kellor's Views," *New – York Tribune,* Feb. 7, 1905, 1
347 "Regulating Employment Agencies," *New York Times,* Mar. 26, 1906, 10
348 "Will Enforce New Law: Employment Agencies to be Directed to Secure License Now Required," *The Washington Post,* June 22, 1906, 14
349 "Frances A. Kellor Sponsored New State Policy Toward Immigrant," *Industrial Bulletin,* (Mar. 1952), 16
350 Agreement attached to letter from Grace Parker to L. Hollingsworth Wood, L. Hollingsworth Wood papers, Haverford College Special Collections, Call No. 1175, Box 66, National Civic League for Immigrants, Feb. 2, 1912
351 Letter from Grace Parker to L. Hollingsworth Wood, L. Hollingsworth Wood papers, Haverford College Special Collections, Call No. 1175, Box 66, Correspondence 1910 - 1911, Dec. 14, 1911
352 "Revised Laws of The Commonwealth of Massachusetts Relating to Public Instructions," Enclosed with letter from Grace Parker to L. Hollingsworth Wood, L. Hollingsworth Wood papers, Haverford College Special Collections, Call No. 1175, Box 66, Correspondence 1910 - 1911, Dec. 14, 1911
353 Letter from Frances Kellor to L. Hollingsworth Wood, L. Hollingsworth Wood papers, Haverford College Special Collections, Call No. 1175, Box 66, Correspondence 1910 - 1911, Dec. 18, 1911
354 "To Protect Immigrants: Civic League Succeeds in Passing Legislative Program," *New – York Tribune,* May 31, 1910, 14
355 Bennett, Helen Christine, *American Women in Civic Work,* (New York: Dodd, Mead and Company, 1915), 170
356 "Thinks Bill Will Pass: Favor Wells Measure," *New – York Tribune,* May 17, 1907, 3
357 "Weekly Report, North American Civic League for Immigrants," L. Hollingsworth Wood papers, Haverford College Special Collections, Call No. 1175, Box 66, Correspondence 1910 - 1911, July 12, 1911, 4
358 Letter from Frances Kellor to L. Hollingsworth Wood, L. Hollingsworth Wood papers, Haverford College Special Collections, Call No. 1175, Box 66, Correspondence 1910 - 1911, Dec. 18, 1911
359 "Work Started During Last Fiscal Year Now in Operation," L. Hollingsworth Wood papers, Haverford College Special Collections, Call No. 1175, Box 66, National Civic League for Immigrants, Correspondence 1912 (September - December), Oct. 14, 1912, 1 (author's pagination)
360 Letter from Frances Kellor to L. Hollingsworth Wood, L. Hollingsworth Wood papers, Haverford College Special Collections, Call No. 1175, Box 66, Correspondence 1910 - 1911, Dec. 18, 1911
361 "Plan in Regard to Education – Extension Work approved by the New York – New Jersey Committee of the North American Civic League for Immigrants, L. Hollingsworth Wood papers, Haverford College Special Collections, Call No. 1175, Box 66, Constitution & re: Corres, 1911, National Civic League for Immigrants," Oct. 14, 1912
362 "North American Civic League for Immigrants, Immigration Council Minutes," New York Jewish Historical Archives, Baron de Hirsch Fund, RG 1-80, Box 24,

Committee for Immigrants in America / North American Civic League for Immigrants, Mar. 2, 1912, 1

363 "New York – New Jersey Committee of the North American Civic League for Immigrants: Constitution and By-Laws," L. Hollingsworth Wood papers, Haverford College Special Collections, Call No. 1175, Box 66, Constitution & re: Corres, 1911, National Civic League for Immigrants, 1911

364 "North American Civic League for Immigrants, Immigration Council Minutes," New York Jewish Historical Archives, Baron de Hirsch Fund, RG 1-80, Box 24, Committee for Immigrants in America / North American Civic League for Immigrants, Mar. 2, 1912, 1

365 Letter from Grace Parker to the Baron de Hirsch Fund, New York Jewish Historical Archives, Baron de Hirsch Fund, RG 1-80, Box 24, Committee for Immigrants in America / North American Civic League for Immigrants, Sept. 14, 1911, 2

366 "North American Civic League for Immigrants, Immigration Council Minutes," New York Jewish Historical Archives, Baron de Hirsch Fund, RG 1-80, Box 24, Committee for Immigrants in America / North American Civic League for Immigrants, Mar. 2, 1912, 3

367 "League to Protect Aliens From Fraud," *New York Times,* (Jan. 10, 1910), 8

368 "Report of Extension Secretary, March 1 – Sept. 30, 1912, L. Hollingsworth Wood papers, Haverford College Special Collections, Call No. 1175, Box 66, Correspondence, 1912 (September to December),

369 "Plan in Regard to Education – Extension Work approved by the New York – New Jersey Committee of the North American Civic League for Immigrants, L. Hollingsworth Wood papers, Haverford College Special Collections, Call No. 1175, Box 66, Constitution & re: Correspondence 1911, National Civic League for Immigrants," Oct. 14, 1912

370 "Report of Education Secretary: October 1, 1911, to October 1, 1912, L. Hollingsworth Wood papers, Haverford College Special Collections, Call No. 1175, Box 66, National Civic League for Immigrants, Correspondence 1912, Oct. 1, 1912, (September - December), 2

371 Letter from Frank Trumbull to L. Hollingsworth Wood, L. Hollingsworth Wood papers, Haverford College Special Collections, Call No. 1175, Box 66, Correspondence 1910 - 1911, National Civic League for Immigrants, Dec. 18, 1911

372 "Report of the Extension Secretary: March 1 – Sept. 30, 1912," L. Hollingsworth Wood papers, Haverford College Special Collections, Call No. 1175, Box 66, National Civic League for Immigrants, Correspondence 1912 (Sept. – Dec.), Sept. 30, 1912, 4

373 "Annual Report of the New Jersey Committee of the North American Civic League for Immigrants," L. Hollingsworth Wood papers, Haverford College Special Collections, Call No. 1175, Box 66, National Civic League for Immigrants, Correspondence 1912, Oct. 1, 1912, (September - December), 3

374 Ibid., 1

375 "Summary of Labor and Living Conditions in Camps and Small Communities," L. Hollingsworth Wood papers, Haverford College Special Collections, Call No. 1175, Box 66, National Civic League for Immigrants, date unknown, but based upon the 1911 Bureau of Industries and Immigration report, 10

376 "Perils of Immigrant Women: Danger Awaits Them on Every Side Says Miss Kellor," *New – York Tribune,* Jan. 30, 1910, C5

377 "League to Protect Aliens From Fraud: New Organization Plans Also to Assist Immigrants in Many Other Ways: Will Urge Distribution," *New York Times*, 10 Jan. 1910, 8
378 "A Good Samaritan for Hapless Alien Hosts is Miss Frances A. Kellor," *New – York Tribune,* May 12, 1912, A4
379 Letter from Mary Dreier to Phyllis Holbrook, November 23, 1960, 4, in possession of Ellen Fitzpatrick.
380 "Frances A. Kellor Sponsored New State Policy Toward Immigrant," *Industrial Bulletin,* (Mar. 1952), 17

------ CHAPTER SEVEN ------

381 Kellor, Frances. Protection of Aliens. As reprinted in the Report of the Immigration Commission. Statements and Recommendations Submitted by Societies and Organizations Interested in the Subject of Immigration. (Washington Government Printing Office, Washington D.C., 1911). 61st Congress 3d Session, Document No. 764. 262-265
382 Kellor, Frances, "Needed – A Domestic Immigration Policy," *North American Review,* Publishing Company, 1911, 1
383 Ibid., 11
384 Ibid., 9
385 Kellor, Frances, "Needed – A Domestic Immigration Policy," *North American Review,* Publishing Company, 1911, 12
386 Ibid., 3
387 Ibid., 7
388 Ibid., 11
389 Ibid., 9
390 Ibid., 8
391 Ibid., 4
392 Ibid., 2
393 Ibid., 4
394 Ibid., 3
395 Kloppenberg, James, *Uncertain Victory: Social Democracy and Progressivism in European and American Thought, 1870 – 1920,* (New York: Oxford University Press, 1986).
396 Mattson, Kevin, *Creating A Democratic Public: The Struggle for Urban Participatory Democracy During the Progressive Era,* (University Park: The Pennsylvania State Press, 1998)
397 Milkis, Sidney M., *Theodore Roosevelt, the Progressive Party, and the Transformation of American Democracy,* (Lawrence: University Press of Kansas, 2009), 161
398 "Colonel's Last Word A Tribute To Women: Because of Them It's Been a Different Campaign Than Any He Ever Saw, He Says," *New York Times*, Nov. 3, 1912, 11
399 Dalton, Kathleen, *Theodore Roosevelt: A Strenuous Life,* (New York: Knopf Publishing Group, 2004), 406
400 "Progressive Platform of 1912," *TeachingHistory.Org,* http://teachingamericanhistory.org/library/index.asp?document=607; Internet accessed, 7 Sept. 2009

401 Kellor to Suffrage Organization, 1912, document 0023, Roll 7 Microfilm, Series One, Jane Addams Papers, Swarthmore College Peace Collection, Swarthmore College
402 "Women as A Factor In the Political Campaign: For the First Time in American History Their Active Support Is Openly Sought by All Parties," *New York Times*, Sept. 1,1912, SM9
403 Maxwell, William J., "Frances Kellor in the Progressive Era: A Case Study in the Professionalization of Reform," (Ed.D. diss., Columbia University, 1969), 189
404 Theodore Roosevelt to Frances Kellor, 4 July 1906, Vol. 82, Reel 65, Series 1, Theodore Roosevelt papers, Collections of the Manuscript Division, Library of Congress.
405 Fitzpatrick, Ellen, *Endless Crusade: Women Social Scientists and Progressive Reform* (Oxford: Oxford University Press, 1990), 140
406 "Colonel's Last Word A Tribute To Women: Because of Them It's Been a Different Campaign Than Any He Ever Saw, He Says," *New York Times*, Nov. 3, 1912, 11
407 Roosevelt, Theodore, *An Autobiography* (New York: The MacMillan Company, 1913), 180
408 Kellor, Frances, "A New Spirit in Party Organization," *North American Review* CXCIX, no. 703 (June 1914): 881
409 Lippmann, Walter *A Preface to Politics,* (New York: Mitchell Kennerley 1913), 2.
410 "The Progressive National Service: What It Is, What It Does, What It Means to You," Box 195, Samuel McCune Lindsay papers, Columbia University Rare Book and Manuscripts Library, 6
411 Jane Addams, *The Second Twenty Years at Hull-House: September 1909 to September 1929: with a Record of a Growing World Consciousness,* (New York: The Macmillan Company, 1930), 40
412 Kellor, Frances, "A New Spirit in Party Organization," *North American Review*, Jun. 1914, Vol. CXCIX, No. 703, 886
413 The Progressive Service of the National Progressive Party, report, Aug. 1913, Exhibit A, Box 195, Columbia University Rare Book and Manuscripts Library, SMLP, 26
414 The Progressive Service of the National Progressive Party, report, Aug. 1913, Exhibit A, Box 195, Columbia University Rare Book and Manuscripts Library, Samuel McCune Lindsay Papers, 27
415 Ward, Lester Frank, "The Psychic Factors of Civilization." (Ginn & Company, Boston. 1893) 330. Herein Ward described 'sociocracy' as government resting, "directly upon the science of sociology, to investigate the facts bearing on every, subject . . . purely and solely for the purpose of ascertaining what is for the best interests of society at large."
416 Ibid., 6.
417 "Minutes of the Meeting of the New York State Progressive Service Board," 1 Aug. 1913, Exhibit A, Box 195, Columbia University Rare Book and Manuscripts Library, Samuel McCune Lindsay Papers, 4
418 Hugh Halbert to Frances Kellor, 27 Jan. 1913, Vol. 81, Reel 382, Series 3A, TRP, Collections of the Manuscript Division, Library of Congress.
419 "Minutes of the Meeting of the New York State Progressive Service Board," 1 Aug. 1913, 7, Exhibit A, Box 195, Series Two, Samuel McCune Lindsay Papers, Columbia University Rare Book and Manuscripts Library, Columbia University
420 Kellor, Frances, "A New Spirit in Party Organization," *North American Review*, Jun. 1914, Vol. CXCIX, No. 703, 887.

[421] "The Progressive Service of the National Progressive Party: Jan. – Aug. 31, 1913," 31 Aug. 1913, Box 195, Samuel McCune Lindsay Papers, Columbia University Rare Book and Manuscripts Library, Columbia University, 23

[422] "The Progressive National Lyceum Service," box 112, Samuel McCune Lindsay Papers, Columbia University Rare Book and Manuscripts Library, Columbia University, 2

[423] "The Progressive Service of the National Progressive Party, Samuel McCune Lindsay Papers, 17

[424] Ibid., 23

[425] "The Progressive National Lyceum Service," Samuel McCune Lindsay Papers, Columbia University Rare Book and Manuscripts Library, Columbia University, 2

[426] "The Progressive Service of the National Progressive Party: Jan. – Aug. 31, 1913," 31 Aug. 1913, 14 – 16, Box 195, Series Two, Samuel McCune Lindsay Papers, Columbia University Rare Book and Manuscripts Library, Columbia University

[427] Maxwell, William J., "Frances Kellor in the Progressive Era: A Case Study in the Professionalization of Reform," (Ed.D. diss., Columbia University, 1969), 205

[428] "The Progressive National Service: What It Is, What It Does, What It Means to You," Box 195, Samuel McCune Lindsay Papers, Columbia University Rare Book and Manuscripts Library, Columbia University, 5

[429] "The Progressive National Service: Samuel McCune Lindsay Papers, 5

[430] "Minutes of the Meeting of the New York State Progressive Service Board," 1, 1 Aug. 1913, Box 195, Series Two, SML Columbia University Rare Book and Manuscripts Library, Columbia University.

[431] Richberg, Donald, *Tents of the Mighty*, (New York: Willett, Clark & Colby, 1930), 48

[432] Frances Kellor to Jane Addams, 3 July 1913, document 7881, Roll 7 Microfilm, Series one, Jane Addams Papers, Swarthmore College Peace Collection, Swarthmore College

[433] "The Progressive Service of the National Progressive Party: Jan. – Aug. 31, 1913," 31 Aug. 1913, Box 195, Samuel McCune Lindsay Papers, Columbia University Rare Book and Manuscripts Library, Columbia University, 4

[434] Davis, Allen, "The Social Workers and the Progressive Party, 1912-1916," *The American Historical Review* 69, no. 3, (Apr. 1964): 687

[435] Ibid., 2.

------ CHAPTER EIGHT ------

[436] "Roosevelt Dines With City Lodgers. "Fine!" His Comment on Supt Whiting's Free Bread, Soup, and Coffee: Woman and Baby Stir Him: Asks Many Questions of the Guests," *New York Times*, Dec. 29, 1914, 1

[437] "Roosevelt Gives Jobless $10,000: Preaches a Sermon, Orders Baskets Passed and Suggests Cures for Unemployment: $14,000 From Audience," *New York Times*, Jan. 27, 1915, 1

[438] "Experts Differ on City's Relief Need," *New – York Tribune*, 17 Dec. 1914, 8.

[439] "How Ellis Island Could Help," *New – York Tribune*, Feb. 1, 1915, 8

[440] Ibid., 8

[441] "Committee for Immigrants in America, Report for Month Ending Mar. 13, 1915," New York Jewish Historical Archives, Baron de Hirsch Fund, RG 1-80, Box

24, Committee for Immigrants in America / North American Civic League for Immigrants, Mar. 31, 1915, 1
[442] "How Ellis Island Could Help," *New – York Tribune,* Feb. 1, 1915, 8
[443] "Social Era Begun at Hotel de Gink," *New York Times,* Feb. 19, 1915, 6
[444] "Bundle Day in New York," *The Independent,* 15 Feb. 1915, 235.
[445] "500,000 Bundles for the Jobless," *New York Times,* 5 Feb. 1915.
[446] Ibid., 235, 235.
[447] "Praise From T.R. Bundle Day Crown," *New-York Tribune,* Feb. 7, 1915, 12
[448] "Bundle Day in New York," *The Independent,* 15 Feb. 1915, 236
[449] Ibid., 236
[450] Frank Trumbull to Society of Jewish Social Workers, 2, Dec. 23, 1915, Box 16, RG 1-88, American Jewish Historical Society, National Association of Jewish Social Workers
[451] Frances Kellor to Theodore Roosevelt, Feb. 3, 1915 Vol. 82, Reel 198, Series 1, TRP, Collections of the Manuscript Division, Library of Congress
[452] "Committee for Immigrants in America, First Semi-Monthly Report," 4, Nov. 30, 1914, "Committee for Immigrants in America / North American Civic League for Immigrants" folder, Box 24, RG 1-80, Baron de Hirsch Fund Papers, New York Jewish Historical Archives
[453] Edward Hartmann, *The Movement to Americanize the Immigrant* (New York: Columbia University Press, 1948), 97
[454] "Committee for Immigrants in America, First Semi-Monthly Report," 4, Nov. 30, 1914, "Committee for Immigrants in America / North American Civic League for Immigrants" folder, Box 24, RG 1-80, Baron de Hirsch Fund Papers, New York Jewish Historical Archives
[455] Kellor, Frances, "National Americanization Day – July 4th," *Immigrants in America Review,* 2, no. 1, (Sept. 1915): 20.
[456] Ibid., 22
[457] Ibid., 5
[458] Kellor, Frances, "National Americanization Day – July 4th," *Immigrants in America Review* 2, no. 2 (Sept. 1915): 20
[459] Hartmann, Edward, *The Movement to Americanize the Immigrant,* (New York: Columbia University Press, 1948), 113
[460] "Jews Make the 4th a Liberty Festival," *New York Times,* July 5 1915, 14
[461] Kellor, Frances, "Americanization Day," *Immigrants in America Review,* 1. no. 2 (June 1915): 75
[462] "Americanization Day in 150 Communities," *The Survey* 34, no. 18 (1915): 390.
[463] "Preliminary Report of National Americanization Day Celebration: Fourth of July, 1915," 8, July 1915, "National Americanization Day, 1915" folder, Box 66, L. Hollingsworth Wood Papers, Haverford College Special Collections, Haverford College.
[464] Ibid., 10
[465] Kellor, Frances, "Americanization Day: The Preliminary Report of the National Committee," *The American Leader* 8, no. 4, 241.
[466] "Preliminary Report of National Americanization Day Celebration: Fourth of July, 1915," 11
[467] Ibid., 24
[468] Ibid., 20
[469] "To Teach Patriotism," *New York Times,* May 30, 1915, 4

470 Kellor, Frances, *Straight America: A Call to Service*. (New York: The MacMillan Company, 1916), 59
471 Kellor, Frances, "Americanization Day," *Immigrants in America Review*, 1, no. 2 (June 1915): 74
472 Roosevelt, Theodore, "Americanization Day," *Metropolitan Magazine*, (July 1915): 1
473 Ibid., 2
474 Ibid., 3
475 Kellor, Frances, "Americanization Day: The Preliminary Report of the National Committee," *AL* 8, no. 4, 240
476 Ibid., 240
477 Kellor, Frances, "National Americanization Day – July 4th," 20
478 "Americanization Day in 150 Communities," *S* 34, no. 18 (1915): 390
479 "Preliminary Report of National Americanization Day Celebration: Fourth of July, 1915," 14, July, 1915, "National Americanization Day, 1915" folder, Box 66, L. Hollingsworth Wood Papers, Haverford College Special Collections, Haverford College
480 Ibid., 15.
481 "Preliminary Report of National Americanization Day Celebration: Fourth of July, 1915," 13, July 1915, "National Americanization Day, 1915" folder, Box 66, L. Hollingsworth Wood Papers, Haverford College Special Collections, Haverford College
482 Olneck, Michael. "Americanization and the Education of Immigrants, 1900-1925: An Analysis of Symbolic Action." *American Journal of Education*, Vol. 97. No. 4. (Aug., 1989): 414
483 "Day-Long Pageant Pictures America United For War: Parade, Sweeping Unceasingly Up Fifth Avenue: Emblematic of the Nation's Spirit," *New York Times*, 5 July 1918, 1
484 Sample Program for Fourth of July Citizenship Celebration. Reprinted in Immigration and Americanization: Selected Readings. Davis, Philip ed. (Boston: Ginn and Company, 1920), 670
485 Letter from Frances Kellor to Theodore Roosevelt, TRP, 21 Jan. 1915, Vol. 82, Reel 197, Series 1, Collections of the Manuscript Division, Library of Congress
486 Fleischman, Henry, "The Educational Alliance." *Immigrants in America Review*, 1, no. 2 (June 1915): 68
487 "Minutes of the Meeting of the Extension Committee of he North American Civic League for Immigrants," 30 May 1913, "National Americanization Day, 1915" folder, Box 66, L. Hollingsworth Wood Papers, Haverford College Special Collections, Haverford College
488 Ibid. 70.
489 Kallen, Horace, "The Meaning of Americanism," *Immigrants in America Review*, 1, no. 4, (Jan. 1916): 12
490 Ibid., 18.
491 Ibid., 15
492 Ibid., 18.
493 Ibid., 19.

-----CHAPTER NINE -----

[494] "American Aid French Artists," *The New York Times,* Aug. 15, 1915, SM21
[495] Ibid., SM21
[496] Benny Bufano, wikipedia, http://en.wikipedia.org/wiki/Benny_Bufano
[497] "Americanization of Immigrants," *The Outlook,* Dec. 15, 1915, 881 - 882
[498] Carlson, Robert. *The Americanization Syndrome: A Quest for Conformity.* (St. Martin's Press: New York, 1987), 84
[499] Review of *Out of Work: A Study of Unemployment,* Alvin Johnson, *The New Republic* 2, no. 24, part 2, 17 (April 1915): 12
[500] Kellor, Frances, *Out of Work: A Study of Unemployment,* (New York: G.P. Putnam's and Sons / The Knickerbocker Press, 1915), 478
[501] Ibid., 373
[502] Ibid., 485
[503] Ibid., 55
[504] Ibid., 57
[505] Ibid., 54
[506] Ibid., 141
[507] Ibid., 135
[508] Ibid., 136
[509] Ibid., 111
[510] Ibid., 147
[511] Ibid., 147
[512] Ibid., 147
[513] Review of Out of Work, *The New Republic,* Apr. 17, 1915, Part Two, No. 24, 12
[514] Review of *Out of Work: A Study of Unemployment,* Ordway Tead, *The American Journal of Sociology* 21, no. 2 (Sept. 1915): 267
[515] Kellor, Frances, *Out of Work: A Study of Unemployment,* (New York: G.P. Putnam's and Sons, 1915), 488
[516] Review of Out of Work, *The New Republic,* Apr. 17, 1915, Part Two, No. 24, 12
[517] Research Department of the Committee for Immigrants, "Citizenship Syllabus: Many People's, One Nation, America," (Albany: New York State Department of Education, 1916), 1
[518] Ibid., 4
[519] Ibid., 2.
[520] Ibid., 4
[521] "The Progressive Service of the National Progressive Party," 6, Box 195, Series 2, Samuel McCune Lindsay Papers, Columbia University Rare Book and Manuscripts Library, Columbia University
[522] Research Department of the Committee for Immigrants, "Citizenship Syllabus: Many People's, One Nation, America," 4
[523] Ibid., 5
[524] Ibid., 7
[525] John Dewey, *Moral Principles in Education,* (Carbondale and Edwardsville: Southern Illinois University Press, 1909), 10
[526] Ibid., 50
[527] Ibid., 27

------ CHAPTER TEN ------

528 Research Department of the Committee for Immigrants, "Citizenship Syllabus: Many People's, One Nation, America," 6
529 "'America First,' Urges Women's Defense Appeal," *New – York Tribune,* Nov. 16, 1915, 3
530 Ibid., 3
531 Kellor, Frances, "The Immigrant and Preparedness," *Immigrants in America Review,* Vol. 1, No. 4, Jan. 1916, 20
532 Kloppenberg, James, *Uncertain Victory: Social Democracy and Progressivism in European and American Thought, 1870 – 1920,* (New York: Oxford University Press, 1986), 388
533 Rossinow, Doug, *Visions of Progress The Left-Liberal Tradition in America,* (Philadelphia: University of Pennsylvania Press, 2008), 37
534 "'America First,' Urges Women's Defense Appeal," *New – York Tribune,* Nov. 16, 1915, 3
535 Letter from Frances Kellor to Theodore Roosevelt, Roosevelt papers, Collections of the Manuscript Division, Library of Congress, Jan. 6, 1913, Reel 382, Vol. 80, Series 3A
536 Letter from Frances Kellor to Theodore Roosevelt, Roosevelt papers, Collections of the Manuscript Division, Library of Congress, Jan. 6, 1913, Reel 382, Vol. 80, Series 3A
537 Hennen, John, *The Americanization of West Virginia: Creating a Modern Industrial State, 1916 – 1925,* (Lexington: The University Press of Kentucky, 1996), 42 – 43
538 Capozzola, Christopher, *Uncle Sam Wants You: World War One and the Making of the Modern American Citizen,* (New York: Oxford English Press, 2008)
539 Higham, John, *Strangers in the Land: Patterns of American Nativism, 1860 – 1925,* (New Brunswick: Rutgers University Press, 1955), *248-249*
540 Ibid., 249
541 Frances Kellor, "The Immigrant and Preparedness," *Immigrants in America Review,* Vol. 1, No. 4, Jan. 1916, 20
542 Kellor, Frances, *Straight America: A Call to National Service,* (New York: The MacMillan Company, 1916), 22 – 23
543 Ibid., 24
544 Ibid., 28
545 Ibid., 66
546 Ibid., 49
547 Ibid., 75
548 Ibid., 76
549 Ibid., 21 - 22
550 Ibid., 22
551 Ibid., 88
552 Quoted in Livingston, James, "War and the Intellectuals: Bourne, Dewey, and the Fate of Pragmatism, *The Journal of the Gilded Age and Progressive Era* 2, no. 4 (Oct. 2003): 448
553 Kellor, Frances, *Straight America: A Call to National Service,* (New York: The MacMillan Company, 1916), 31

554 Ibid., 175
555 Ibid., 97
556 Ibid., 113-114
557 Ibid., 51
558 Ibid., 51 - 52
559 Ibid., 52 - 53
560 Ibid., 53
561 Ibid., 139 – 140
562 Ibid., 140
563 Ibid., 141
564 Ibid., 142
565 Ibid., 143
566 Ibid., 143
567 Ibid., 141
568 Ibid., 175
569 Ibid., 176
570 Ibid., 177
571 Hansen, Olaf, "Randolph Bourne: The Radical Will: Selected Writings, 1911 – 1918," 48
572 James, William, "The Moral Equivalent of War," *Emory University*, http://des.emory.edu/mfp/moral.html, Accessed 6 June 2009
573 Dewey, John, "Universal Service as Education," *New Republic 7*, (22 April 1916): 471
574 Ibid., 471
575 Bourne, Randolph, "A Moral Equivalent for Universal Military Service," *National Review*, 7, no. 87 (1 July 1916): 218
576 Ibid., 218.
577 Bourne, Randolph, "Americanism," *National Review*, 3, no. 99 (23 Se1916): 197
578 Ibid., 197
579 Ibid., 197
580 Kellor, Frances, "A Conservation Policy for Industry," *Annals of the American Academy of Political and Social Science* 65, (May 1916): 244
581 Kellor, Frances, *Straight America: A Call to National Service*, (New York: The MacMillan Company, 1916), 44
582 Ibid., 177-178
583 Ibid., 177
584 Ibid., 178.

------ CHAPTER ELEVEN ------

585 As quoted in the advertisement entitled, "Our National Problems Frances A. Kellor's New Book: Straight America, Straight America," *The Independent*, Aug. 14, 1916, 232
586 "Son of Hughes Carries Luck on Visit to Campaign Shop," *New - York Times*, Sept. 19, 1916, 4
587 "Women to Run Train for Hughes," *Chicago Daily Tribune*, Sept. 8, 1916, 1
588 "Hughes Women Sing as they Reach City," *New York Times*, Nov. 4, 1916, 6
589 Ernestine Evans, "Hughes Women Campaigners Home After 11,075 Mile Trip," *New – York Tribune*, Nov. 4, 1916, 6
590 "Women's Special Great Success," *Los Angeles Times*, Oct. 12, 1916, 15

591 "Tells Why Hughes Asks Women's Aid," *New York Times,* Aug. 7, 1916, 9
592 "Women's Campaign Train Speakers on Job at 6 A. M.," *New – York Tribune*, 4 Oct. 1916, 6
593 "St. Paul Men Scarce at Women's Meeting," *New York Times,* Oct. 8, 1915, 4
594 "Just What Happened on the Ill – Fated 'Golden Special,'" *The Washington Post,* Dec. 24, 1916, MT8
595 "Women to Run Train for Hughes," Chicago Daily Tribune, Sep. 8, 1916, 1
596 "Hughes Women Sing as they Reach City," *New York Times,* Nov. 4, 1916, 6
597 "Hughes Irons Out Opposition to Ickes," *New York Times,* July 20, 1916, 5
598 "Tells Why Hughes Asks Women's Aid," *New York Times,* Aug. 7, 1916, 9
599 Letter from Katherine Edson to Mrs. Lyndsay Van Rensslaer, Dec. 4, 1914, folder 4, Box 1, KEP, University of California at Los Angeles, Department of Special Collections, University of Los Angeles at California
600 "Hughes Sees 20 Women Enter Nation-wide Campaign for Him," *New – York Tribune,* July 8, 1916, 4
601 "City Acclaims Hughes," *New – York Tribune,* Nov. 5, 1916, 1
602 Ibid., 5.
603 Evans, Ernestine, "Hughes Women Campaigners Home After 11.075 Mile Trip," *New – York Tribune,* Nov. 4, 1916, 6
604 "Campaign Weekly to Boost Hughes," *New – York Tribune,* Aug. 6, 1916, 8
605 "Mr. Hughes on Tour," *NR,* Aug. 19, 1916
606 "Hughes Indorsement Gives Suffrage Forces New Vigor," *New – York Tribune,* Aug. 3, 1916, 5
607 Letter from Edwin Rowell to Katherine Edson, 2, July 6, 1916, folder, 3 Box 5, KEP, University of California at Los Angeles, Department of Special Collections.
608 "Hughes Gets Plans of his Women Aids," *New York Times,* July 8, 1916, 5
609 "St. Paul Men Scarce at Women's Meeting," *New York Times,* Oct. 8, 1915, 4
610 "Hughes Women Reach Chicago This Morning," *CDT,* Oct. 5, 1916, 5
611 Ernestine Evans, "Baltimore Hears Hughes Women," *New – York Tribune*, 3 Nov. 1916, 4
612 "Just What Happened on the Ill – Fated 'Golden Special,'" *The Washington Post*, 24 Dec. 1916, MT8
613 Kellor, "Women in the Campaign," *Yale Review*, Jan. 1917, 11
614 Kellor, Frances, "Cloisters in American Politics: Rough Draft," folder 12, Box, 4, Ethel Eyre Valentine Dreier Papers, Sophia Smith Collection, Smith College
615 Evans,"Hughes Women Campaigners Home After 11,075 Mile Trip," 6
616 Kellor, Frances, "Women in the Campaign," *Yale Review*, Jan. 1917, 13 – 14
617 "Tells Why Hughes Asks Women's Aid," *New York Times,* Aug. 7, 1916, 9
618 Ibid., 5.
619 "Hughes Indorsement Gives Suffrage Forces New Vigor," *New – York Tribune*, Aug. 3, 1916, 5.
620 Evans, Ernestine, "Women's Train Wins Uncle Joe," *New-York Tribune,* Oct. 31, 1916, 4
621 "Mrs. E. N. Monroe Introduces Speakers," *Elizabeth Freeman Website,* unidentified newspaper clipping, http://www.elisabethfreeman.org/PDF/hughes/francesKellor_big.pdf; Internet accessed, May 16, 2009
622 Ernestine Evans, "Women's Train Wins Uncle Joe," *New-York Tribune*, 31 Oct. 1916, 4.

623 Milkis, Sidney M., *Theodore Roosevelt, the Progressive Party, and the Transformation of American Democracy,* (Lawrence: University Press of Kansas, 2009), 172

624 Butcher, Fanny, "Hughes Women Invade Dakota," *Chicago Daily Tribune,* Oct. 9, 1916, 10

625 "Hughes Women Want No Hyphen," *New – York Tribune,* July 13, 1916, 6

626 "Tells Why Hughes Asks Women's Aid," *New York Times,* Aug. 7, 1916, 9

627 Evans, Ernestine, "Hughes Women on Bryan's Trail," *New – York Tribune,* Oct. 30, 1916, 5

628 Evans, Ernestine, "Friends and Foes in Chicago Keep Hughes Women on Jump," *New – York Tribune,* Oct. 6, 1916, 5

629 Evans, Ernestine, "Friends and Foes in Chicago Keep Hughes Women on Jump," *New – York Tribune,* Oct. 6, 1916, 5

630 "Hughes Women's Special Makes Four Oregon Towns," *CDT,* Oct. 16,1916, 9

631 Kellor, Frances, "Women in the Campaign," Yale Review, Jan. 1917, 11

632 "Just What Happened on the Ill – Fated 'Golden Special,'" *The Washington Post,* Dec. 24, 1916, MT8

633 Evans, Ernestine, "Friends and Foes in Chicago Keep Hughes Women on Jump," *New – York Tribune,* Oct. 6, 1916, 5

634 "Women on Western Campaign Win Mrs. Hughes's Gratitude," *New –York Tribune,* Oct. 20, 1916, 4

635 Ernestine Evans, "Miss Kellor Wins Skirmish Against Hecklers in Toledo," *New – York Tribune,* Oct. 5, 1916, 1

636 "Toledans Heckle Women Spellbinder," *New York Times,* Oct. 5, 1916, 3

637 Ernestine Evans, "Miss Kellor Wins Skirmish Against Hecklers in Toledo," *New – York Tribune,* Oct. 5, 1916, 1

638 "Toledans Heckle Women Spellbinder," *New York Times,* Oct. 5, 1916, 3

639 Ibid., 3.

640 "Hughes Women Reach Chicago This Morning," *Chicago Daily Tribune,* Oct. 5, 1916, 5

641 Evans, Ernestine, "Miss Kellor Wins Skirmish Against Hecklers in Toledo," 1

642 "Toledans Heckle Women Spellbinder," *New York Times,* Oct. 5, 1916, 3

643 "Hughes Women Reach Chicago This Morning," *Chicago Daily Tribune,* Oct. 5, 1916, 5

644 "N.Y. Women New Factor in Campaign," *New – York Tribune,* July 21, 1916, 1

645 "National Hughes Alliance: Work Being Done by Women's Committee," July 6, 1916, folder 3, Box 5, KEP, University of California at Los Angeles, Department of Special Collections, University of California at Los Angeles

646 "Chicago Women Plan Big Day for Hughes Speakers," *CDT,* Oct. 4, 1916, 17.

647 "Women to Run Train for Hughes," *Chicago Daily Tribune,* Sept. 8, 1916, 1

648 Evans, Ernestine, "Women of Hughes Train Win 2,000 Sisters in St. Paul Rally," *New – York Tribune,* Oct. 8, 1916, 6

649 "Women on Western Campaign Win Mrs. Hughes's Gratitude," *New –York Tribune,* Oct. 20, 1916, 4

650 Evans, Ernestine, "Hughes Women Capture Joliet," *New – York Tribune,* Nov. 1, 1916, 6

651 Evans, Ernestine, "Hughes Women On Bryan's Trail," *New – York Tribune,* Oct. 30, 1916, 5

652 Ernestine Evans, "Baltimore Hears Hughes Women," New – York Tribune, 3 Nov. 1916, 4

653 Butcher, Fanny, "Hughes Women Invade Dakota," *Chicago Daily Tribune,* Oct. 9, 1916, 10

654 "Chicago Women Plan Big Day for Hughes Speakers," *Chicago Daily Tribune,* Oct. 4, 1916, 17.

655 Butcher, Fanny, "You and Hughes, Iowa's Welcome To Women Train," *Chicago Daily Tribune,* Oct. 7, 1916, 15

656 "T.R. And 12,000 Welcome Women," *New – York Tribune,* Nov. 4, 1916, 2.

657 "Tells Why Hughes Asks Women's Aid," *New York Times,* Aug. 7, 1916, 9

658 Letter from Frances Kellor to Katherine Edson, 1, Dec. 22, 1916, folder 3, Box 5, Katherine Edson Papers, University of California at Los Angeles, Department of Special Collections, University of California at Los Angeles

659 Letter from Katherine Edson to Frances Kellor, 1, Dec. 12, 1916, folder 4, Box 1, Katherine Edson Papers, University of California at Los Angeles, Department of Special Collections, University of California at Los Angeles.

660 Letter from Edwon Rowell to Katherine Edson, 2, July 6, 1916, folder 3, Box 5, Katherine Edson Papers, University of California at Los Angeles, Department of Special Collections, University of California at Los Angeles.

661 "Just What Happened on the Ill – Fated 'Golden Special,'" *The Washington Post,* Dec. 24, 1916, MT8

----- CHAPTER TWELVE ------

662 "State War Census to List All from 16 to 64 Years of Age," *New-York Tribune,* April 12, 1917, 3

663 "Calls Zone System Wrong," *New York Times,* Nov. 11, 1917, 10

664 "Central Federal Agency Advocated for Aliens," *New York Times*, July 15, 1917, 68

665 "Calls Zone System Wrong," *New York Times,* Nov. 11, 1917, 10

666 "Central Federal Agency Advocated for Aliens," *New York Times*, July 15, 1917, 68

667 Maxwell, William J., "Frances Kellor in the Progressive Era: A Case Study in the Professionalization of Reform," (Ed.D. diss., Columbia University, 1969), 246

668 "The Friendly Alien a Big War Problem: Miss Kellor Sees More Danger in Industrial Unrest that in German Activities: Would Raise His Standards: No Chance for Enemy Propaganda Where Labor is Contented with Fair Treatment," *New York Times*, July 29, 1917, 6

669 Ibid., 6

670 "Alien Board as Preparedness Measure Urged," *Christian Science Monitor*, Mar. 8, 1917, 6

671 Hill, Howard, "The Americanization Movement," *The American Journal of Sociology* 24, no. 6, (May 1919): 627

672 Letter from Frances Kellor to Philander Claxton, 10 April 1918, "Americanization" folder, Box 7, Records of the Office of Education, Records of the Office of the Commissioner, Record Group 12, National Archives.

673 Ibid., Kellor to Claxton, 27 Apr. 1918

674 Ibid., Claxton to Kellor, 20 Mar. 1918

[675] Documents concerning Frances Kellor organized by Claxton, Indexed item 'A,' 16 April 1918, "Americanization" folder, Box 7, Records of the Office of Education, RG 12, NA.
[676] Documents concerning Frances Kellor organized by Claxton, 16 April 1918, Indexed item 'B,' Folder Americanization, Box 7, Records of the Office of Education, RG 12, NA.
[677] Documents concerning Frances Kellor organized by Philander Claxton, Indexed item 'C,' 16 April 1918, "Americanization" folder, Box 7, Records of the Office of Education, Record Group 12, NA.
[678] Ibid, indexed item 'B.'
[679] *Americanization Bulletin* 2, no. 3 (Nov. 1919): 1, "Americanization" folder, Box 44, Records of the Office of the Commissioner, RG 12, NA.
[680] Ibid., 2.
[681] "Elementary Civics for Immigrants," 1918, "Americanization" folder, Box 44, Records of the Office of the Commissioner, RG 12, NA
[682] Letter from Frank Trumbull to Claxton, 3, 1 Apr. 1919, "Americanization" folder, Box 7, Entry 6, File 106, Historical File, 1870 – 1950, Records of the Office of Education, Records of the Office of the Commissioner, RG 12, NA
[683] Department of the Interior, Bureau of Education and Council of National Defense, Schedule 9, Box 12, Records of the Office of Education, RG 12, NA, 2
[684] Enclosed with Frances Kellor to Claxton, June 24, 1918, "Americanization" folder, Box 7, Records of the Commissioner of Education, RG 12, NA
[685] Letter from Frances Ramsey to Claxton, 12 June 1918, "Americanization" folder, Box 7, Records of the Commissioner of Education, RG 12, NA.
[686] Letter from Claxton to Frances Kellor, 13 June 1918, "Americanization" folder, Box 7, Records of the Commissioner of Education, RG 12, NA.
[687] Letter from Frances Rumsey to Claxton, 3 July 1918, "Americanization" folder, Box 7, Records of the Commissioner of Education, RG 12, NA.
[688] Kellor, Frances, *Neighborhood Americanization: A Discussion of the Alien in a New Country and of the Native in His Home Country*, An address to the Colony Club in New York City, Feb. 8, 1918; in Wisconsin State Historical Society Pamphlet Collection #54-997, 8
[689] Ibid., 8
[690] Ibid., 18
[691] "Rich and Poor in Astor Home," *New – York Tribune,* Jan. 25, 1917, 1.
[692] Ibid., 17.
[693] Kellor, Frances, "Americanization of Women: A Discussion of an Emergency Created by Granting the Vote to Women in New York State," Address delivered before the New York State Woman's Suffrage Party in New York City, Jan. 17, 1918, 7
[694] Ibid., 7.
[695] Kellor, Frances, *Neighborhood Americanization: A Discussion of the Alien in a New Country and of the Native in His Home Country*, An address to the Colony Club in New York City, Feb. 8, 1918; in Wisconsin State Historical Society Pamphlet Collection #54-997, 23
[696] Ibid., 17
[697] Ibid., 12
[698] Ibid., 13
[699] Ibid., 8
[700] Ibid., 11

[701] Kellor, Frances, "Americanization of Women: A Discussion of an Emergency Created by Granting the Vote to Women in New York State," Address delivered before the New York State Woman's Suffrage Party in New York City, Jan. 17, 1918, 8
[702] Ibid., 8
[703] Kellor, Frances, *Neighborhood Americanization: A Discussion of the Alien in a New Country and of the Native in His Home Country*, An address to the Colony Club in New York City, Feb. 8, 1918; in Wisconsin State Historical Society Pamphlet Collection #54-997, 18
[704] Ibid., 17.
[705] Ibid., 22.
[706] Kellor, Frances, "Americanization of Women: A Discussion of an Emergency Created by Granting the Vote to Women in New York State," Address delivered before the New York State Woman's Suffrage Party in New York City, Jan. 17, 1918, 5
[707] Ibid., 10.
[708] Kellor, Frances, *Neighborhood Americanization: A Discussion of the Alien in a New Country and of the Native in His Home Country*, An address to the Colony Club in New York City, Feb. 8, 1918; in Wisconsin State Historical Society Pamphlet Collection #54-997, 24
[709] "Americanization of Immigrants, *Christian Science Monitor,* Dec. 14, 1917, 9
[710] Hartmann, Edward, *The Movement to Americanize the Immigrant,* (New York: Columbia University Press, 1948), 132
[711] Lape, Esther, 'The 'English First' Movement in Detroit," *Immigrants in America Review* 1, no. 3, (Sept. 1915): 46
[712] Ibid., 47
[713] Ibid., 50
[714] "Americanizing a City." A pamphlet by the National Americanization Committee and the Committee for Immigrants in America. New York, (15 Dec. 1915): 11, "Americanization" folder, Box 7, Records of the Office of Education, Records of the Office of the Commissioner, Record Group 12, National Archives
[715] Ibid., 11
[716] "Chambers of Commerce and Alien Workmen," *Nation's Business,* Dec. 1915, Vol. 3, No. 12, 20
[717] Hartmann, Edward, *The Movement to Americanize the Immigrant,* (New York: Columbia University Press, 1948), 130
[718] Brophy, Anne, "'The committee … has stood out against coercion': the reinvention of Detroit Americanization, 1915," *Michigan Historical Review* 29, no. 2 (22 Sept. 2003): 2
[719] Carlson, Robert, "Americanization as an Early Tweintieth-Century Adult Education Movement," *History of Education Quarterly* 10, no. 4 (Winter, 1970): 455.
[720] Barrett, James, "Americanization from the Bottom Up: Immigration and the Remaking of the Working Class in the Unites States, 1880 -1930, *The Journal of American History* 79, no 3 (Dec. 1992): 1009
[721] Ibid., 1013
[722] "Chamber Welcomes Woman," *Los Angeles Times,* Oct. 30, 1913, II5.
[723] "Chambers of Commerce and Alien Workmen," *Nation's Business,* Dec. 1915, Vol. 3, No. 12, 18

[724] Higham, John, *Strangers in the Land, Patterns of American Nativism, 1860 – 1925,* (New Brunswick, Rutgers University Press, 1955), 244
[725] Letter from Frank Trumbull to Claxton, 5 Dec. 1918, Folder Americanization, Box 7, Records of the Office of Education, Record Group 12, NA, 2
[726] "Chambers of Commerce and Alien Workmen," *NB* 3, no. 12 (Dec. 1915): 18
[727] Ibid., 19
[728] "Engineers and the New Nationalism," *Engineering Record* 74, no. 1 (1916): 12
[729] "Engineers and the New Nationalism," *Engineering Record* 74, no. 1 (1916): 12
[730] Ibid., 12.
[731] Ibid., 12.
[732] "Better Homes for the Immigrant Workman," *NYT,* 28 May 1916, SM12
[733] "Engineers and the New Nationalism," *Engineering Record* 74, no. 1 (1916): 12
[734] Ibid., 13.
[735] Kellor, Frances, "Machinery and Men," *The Independent,* July 21, 1917, 106
[736] Kellor, Frances, "Engineering Methods Must Replace Paternalism in the Handling of Labor," *Engineering News- Record,* 12 Apr. 1917, 6
[737] Ibid., 7
[738] Ibid., 6
[739] Frances, Kellor, "Industrial Americanization: A Discussion of the Conditions of the Labor Market Now and After the War," address delivered at a conference of that national association of Cotton Manufacturers in Boston, Copley – Plaza Hotel, 18 Jan. 1919, 16
[740] Ibid., 10
[741] Kellor, Frances, "A Leaf From Lenin's Policy on Manpower," *Engineering News – Record,* March 11, 1920, 517
[742] Ibid., 519
[743] Haber, Samuel, *Efficiency and Uplift,* (Chicago: University of Chicago Press, 1964), 67
[744] Montgomery, David, *Fall of the House of Labor: The Workplace, the state, and American labor activism, 1865 – 1925,* (Cambridge: Cambridge University Press, 1987), 254
[745] Ibid., 247.
[746] Haber, Samuel, *Efficiency and Uplift,* (Chicago: University of Chicago Press, 1964), 19
[747] Kellor, Frances, "Industrial Americanization and National Defense," *North American Review,* No. 205. (Jan. / Jun., 1917), 727
[748] Kellor, Frances, "Engineering Methods Must Replace Paternalism in the Handling of Labor," *Engineering News- Record,* 12 Apr. 1917, 6
[749] Kellor, Frances, "Industrial Americanization and National Defense," *North American Review,* No. 205. (Jan. / Jun., 1917), 732
[750] Kellor, Frances, "Welfare or Manpower Engineering?," *National Efficiency Quarterly* 1, no. 3, (Nov. 1918): 127
[751] Ibid., 129.
[752] Letter from Frank Trumbull to Claxton, Apr. 1, 1919, "Americanization" folder, Box 7, Records of the Commissioner of Education, Record Group 12, NA. 1
[753] Hartmann, Edward, *The Movement to Americanize the Immigrant,* (New York: Columbia University Press, 1948), 101
[754] "The Friendly Alien a Big War Problem: Miss Kellor Sees More Danger in Industrial Unrest that in German Activities: Would Raise His Standards: No Chance

for Enemy Propaganda Where Labor is Contented with Fair Treatment," *New York Times*, July 29, 1917, 6

755 Letter from Frank Trumbull to Claxton, Apr. 1, 1919, "Americanization" folder, Box 7, Records of the Commissioner of Education, RG 12, NA. 1

756 Letter from Samuel Gompers to Claxton, May 8, 1918, "Americanization" folder, Box 7, Records of the Commissioner of Education, RG 12, NA

757 "Urges Americanization Bill," *New York Times*, Jan. 17, 1920, 10

758 Letter from Frank Trumbull to Claxton, 1 April 1919, "Americanization" folder, Box 7, Records of the Commissioner of Education, Record Group 12, National Archive. 1

----- CHAPTER THIRTEEN ------

759 "Council is Formed Here to Aid Lane's Melting Pot Plans," *New – York Tribune*, 17 Jan. 1919, 2

760 Ibid., 2

761 Inter-Racial Council, Brief in Opposition to the Exclusion of Foreign Language Newspapers from Second Class Mailing Privileges, 1921 [in regard to Senate Bill 3718, entitled "A Bill to Exclude Certain Foreign Publications from 2nd Class Mailing Privileges", 66:3rd Sess. 2., 110

762 House Committee on Immigration and Naturalization, *Proposed restriction of Immigration*, 66th Cong., 2nd sess., April 22, 1920, 85

763 "To Foster Americanism," *NYT*, Mar. 28, 1919, 18

764 Third Astor Uplift Dinner: Prominent Persons Hear More of Americanization Campaign, *New York Times*, Feb. 14, 1917, 9

765 House Committee on Immigration and Naturalization, *Proposed restriction of Immigration*, 66th Cong., 2nd sess., Apr. 22, 1920, 127

766 Kellar, Alice, "Coldwater, Michigan," *Coldwater Republican*, July 7, 1893, 3

767 "Gather Data Here for Senate Inquiry," *New York Times*, Nov. 29, 1918, 7

768 "Hammerling's Deals Bared by Becker," *New York Tribune*, Nov. 29, 1918, 12

769 Ibid., 7.

770 Ibid., 12

771 "Foreign – Language Papers Organize," *Christian Science Monitor*, Mar. 29, 1919, 6

772 "The American Press in Foreign Languages," *New York Times*, June 18, 1919, 13

773 Ibid., 6.

774 "Foreign Press Here Attacks 'Red Menace," *New- York Tribune*, Mar. 28, 1919, 10

775 "Foreign – Language Papers Organize," *Christian Science Monitor*, Mar. 29, 1919, 6

776 Kellor, Frances, "Advertising to Foreign Born Buyers in America," *Advertising and Selling*, (June 14, 1919): 19

777 "Central Federal Agency Advocated For Aliens," *New York Times*, July 15, 1917. 68.

778 Kellor, Frances, "The Place and Purpose of American Association of Foreign Language Newspapers," *Advertising and Selling*, (July 5, 1919): 5

779 "Against Alien Press Bill," *New York Times*, Mar. 4, 1920, 10

780 Ibid., 10

[781] Hartmann, Edward, *The Movement to Americanize the Immigrant,* (New York: Columbia University Press, 1948), 225

[782] "Summary of Attacks Against the 'Russkoye Slovo'," 1, folder 4, Box 2, Felix M. Warburg Collection, American Jewish Archives

[783] House Committee on Immigration and Naturalization, *Proposed restriction of Immigration,* 66th Cong., 2nd sess., Apr. 22, 1920, 114

[784] Ibid., 114

[785] Ibid., 114

[786] Ibid., 115

[787] "Meet to Formulate Immigration Policy," *New York Times,* Apr. 8, 1920, 19

[788] "Immigration a Necessity," *The Washington Post,* Apr. 11, 1920, 26

[789] "Cut in Immigration Hits Labor Market," Jan. 1, 1920, *New York Times,* 27

[790] "Need of Immigration," Feb. 10, 1920, *New – York Tribune,* 10

[791] "Our Immigration Dilemma" *New York Times,"* May 2,1920, XX4

[792] Park, Robert, *The Immigrant Press and Its Control* (New York: Harper and Brothers Publishers, 1922), 452

[793] "Offset to Propaganda," *Christian Science Monitor,* Jan. 19, 1920, 1

[794] "Racial Council to Explain to Aliens Deportation Causes," *New – York Tribune,* Jan. 18, 1920, C5

[795] Ibid., C5.

[796] "Alien Labor Flees U.S. Terrorized by Wholesale Raids," *New – York Tribune,* Jan. 18, 1920, 12

[797] "Red Raids Making Alien Born Panicky," *The Los Angeles Times,* Jan. 18, 1920, IV13

[798] Kellor, Frances, "The Place and Purpose of American Association of Foreign Language Newspapers," *Advertising and Selling,* (July 5, 1919): 6

[799] Ibid., 1

[800] Ibid., 6

[801] Kellor, Frances, "Advertising to Foreign Born Buyers in America," *Advertising and Selling,* (June 14, 1919): 19

[802] "The Foreign Market in the United States," *Chicago Daily Tribune,* Jul. 11, 1919, 32

[803] House Committee on Immigration and Naturalization, *Proposed restriction of Immigration,* 66th Cong., 2nd sess., Apr. 22, 1920, 104

[804] Kellor, Frances, "Advertising to Foreign Born Buyers in America," *Advertising and Selling,* (June 14, 1919): 20

[805] "The Foreign Market in the United States," *Chicago Daily Tribune,* Jul. 11, 1919, 32

[806] Ibid., 32

[807] Kellor, Frances, "Advertising to Foreign Born Buyers in America," *Advertising and Selling,* (June 14, 1919): 20

[808] House Committee on Immigration and Naturalization, *Proposed restriction of Immigration,* 66th Cong., 2nd sess., Apr. 22, 1920, 105

[809] Kellor, Frances, "The Place and Purpose of American Association of Foreign Language Newspapers," *Advertising and Selling,* (July 5, 1919): 6

[810] Ibid., 6

[811] Letter from Coleman DuPont to Felix Warburg, Jan. 4, 1919, folder 4, Box 2, Felix M. Warburg Collection, American Jewish Archives

[812] House Committee on Immigration and Naturalization, *Proposed restriction of Immigration,* 66th Cong., 2nd sess., Apr. 22, 1920, 123

813 Hennen, John, *The Americanization of West Virginia: Creating a Modern Industrial State, 1916 – 1925,* (Lexington: University Press of Kentucky, 1996)
814 Letter on Inter-Racial Council stationary, 4, Nov. 19, 1919, folder Box 2, 4, Nov. 19, 1919, Felix M. Warburg Collection, American Jewish Archives

------ CHAPTER FOURTEEN ------

815 Kellor, Frances, *Immigration and the Future,* (New York: George H. Doran Company, 1920)
816 Kellor, Frances, *The Federal Administration and the Alien: A Supplement to Immigration and the Future,* (New York: George H. Doran Company, 1921)
817 Abbott, Edith, review of "Immigration and the Future, The Federal Administration and the Alien," *The Journal of Political Economy* 30, no. 2 (April 1922): 312
818 "Miss Kellor Condemns Our Haphazard Immigration Policy," *New – York Tribune,* Jan. 2, 1921, E8
819 "Miss Kellor Condemns Our Haphazard Immigration Policy," *New – York Tribune,* Jan. 2, 1921, E8
820 Kellor, Frances, *Immigration and the Future,* (New York: George H. Doran Company, 1920), 118
821 Ibid., 147
822 Kellor, Frances, "What is Americanization?," *Yale Review,* Vol. 3, 1919, 285
823 Ibid., 286
824 Ibid., 295
825 Ibid., 287
826 Kellor, Frances, "Immigration in Reconstruction," *North American Review* 209, no. 759 (Feb., 1919): 200
827 Kellor, Frances, "How Shall the Alien Be Made Into a Good American?," *New – York Tribune,* Apr. 4, 1920, E6
828 Kellor, Frances, "Americanizing the Aliens," *New York Times,* Feb. 29, 1920, XX12
829 Kellor, Frances, "What is Americanization?," *Yale Review,* Vol. 3, 1919, 289
830 Kellor, Frances, "Americanizing the Aliens," *New York Times,* Feb. 29, 1920, XX12
831 Kellor, Frances, "What is Americanization?," *Yale Review,* Vol. 3, 1919, 295
832 Kellor, Frances, *Immigration and the Future,* (New York: George H. Doran Company, 1920), 176
833 Kellor, Frances, "What is Americanization?," *Yale Review,* Vol. 3, 1919, 287
834 Ibid., 296
835 Kellor, Frances, *Immigration and the Future,* (New York: George H. Doran Company, 1920), 46 - 47
836 Ibid., 265
837 Ibid., XV.
838 Ibid., 265
839 Ibid., 256
840 "Creation of Board for Distribution of Aliens Urged," *New – York Tribune,* Jan. 14 1921, 4
841 Kellor, Frances, "Future Immigration," *North American Review,* 214, no. 788 (July 1921): 13

842 Ibid., 15.
843 "Creation of Board for Distribution of Aliens Urged," *New – York Tribune,* Jan. 14 1921, 4
844 "Emigration Policy of Europe Hits U.S.," *New York Times,* Aug. 1, 1920, 25
845 Kellor, Frances, "Future Immigration," *North American Review,* 214, no. 788 (July 1921): 13
846 Ibid., 18 – 19
847 Kellor, Frances, *Immigration and the Future,* (New York: George H. Doran Company, 1920), 70
848 "Emigration Policy of Europe Hits U.S." *New York Times,* Aug. 1, 1920, 25
849 Kellor, Frances, *Immigration and the Future,* (New York: George H. Doran Company, 1920), 47
850 Kellor, Frances, "Immigration in Reconstruction," *North American Review* 209, no. 759 (Feb., 1919): 207
851 Kellor, Frances, *The Federal Administration and the Alien: A Supplement to Immigration and the Future,* (New York: George H. Doran Company, 1921), 48
852 Ibid., 48
853 Ibid., 49.
854 Kellor, Frances, *Immigration and the Future,* (New York: George H. Doran Company, 1920), 192
855 Ibid., 197
856 Kellor, Frances, *The Federal Administration and the Alien: A Supplement to Immigration and the Future,* (New York: George H. Doran Company, 1921), 67
857 Kellor, Frances, "Immigration in Reconstruction," *North American Review,* 209, no. 759 (Feb., 1919): 203
858 Kellor, Frances, *Immigration and the Future,* (New York: George H. Doran Company, 1920), 65
859 Kellor, Frances, *The Federal Administration and the Alien: A Supplement to Immigration and the Future,* (New York: George H. Doran Company, 1921), 37
860 Ibid., 38
861 Ibid., 45
862 Ibid., 69
863 Ibid., 70
864 Ibid., 72
865 Kellor, Frances, "Immigration in Reconstruction," *North American Review* 209, no. 759 (Feb., 1919): 200
866 Ibid., 206
867 Frances Kellor, *The Federal Administration and the Alien: A Supplement to Immigration and the Future,* (New York: George H. Doran Company, 1921), 80.
868 Corbin, John, "Along the Thorny Path to Peace," *New York Times,* Jan. 18, 1925, BR10
869 "Frances Kellor," *Coldwater Daily Republican,* May, 4, 1961, 1
870 Florence Allen, Memorial Address for Frances Kellor Hall, Rockefeller Plaza, New York, Nov. 19, 1953, in possession of Holbrook Heritage Room, Coldwater Public Library, 2
871 Ibid., 2
872 Kellor, Frances, *The Federal Administration and the Alien: A Supplement to Immigration and the Future,* (New York: George H. Doran Company, 1921), 49
873 Kellor, Frances, "Humanizing the Immigration Law," *North American Review,* 211, no. 775, (June 1923): 769

874 Ibid., 784

------ CHAPTER FIFTEEN ------

875 Kellor, Frances, "Cloisters in American Politics: Rough Draft," 11, folder 12, Box 12, Ethel Eyre Valentine Dreier Papers, the Sophia Smith Collection, Smith College
876 Kellor, Frances, "Cloisters in American Politics: Rough Draft," Sophia Smith Collection, Smith College, 4
877 Ibid., 3
878 Muncy, Robyn, *Creating a Female Dominion in American Reform, 1890 – 1935*, (New York: Oxford University Press, 1991)
879 Ibid., 6
880 Kellor, Frances, "Women in British and American Politics," *Current History*, Feb. 1923, 834
881 Kellor, Frances, "Cloisters in American Politics: Rough Draft," Sophia Smith Collection, Smith College, 5
882 Ibid., 8
883 Ibid., 9
884 Kellor, Frances, "Cloisters in American Politics: Rough Draft," Sophia Smith Collection, Smith College, 4
885 Ibid., 9
886 Ibid., 10
887 Ibid., 7
888 Ibid., 10
889 Frances Kellor to Katherine Edson, 1, Dec. 22, 1916, folder 3, Box 5, Katherine Edson Papers, University of California at Los Angeles, Department of Special Collections, University of Los Angeles at California
890 Kellor, Frances, "Cloisters in American Politics: Rough Draft," Sophia Smith Collection, Smith College, 11
891 Ibid., 10
892 Kellor, Frances, "Arbiters Give Services Under American Plan," *Christian Science Monitor*, Feb. 10, 1930, 3
893 Kellor, Frances, *American Arbitration: Its History, Functions and Achievements*, (New York: Harper & Brothers Publishers, 1948), 658
894 "Arbitrators Honor Woman Associate," *New York Times*, November 20, 1953, 25
895 American Arbitration Association, "A Brief Overview of the American Arbitration Association," http://www.adr.org/Overview ,Accessed December, 2006
896 Florence Allen, Memorial Address for Frances Kellor Hall, Rockefeller Plaza, New York, Nov. 19, 1953, in possession of Holbrook Heritage Room, Coldwater Public Library, 2
897 Kellor, Frances, "Arbiters Give Services Under American Plan," *Christian Science Monitor*, Feb. 10, 1930, 3
898 Kellor, Frances, "Trade Impasse Found Leading to Most Wars," *Christian Science Monitor*, Feb. 8, 1930, 3
899 Kellor, Frances, "Arbitration in the New Industrial Society," (New York: McGraw – Hill Book Company, Inc., 1934), vi
900 "Arbitration Held Judicial Process," *New York Times*, Dec. 2, 1941, 14

[901] O'Connell, Lucille, *Notable American Women: The Modern Period, A Biographical Dictionary,* Eds. Sicherman, Barbara, Green, Carol, (Cambridge: The Belknap Press of Harvard University Press, 1980), 395

[902] Kellor, Frances, "American Arbitration: Its History, Functions and Achievements," (New York: Harper & Brothers Publishers, 1948), 158

[903] Kellor, Frances, *Immigration and the Future,* (New York: George H. Doran Company, 1920), 268

[904] Moyer, Imogene, *Criminological Theories: Traditional and Nontraditional Voices and Themes,* (Thousand Oaks: Sage Publications, 2001), 30

[905] Faderman, Lillian, *To Believe in Women: What Lesbians have Done for America – A History,* (Boston: Houghton Mifflin Company, 1999), 140

[906] Carlson, Robert, "Americanization as an Early Tweintieth-Century Adult Education Movement," *History of Education Quarterly* 10, no. 4 (Winter, 1970): 455.

[907] "Will Enforce New Law: Employment Agencies to be Directed to Secure License Now Required," *The Washington Post,* June 22, 1906, 14

[908] Review of *Out of Work: A Study of Unemployment,* Ordway Tead, *The American Journal of Sociology* 21, no. 2 (Sept. 1915): 267

www.ingramcontent.com/pod-product-compliance
Lightning Source LLC
Chambersburg PA
CBHW031230290426
44109CB00012B/238